FRANCIS OF ASSISI

FRANCIS

OF

ASSISI

THE LIFE OF A RESTLESS SAINT

VOLKER LEPPIN

Translated from the German by Rhys S. Bezzant

Yale
UNIVERSITY PRESS
NEW HAVEN & LONDON

Published with assistance from the Mary Cady Tew Memorial Fund.

Yale University Press books may be purchased in quantity for
educational, business, or promotional use. For information, please email
sales.press@yale.edu (U.S. office) or sales@yaleup.co.uk (U.K. office).

Set in Spectral type by Newgen.
Printed in the United States of America.

Library of Congress Control Number: 2024944768
ISBN 978-0-300-26380-0 (hardcover: alk. paper)

A catalogue record for this book is available from the British Library.

This paper meets the requirements of
ANSI/NISO Z39.48-1992 (Permanence of Paper).

10 9 8 7 6 5 4 3 2 1

Contents

Translator's Foreword

IT HAS BEEN ENORMOUSLY SATISFYING TO UNDERTAKE THIS translation of Volker Leppin's book *Franziskus von Assisi*, published originally in 2018 by the Wissenschaftliche Buchgesellschaft, Darmstadt, Germany. Not only is Leppin an outstanding scholar of the late medieval and early modern period, his German prose is fresh and vital, inviting the reader into an adventure that isn't merely academically considered but is also spiritually and emotionally engaging. I have read his books with great profit as an English-speaking Australian and offer my translation here as a token of my appreciation, accompanied by my prayer that many others would read church history, especially the biographies of leaders of the church in ages past, with the expectation of personal growth and deepening joy.

Of course, Leppin's style is not always easy to capture in English idiom, but I trust this translation will both excite and inform the reader. Many of Leppin's secondary sources, some of which are referenced in the endnotes, were written in German or Italian, which will not be of great help to the English-speaking readers of this translation. Thankfully Leppin also drew on English-language material to explain his conclusions and to navigate scholarly debates, and he also quoted from several books on Francis that have been translated into English. Thus this book will make a powerful contribution to reflection and research on the life and ministry of Francis in the English-speaking world—and beyond.

Where possible, I have sourced primary material from Marion Habig's extraordinary book *St Francis of Assisi: Writings and Early Biographies: English Omnibus of the Sources for the Life of St Francis.* Unfortunately, Habig's book uses numeration in ways that vary between texts, with chapter numbers, paragraph numbers, and page numbers not always used consistently and not always with arabic numerals, and without using line numbers that prove useful in some other primary document source books. I have tried to standardize here by offering simply the title of the text (or a summary title), the paragraph or section being quoted before a colon, with the page number after the colon. Finding the page, then the subdivision on that page, will lead the interested reader successfully to the relevant text. This will be my approach to other primary document texts too. Where the author quotes from the Scriptures, I have used the New Revised Standard Version for texts in English. Names of churches are chiefly rendered in Italian, though place names and personal names will be rendered with common English names when they have one. American spelling has been used, except in direct quotations from British sources.

I'd like to express my gratitude to Jennifer Banks at Yale University Press for her encouraging support for the project. As well, I wish to thank Michael Hilton for his help with Latin texts and Patrick Maisch for his assistance finding primary source material—both relieving me of great anxiety—along with the good people of St. Leonard's Anglican Church in Assisi, who were kind and welcoming during a period of chaplaincy in their glorious town in December 2022. I learned so much there during a very productive period of translating. Finally, I want to express my sincere love and heartfelt gratitude to my exchange student family in Germany, the Lenzes, for all their patience and laughter while training me in German over so many years! They have been so good to me. And in special remembrance of Fritz Lenz, who died during production of the final draft of this book, I dedicate this translation to him. *Pace e bene.*

Rhys S. Bezzant
Ridley College (Australian College of Theology)
Melbourne, Australia

Preface

BEHIND THE HIGH ALTAR OF THE ELIZABETH CHURCH IN Marburg, central Germany, the sun shines through wonderful stained-glass windows crafted in the thirteenth century. We see there the figure of Elizabeth of Thuringia (often known as Elizabeth of Hungary), after whom the church was named when it was founded in the Middle Ages, though for centuries now it has celebrated Protestant rites. Alongside her, we can also see Francis of Assisi, a man whom she never met but who nonetheless influenced her greatly. It was here that I met Francis myself for the first time. I grew up in that church as the pastor's son, so I was very familiar with the saints depicted in the windows, without ever asking if they were Catholic or Protestant. Since those days, I have often thought about Francis and have tried to imagine what he was really like. So this book is my attempt to pull the pieces together, for I have never really been able to shake myself free from my fascination with the man.

Indeed, the challenges in reconstructing Francis are part of what drew me to him in the first place, as many other biographers over the centuries have discovered in studying the *poverello* (the "poor little man") from Assisi. He is stimulating, irritating, sometimes even disturbing. And we can thank a recent pope for helping us to ask questions about the *poverello* again, and for allowing him to ask questions of us. This book is part of that larger conversation. In this book, I went in search of the man, and I found someone who was himself a seeker.

This book was first published in German. Rhys Bezzant (Ridley College, Melbourne, Australia) has translated it into English with unstinting effort. Working with him was a great pleasure, both professionally and personally. Patrick Maisch (Yale/Tübingen) has rendered sterling assistance in checking quotations. Thanks to Peter Palm for the map. From the very beginning, collaborating with Jennifer Banks of Yale University Press has been an exceptionally enjoyable experience. I thank them all most sincerely for their help on this project, which now represents my move to the United States from Germany not just geographically but linguistically too.

Volker Leppin
Horace Tracy Pitkin Professor of Historical Theology
Yale Divinity School
New Haven, Connecticut

The Papal States in the time of Innocent III

FRANCIS OF ASSISI

CHAPTER 1

Getting Close to Francis

RANCIS OF ASSISI: A MAN AND A SAINT FROM THE Middle Ages, yet for some almost a contemporary. This development has been impressively illustrated by Patricia Appelbaum in her book *St. Francis of America*. Ever since Protestants discovered Francis in the second half of the nineteenth century in search of their premodern roots, he has served as a form of identification for generations of Christians from different denominations, and their enthusiasm has taken many different forms. In 1938, the magazine *House and Garden* featured an advertisement for a garden statue of the saint. A generation later, he became the "hippie saint" and patron of the 1967 "Summer of Love" in San Francisco, the city that bears his name. In the same year, another reason for his immense popularity arose: his view of nature gave solace and encouragement to those who feared ecological catastrophe. Pope Francis shared a similar outlook in his encyclical "Laudato Si'" of 2015, in which the head of the Roman Catholic Church refers to his namesake when addressing his concerns about climate catastrophe.[1]

Indeed, the title of this encyclical quotes a poem by the Assisi saint: *The Canticle of Brother Sun*. In this song and in many stories about him, we appreciate his close connection with nature. It is said that he spoke to the birds, and legend has it that in Gubbio he even tamed a wolf. He praised the sun, the moon, and the stars. He might be the saint *for* our time, but he is not *of* our time. He knew nothing about the climate catastrophe and the modern world that brought it about. And in fact, we don't know all that much about him anyway. We rely mainly on the late collection of legends called the *Fioretti* (*Little Flowers of St Francis*), in which we find, for example, the story of the wolf. For a long time it was thought that the *Life* of Francis by the Franciscan minister-general Bonaventure (d. 1274) was a kind of biography, and it has certainly shaped the way memory of him is preserved in both its long and short versions (*Legenda maior* and *minor*). It was also the basis of the famous frescoes that Giotto painted on the walls of the Basilica of San Francesco in Assisi. The impression they make even today is overwhelming, combining as they do both the aura of the humanity and the holiness of Francis. But modern scholars have found it increasingly difficult to trust Bonaventure's account since the Protestant historian Paul Sabatier (1858–1928) raised in his *Life of St Francis of Assisi* the explosive "Franciscan question," a highly complex technical debate about the reliability of the early sources, which no biographer of Francis can ignore. It arises from the insight that the early biographies have always pursued a specific agenda. When Bonaventure led the Franciscan Order in a delicate period of its life, it is evident how he built on others' works, as well as attempting to paint the image of the founder in such a way that his priorities could encompass the divergent Franciscan branches. His biography very obviously did not serve primarily as a historical narrative about the life of Francis of Assisi, but instead served the needs of Bonaventure in his own social and political context.[2]

But it is not only Bonaventure's biography that we should approach with caution. Even before its composition, the Franciscan question had begun with the death of the saint, which marked the beginning of widespread devotion to him. Shortly after Francis's death, Pope Gregory IX commissioned a biography of Francis by Thomas of Celano (d. 1260). This project would serve Gregory's own fame, since he himself appeared as an incidental figure in the story. Before being elected pope, when he was still Cardinal Hugolino of Ostia, he had been the protector of the new order and had supported Francis of Assisi over an even longer period. Therefore it will come as no surprise that the splendor of Francis's biography would also irradiate the glory of the one who had commissioned it. The author himself, Thomas of Celano, was not exactly someone from whom distance should be expected either for it was assumed that medieval biographers would recount a life for readers to emulate. Celano was already a follower of Francis of Assisi during his lifetime and had been a superintendent of the Franciscan communities in the Rhineland since 1223. His work served to justify and propagate the veneration of the founder of the order, who was quickly canonized just two years after his death on October 3, 1226, and its composition was certainly intended to smooth out the process of leadership succession in the order. All this makes the oldest *Life* of Francis at least as much a document reflecting its author's immediate needs as a testimony to the life it is intended to portray, expressing the tension so characteristic of the Franciscan question.[3]

It is evident that the authors of the early sources depicting the life of Francis of Assisi had different intentions from those pursued by contemporary historians, for they were not seeking to compose a biography in the modern sense of the word; their goal was to present the legend of a saint. Medieval hagiography is not modern scholarship. This might make it more difficult to use the biographies for historical reconstructions, but research suggests that it is not impossible. Through the individual prayers and writings that Francis composed, we have a reasonably secure basis for understanding his spiritual concerns, but when biographers today refer to the less secure texts of the early *Lives*, they have to weigh carefully the evidence. How closely Celano's text and the veneration of Francis were linked is shown by the fact that soon after his *Life* was written, he went on to write a work that has the word *legend* in its title: *An Umbrian Choir Legend,* though the English word *chancel*, referring to that architectural space of the church building where the clergy sit, might be a better translation than "choir," which suggests a group of singers. Of course, "legenda" in Latin does not represent a statement about (doubtful) reliability as it might in today's usage but means quite literally that the text was intended to be read; this short work was divided into nine readings. It was intended to respond to the new mandate from Benedict of Arezzo, head of the Franciscan province of Romania and Greece, that every brother should have the opportunity to read the abridged version of Francis's life in his own breviary, a common and condensed collection of liturgical texts that the brothers normally carried with them. In this way, the brothers were regularly able to hold before their eyes the life of the founder of the order, which Celano summarized for this purpose using his previously written *Life* as his guide. Of course, such texts were used not only for individual purposes but also for the common liturgy. We have an impression of this from the chronicle of Thomas of Eccleston (d. after 1258) about the beginnings of the Franciscans in England. For the year 1235 he reports: "Brother Augustine . . . related publicly in the convent at London that he had been in Assisi for the feast of St Francis and that Pope Gregory was there; when the pope went up to preach, the brothers chanted: 'This one the saint chose as his father, when he ruled over a lesser church,' and the pope smiled." Indeed, he did have a reason to smile, because the person elected as Pope Gregory had been Francis's spiritual father, the former Cardinal Hugolino. The song the brothers sang came from the *Office of St Francis*, which the former French court music director Julian of Speyer (d. c. 1250) had composed in the early 1230s. Now he served the Friars Minor instead of the king of France, and not just as a musician. Around the same time as he wrote the *Office*, he also wrote a biography of the founder of the order, largely using Celano's work as his template.[4]

However, Celano continued to be active as a writer himself. Thanks to the research of Jacques Dalarun, we discovered just a few years back that Celano wrote another, even shorter version of his *Life*, but despite the significance of the find, Celano's so-called *Second Life* from the early 1240s is more important still. At the General Chapter of the Franciscans on October 4, 1244, the general of the order, Crescentius of Jesi, who served in that role from 1244 to 1247, called for the collection of "signs and wonders of our blessed Father Francis," whereupon Celano received a new commission from the general, asking that it be "set down in writing for the consolation of those living and for a remembrance for those to come." Again, for today's historiography, the question remains of how to deal with the resulting text. Crescentius's call to collect memories may at first glance raise the hope that the *Second Life* will contain new insights, and that is of course possible. But almost twenty years after the death of the saint, the narrative traditions were likely to have changed and grown. Perhaps memories had faded, but more likely just the opposite had happened: they had become brighter. It had become increasingly obvious in the meantime that the memories concerned not just a young fellow citizen but now a revered and venerable saint. In addition, Crescentius's appeal clearly had the aim of calming the turmoil in which the order was embroiled, given the dispute about Francis's legacy and the growing expectation of an imminent apocalyptic event. Celano's commemorative commission served not to clarify the past but to provide orientation in the present. In extended sections of the work, his *Second Life* reads almost like a commentary on the validity of the Franciscan rule and how it was to be implemented. The consolation of contemporaries focused on the very concrete impact it could have on the internal peace of the order. In short, one does not have to approach this *Life* overcritically, but one does have to use it cautiously. The "veil of remembrance" is likely to have settled over some things here too, and the very real political intentions of the order would have colored the way other events were presented.[5]

Unfortunately, this disclaimer also applies to another work connected with Crescentius's appeal which, strictly speaking, consists of two documents that have been handed down together. The first is a letter from three of the founder's companions, Leo, Rufino, and Angelo, in which they announce that, following Crescentius's lead, they want to collect stories of miracles and signs of Francis's holy life, not in the sense of a detailed legend but like "a few flowers from a lovely meadow." This letter has been handed down in the manuscripts together with a second text, which offers a comprehensive biography. If both belong together, and the tradition clearly speaks for it, then in some respects this would be the most authentic report about the *poverello,* written by people who were close to him from the beginning. But even this is not so simple. Leonhard Lehmann, himself a Capuchin member of the Franciscan tradition and an outstanding expert on the problems of the sources, aptly summarized the difficulties of the *Legend of the Three Companions*: "Whether it is complete or 'mangled' . . . ; whether or not it belongs to the letter signed by the Three Companions, Leo, Rufino, and Angelo, written in Greccio on August 11, 1246; whether the three mentioned are really the authors or not; whether the work was completed by August 11, 1246, or was supplemented later; whether it was only written in the 1360s or even at the beginning of the fourteenth century."[6]

Given current contentious debates among researchers in the field, one cannot avoid using the *Legend of the Three Companions* with the same caution as all the other sources, even if one traces it back to Leo and Francis's two other friends. It has great merit nonetheless. The fact that it contains information beyond Celano's account is undisputed, but it is still the case that it was written twenty years after the death of Francis. Even friends can suffer from failures of memory or embellish things too much. Indeed, friends in particular may tend to emphasize the strengths of their former companion more than a sober observer would in their biographical descriptions. In short: the Franciscan question remains open and every biographer must deal with it anew.

This also applies to another very exciting source, which may have been composed before 1241 within Gregory IX's lifetime: the records of the so-called Anonymus Perusinus, who can probably be identified as John of Perugia and who seems to have collected stories about Francis. This long-lost and little-noticed text belongs to a series of very early testimonies that lead us very close to the phase of personal recollections of Francis himself. Perhaps, as Leonhard Lehmann suspects, it even served as a model for the *Legend of the Three Companions,* or at least as a helpful resource. If so, however, it also sheds light on what counts as memory: if the Three Companions themselves (assuming they were the authors of the legend that bears their name) used a template, they didn't rely on their memory alone. The report by John of Perugia does not lead us out of the thicket, but rather deeper into it.[7]

In short, much has been written about the life of Francis, and yet not much can be assumed as certain. The little that can be recounted we might summarize in this way: the son of a merchant, born around 1181/82, he turned to those who were sick and abandoned in his hometown of Assisi, and thus set himself apart from the merchant class from which he came. He revolted more and more against his parents' wealth, urging them to live in apostolic imitation of Christ instead. Already during his lifetime, but even more so after his death, he became a symbol of poverty, and was nicknamed the *poverello.* And yet, unlike many who had walked the apostolic path before him, he was able to remain at peace with the church. Although he did not want to join any traditional religious order, he founded a brotherhood and managed to have it recognized in 1209 by Pope Innocent III, one of the most powerful popes of the Middle Ages. His community flourished, gradually found its legal basis as a mendicant order, and spread throughout Europe. Many of the younger generation seem to have joined this movement, perhaps representing the counterculture of the age, just as hippies of the twentieth century demonstrated great affection for Francis too. In any case, he seems to have given expression to the mood of his time. His journey to Sultan al-Malik al-Kamil in 1219/20 shows how wide his own imagination could venture, though we don't know a great deal about the encounter—we should be satisfied that it took place at all. In the period following his journey, Francis became increasingly burdened by the success of his movement. In 1220 he resigned from the leadership of the order and seems to have withdrawn more and more into solitude. Emaciated and plagued by illness, he died in 1226.

Of course, there are some episodes in Francis's life about which we do know more, propelling further detailed discussion, especially the question of whether he experienced the miracle of stigmatization in 1224. This book is intended to cover those details as well. But perhaps more important still is what we can learn about his inner biography, his spirituality, and ultimately the life of his soul, which is more reliably substantiated by the sources. After all, in some writings—not least the already mentioned *The Canticle of Brother Sun*—his own hand has been preserved. They provide important clues for reconstructing his journey of faith. For this reason, the inner biography takes up a significant place in the following pages. The emotional and spiritual world of Francis forms this biography's backbone, so we will come back to it time and time again. But one cannot recount the inner biography without the outer one. Yet even to capture the historical facts of his life, we need to consult his testimonial writings, although a certain amount of caution applies here as well, because we have hardly any letters of the kind that are normally available as reliable testimonies of someone's life. But at least we do have an extremely important text from his own hand relating his autobiography, which he deliberately composed as part of his legacy. Shortly before his death in 1226 he wrote his so-called *Testament,* a text that combines—albeit very briefly—a review of his life and an interpretation of the present state of his order along with admonitions to the brothers. The autobiographical parts in it are pointed and demonstrate a clear set of priorities. Francis names a few episodes and shortens them, making clear that what is true generally about people's memories can also apply to autobiographical fragments. The way we remember our own life and the way we want our own life to be remembered shift. In concrete terms, this means that Francis did not write the *Testament* merely to assemble memories, but to present his own life as a model for his contemporary community of the brothers. Such intent can stain memories. The *Testament* is undoubtedly the most important testimony to Francis's story, but due to its succinctness and its purpose, it unfortunately does not offer the decisive solution to the problems of a biography of Francis of Assisi.[8]

If we take a closer look at the sources, it is true that anyone who sets out to tell the life of Francis of Assisi today, whether they like it or not, is part of a double tradition, which is characterized on the one hand by the hagiographies on which everyone who wants to recount the life of Francis remains dependent. And on the other hand, biographers are dependent on the tradition of intensive research, for which a critical approach to precisely these sources has become a matter of course, and which has done a lot to open our eyes to their problems. Criticism does not mean that the hagiographers' statements should be dismissed in their entirety. As has been shown, they are close in time to the events and are so intertwined with the threads of memory that they bring us very close to the subject of the story, to Francis himself. But one must use them carefully and weigh them against each other. The path back from hagiography to historical events is difficult, but not impossible.[9]

Upon further reflection, it may dawn on us to ask the question of whether the story of the man from Assisi can be told at all, and whether we can reach any conclusion at the end of a Francis biography that allows the life of this man to be summarized in one sentence, even in one word. But it should be said from the outset that this is not exactly the aim of this book. It is a biography, and yet at the same time it is a book about the difficulties of writing a biography, and specifically a biography of Francis of Assisi. A radical position would be to consult only those few fragments that expressly treat details of his life in his own hand, but even these, as pointed out above, are not simple reflections of reality. Everything else is secondhand and follows the different vested interests of the authors in forming "their" Francis. If one were to pursue this radical posture, the pleasure of writing or reading a Francis biography would quickly come to an end. But if this approach proves dissatisfying, and an author is prepared to risk including other accounts as reflections of Francis's life, a necessary consequence will be the inevitable struggle to assess the sources and weigh up the different traditions.

The fact that some biographies have hagiographical purposes does not mean that they contain no historically valuable material. They may be presented according to some literary design, but this is not the same as invention. Perhaps their interest could also be realized through the way in which they rearranged existing material in a new way and in their own way. Importantly, the degree of poetry in the accounts is likely to be higher in those texts that are closer to the action. We should not underestimate the people of the Middle Ages. Even in the thirteenth century, there existed doubts about miraculous reports, and the biographers of Francis were aware of such suspicions, sometimes even tracing them back to the devil. There were limits to what could be conceived, but the narrative was made up not only of inventions but also of reports and memories that were then brought into a new order. When a narrative obviously serves the overall flow of a biography, greater skepticism is appropriate than when it appears to coincide with or even contradict this flow.[10]

With this in mind, we observe how the *First Life* of Celano and the *Legend of the Three Companions* present the smallest amount of tension with Francis's *Testament*. They will therefore be the most important sources in what follows, together with the few other testimonies that Francis himself left behind, for example, prayers, letters, and rules. For each stage in Francis's life, we still have to ask how reliably we can approach each document, and the sobering result remains that we still can't know precisely all the facts. The following pages will only be able to provide many of the episodes from Francis's life with a big question mark looming overhead. Whether we are investigating the commission that Francis is said to have received from the crucifix in the church of San Damiano, or how his first encounter with Pope Innocent III proceeded, it becomes clear again and again that some influential narratives, especially when they are supposed to legitimize events through supernatural interventions in earthly reality, go back more to the construction of their narrators than to the memory of observers. There is no doubt that for medieval people the world was permeated by God's rule and that he was able to reveal himself to people in visions, dreams, and revelations—such stories would not work if they were not believed. Rather, the complex source situation repeatedly suggests that something that was perceived as truth was presented even more starkly as an expression of divine guidance through added episodes than was the case for the earliest layers, which is typical for hagiographies. These literary observations then ensure that occasionally we can remove the question mark behind one or another story. However, it should also be emphasized that to highlight the function of literary insights is not to try to correct the medieval belief in miracles measured by modern assumptions. On the contrary, a full understanding of Francis's biography also includes the fact that he was perceived and revered as a miracle worker, regardless of how we interpret those events today, and that his miracles shouldn't necessarily be seen as inventions. Where the history of a text gives the impression that a narrative has been fashioned over time, there are good reasons to exclude such episodes from historical reconstruction as inventions. Pious inventions, of course, but inventions nonetheless.[11]

Such interpretations are the usual business of the work of historians, drawing conclusions from the long, intense history of research on Francis, with scholarly skepticism part of the mix. As should become clear when reading the following pages, they serve not to diminish the importance of

Francis but to work out his human greatness. The difficulty of writing a consistent biography applies not only to Francis, but in general to every life that has been lived. In dealing with modernity, the Protestant theologian Henning Luther developed the idea that life is ultimately a fragment. We live and experience our biography as a chain of moments shaped by what has gone before, and yet looking back on our lives there may not be an evident red thread that ties all the loose ends together. The meaning of our lives does not simply emerge from within our experience of life but is imputed to us. We might try to determine the meaning of our lives for ourselves and for others through narration and interpretation, and others may try to determine ours by merging all the parts together into a whole.[12]

Understood in this way, Francis's early biographers also tried to do one thing above all: to interpret the life of Francis, handed down to them in fragments, in a meaningful way. The fact that they did this within the horizon of his holiness was a matter of course for them and does not automatically render their reports historically useless. If that were the case, one would have to give up even trying to write a biography of Francis before one had even begun. But the early hagiographers looked at the traditions at their disposal from a certain perspective, that of light and darkness, for the saint who was to ascend to the splendor of heavenly glory was so portrayed that precisely that glory was already visible here on earth, at least as a reflection. From this vantage point, the counter-image appears all the more sinister, whether the darkness was focused on "the world" with its seductions, or especially for Francis on his father, from whom he broke away in disputes (though this rupture was no doubt difficult for both sides). Not only was the writing of the lives and legends to be characterized by this contrast between light and darkness, so also was the prior collection of the material, perhaps even its origins. The miracle books about Francis of Assisi, one of which had already emerged from the labors of Thomas of Celano, bear witness to this. The imagination of Francis's contemporaries kept adding one story after another, often lovingly told and not with the intention of inventing untruths but of expressing ever better narratively what was felt to be the deeper truth in the life of the saint.[13]

It is self-evident for modern research that one is not constrained by these accounts, for research of the Franciscan order itself has set standards here. Conversely, it is also true that the stories should not be dismissed out of hand. Modern interpretation cannot simply disregard the early descriptions but has the task of searching through them for those fragments that might be able to create another story, one that history has over the centuries ignored or overlooked. But together they don't add up by themselves to form a different story, and the modern interpreter would be well advised not to make a complete counter-image out of such opposing fragments. Any interpretation must join what seems most likely from today's perspective with—more precisely—what one can imagine to have happened in the thirteenth century. Seen in this way, modern biography creates meaning from the fragments and yet has to live with the fact that some elements remain questionable.

However, it is still possible to retrieve some plausible narrative from the quandary. Though we might not know exactly what happened in the life of Francis, we nonetheless resolve to tell his story as seems most responsible according to today's critical view of the sources, perhaps requiring that some solid pieces of cultural memory concerning Francis must be called into question. Methodologically, this biography thus accepts the view that tensions between the sources may well provide the most productive lines of inquiry, for Francis was at times very different from what his legend might have required. As a saint, he was a fool for Christ—but in the eyes of many contemporaries he was simply mad. Where the early biographers chose to see him as a benevolent leader of his fraternity, lying behind their depiction some conflicts may still have lurked. And perhaps that is why biographers attached such great importance to the spiritual character of his relationship with Clare di Offreduccio, precisely because the way they behaved toward each other was repugnant to the norms of interaction between young women and men.

The latter example in particular shows the limits of this search for fragmentary evidence beyond the legend of the saint. The indications in the early biographies are not always sufficient to assert with great certainty an alternative biography to them. The complicated tradition leads not to new unambiguous clarity but to a generative web of allusions and ambivalences. That is exactly the aim of this book: to show the many possible facets of the life of Francis of Assisi, and to indicate what possibilities the fragments of a life and above all the reports about it open up for us. The notion that the historian could tell "how it really happened" has long been abandoned by historical scholarship, and the impressive history of research into the Franciscan question has emphatically underlined this in the case of the man from Assisi. Behind the one face that people have repeatedly tried to draw, historical research can trace the many faces that could also depict it. And perhaps such an approach does more justice to the fragmentary nature of life than any attempt to pin it down to just one of the many possibilities.[14]

However, the search for the person behind the many faces is not entirely fruitless, for as varied as they are, some sketches may well present him better than others. One thought that turned out to be a leading notion for the book that follows is that Francis's quest to find his way in the world began with a moment of great clarity when he experienced rejection and the break with his parental home. However, the most we can say at the outset is that there was for him in the beginning no clear orientation toward Christ, just a clear rejection of his father. Only gradually did he feel in Christ the counterpart to the rejected family home, and that rupture became a point of renewal that led finally to his mission in the world, even to the ends of the world when he met the sultan, to become eventually the most popular saint in the United States today. To emphasize that we know little about him does not mean to dismiss the images that the present has of him. Francis is not the same as some today would want to depict him. In the end, he isn't just the person this biography makes him out to be either. Every historical reconstruction is always just an attempt to approach him, and every spiritual contact with him is subject to the proviso that "the historical Francis . . . remains elusive in detail." Whoever honors Francis in their writing must be aware that knowledge can only be fragmentary. And yet we cannot avoid using the fragments and putting them together. So in this book, from the many fragments there is a story that, like all stories about Francis's life, remains a gamble, and that has its surest basis where the preserved original texts by his hand contain something about Francis himself and the depths of his soul, always looking and searching for God. If you look at his intense faith in Christ and his love of the Bible that can be seen through it, he might have approved a confession of the fragmentary nature of life on this earth in the words of the apostle Paul: "For now we see in a mirror dimly, but then face to face" (1 Corinthians 13:12).[15]

CHAPTER 2

Rupture

A Son from a Good Home

E WAS CALLED FRANCIS. FRANCESCO.
There is normally nothing easier in beginning a biography than to investigate a person's name. But in the case of Francis, even here problems await us. According to the reports of the Three Companions and of Bonaventure in his *Legenda Minor,* his mother first named him John, but it was his father, Pietro Bernardone, who called him Francis, not a name without precedent but still an unusual choice. As the Three Companions point out, his father wanted to draw a connection with the country of France, for Pietro was on a business trip there when his son was born around 1181/82. Indeed, several times in their account, it appears that the Companions want to make connections with France, for example, the role that French played in the Bernardone home, and how Francis enjoyed speaking the language, "though he did not know it very well." On one occasion, Francis's brother, Angelo, teased him, and it was said that Francis responded in French. On another occasion, according to Celano, Francis was said to have sung God's praises in French as he walked in the woods. Perhaps John was called Francis by the townsfolk because of his love for the French language, sidelining altogether the story of his father's role in naming him.[1]

But as easy as it might be to dismiss the connection between Francis's father's love for all things French and the name of his son, we should not rush to draw conclusions. His business interests in France were notable, for northern Italy and the city of Assisi had experienced a rapid rise in fortunes in the early thirteenth century due to the growth of trade and the money economy, contributing not just to their economic growth but also to social dislocation. The traditional rights of the nobility increasingly counted for less, while the energy and influence of merchants like Pietro Bernardone counted for more. Francis's path of discipleship into physical and spiritual poverty should be understood against the social tensions that the rapid rise of wealth in Assisi caused, as it created a new basis for right and might.

During Francis's childhood, social relations reflected earlier assumptions, were easier to navigate, and were more visible. Above the town ruled the Rocca Maggiore, a dominating castle that was the occasional home of the Duke of Spoleto, under whose jurisdiction Assisi belonged. It was during the rule of the German emperor Frederick I, nicknamed Barbarossa (r. 1155–90), that Konrad von Urslingen (r. 1176/77–1198/1202) had acquired the title of Spoleto. His rule was destabilized when the line of imperial succession was challenged on the death of the German king Henry VI (r. 1191–97), and when the new pope, Innocent III (r. 1198–1216), began to exercise his influence in Umbria more aggressively. The citizens of Assisi leveraged such competition for power in the years 1197/98 to rise up against the ruling nobility. They drove Konrad from the castle, plundered the possessions of the nobles, and eventually drove them all—including the knightly family of Offreduccio di Bernardino, with their daughter Clare, the future companion of Francis—out of the city. The nobility reacted not just to their expulsion but to the imposition in Umbria of legal norms from northern Italy that curtailed more traditional liberties. It took awhile for conditions to calm down. In two stages, in the years 1203 and 1210, peace treaties were concluded, the first a decree of the victorious nobility over the vanquished, while the second made more space for the developing rights of the bourgeoisie. It was in this very period of instability that the conversion of Francis—if the more particular date of 1206 is not accepted—took place. The treaty of 1210 reflected both the antagonisms of the period and a measure of reconciliation, as both groups committed themselves afresh to pursuing the welfare of the city.[2]

The nobility and the bourgeoisie were now committed to a relationship based not on birth alone, which had privileged the nobility, but one that recognized the role of money. Merchants could now buy their freedom from noble overlords, and the rights of citizens would increasingly be determined through property rights. Dominant in the new social relationship was application of the words *maiores* or *minores*, major or lesser, to describe different social groups; belonging to the upper class of citizens was defined by wealth.

Money might not have ruled the whole world, but in Assisi it represented upward social mobility and success. We don't know to what degree Bernardone was involved in these conflicts, but he certainly was destined to profit from the new arrangements. Francis's father was a representative of this upwardly mobile section of commercial society defined around the pursuit of money, and it is even possible that Francis's father's business trip to France kept him away from the birth and baptism of his first son. Helmut Feld has argued that such a journey could mean up to a year away from home, in which case Bernardone might well have rushed home on news of his son's birth if rumors had spread of the possibility of doubtful paternity. Indeed, rumors like these do make an appearance in accounts of Francis's life. For example, Celano notes that others in the circle of his extended family had asked if his parents were truly his biological parents. In the *Legend of the Three Companions*, it was Francis's parents who questioned whether "his style of living made him appear not so much their son as the son of some great prince." The overall impression from these accounts is that Francis's later sanctity can't be traced back to his early life, and nor was his holy character of human origin.[3]

The theological values undergirding these accounts interact with social reality too. The Three Companions are unusual in their account, for they are unclear in ascribing paternity; they don't refer to the father by name but instead allow for some ambiguity by referring to a *magnus princeps*, a great prince, nor do they use the plural form, which could raise questions concerning Francis's mother. If we follow the legal principle that the mother of a child is always certain, then the background to the accounts must refer to the insinuation that Francis's mother likely—perhaps, with all we know about conflict in Assisi, probably—became pregnant by a nobleman, in which case naming her son "Francis" had other functions, either ironic or demonstrative. It is plausible that Bernardone wanted to defend the notion that he impregnated his wife miraculously from France by insisting on this name, or that the rumors were untrue despite the recognition of his prolonged absence. It is surprising that the biographers of Francis would make any reference, even veiled, to the legitimacy of his conception, which in the medieval mindset would stain Francis as well as his parents. Or perhaps mention of his paternity was intended as a contrast with his holiness, but this pushes us toward the limits of credulity. We note that the identity of Francis's father was not formally reported but emerged as a perception of the interested parties, which suggests that rumors were floating around Assisi. And with rumors the truth is always hard to recover, especially when it is indisputably true that Bernardone had been absent. We could perhaps reconstruct the story to suggest that wicked tongues had invented the story that Francis was born illegitimate, but it just can't be substantiated. Recalling our earlier methodological observations, we surmise that both cited statements, fragmentary in nature, give cause to reflect on Francis's origin story, but in the end fail to provide a clear alternative scenario or aren't enough to create a scandal in the first place. We conclude—the most plausible conclusion—that Francis was the son of Pietro Bernardone and his wife, known as Pica.

The name Francis itself conjures up a range of associations or possibilities for explanation. But it is more complicated still when we return to the name of John. In the early biographies, the name of John was given to Francis at his baptism, whereas the name by which he has been known for centuries since was more like a nickname given to him later, pushing out "Giovanni" from the records. Celano notes that Francis would never forget his relationship with John the Baptist, whose feast day he would celebrate above all others. Even though there are no liturgical records in which Francis draws out any special relationship with the Baptist, this does not necessarily call into question the truth of the claim.[4]

Nonetheless, there are still reasons to doubt that Francis was baptized with the name John. First of all, this information only comes to hand after Crescentius's appeal for memories to be compiled, which the *Legend of the Three Companions* relates. If this legend had its origin in a later period, it would be certain that Celano's *Second Life* would be the earliest evidence of his baptismal name of John, for in his *First Life* he appears not to know about it, but this doesn't mean much. It would be perfectly possible to believe that the name Giovanni was entirely displaced by the name Francesco, and that those good friends who were with him from the beginning, putatively the authors of the *Legend of the Three Companions,* had preserved the memory and passed it on to Celano. This is certainly possible, but not necessarily so.[5]

There is one factor that rubs up against this theory. With Celano's use of the name John, a new theological layer is introduced into his identity. While the name Francis points to his growing reputation as a saint, the name John, on the other hand, points to his service for the Lord. How exactly Celano understands the name Francis is not clear. It is just possible that he wanted to suggest that the reputation of Francis had now reached as far as France.

In the *First Life*, he connects the name of Francis with the sense of someone who has an outspoken (*francus*) and noble heart, although the meaning of the name John is much more easily connected to the mission of Francis, for John the Baptist came preaching the arrival of Christ on earth, and since that time Christians have been trained to look forward to Christ's Second Coming on the Day of Judgment. Francis also took up the role of preaching Christ's return as Judge. And he did this by calling his hearers to repentance, as we shall see, which had been exactly John the Baptist's task too. Francis was to occupy a place in salvation history similar to John, recounted in a *Life* that was written to explain how the different perspectives on the legacy of Francis's order might be reconciled. Celano's *Second Life* was not simply about the details of Francis's life but more the place of his life in the purposes of God for humankind. Just as John in Matthew 11:11 was described as the greatest born of women, so Celano wanted to portray Francis as the most perfect founder of a medieval order. This is made more likely if we grasp how Celano wrote his account at just that time when Crescentius came looking to find out more about Francis, and when in Francis's order the writings of Joachim of Fiore (d. 1202) were becoming known. His understanding of world history was interpreted to make Francis of Assisi the beginning of the third age of salvation history, namely, the age of the Holy Spirit, which would shape monks and orders for the future. And even if this reference to the ideas of Joachim doesn't ultimately hold up, Celano's more moderate analogical connection between John and Francis does suggest some apocalyptic intent. He would not be able to hold back more radical conceptions in which Francis's association with a soon to arrive glorious Kingdom of Christ on earth was expected. In either case, the name of John fits well with any attempt to situate Francis as a forerunner to Christ's appearance in salvation history.[6]

However, the convenience of this association is still no reason to doubt it. It would not be anything out of the ordinary for the Bernardones to have named their son John, and it might actually reflect accurately someone's memory. But there is another detail that fits remarkably well—perhaps too well, creating suspicion. An account of two names belongs not just to Francis but to John the Baptist as well! The New Testament describes the assumption by John's family that their son would be called Zechariah after his father, although Zechariah in Luke's Gospel was not able to contribute to the conversation for he had been struck dumb as a consequence of his unbelief when he heard that in old age he would sire a son. His wife resisted the call to name her son after his father, insisting instead on the name John. So Zechariah was called in to adjudicate the disagreement by writing on a tablet his preferred name, which he decided should be John (Luke 1:57–64). Perhaps because Francis's parents were in disagreement over the name of their own son, the name of John the Baptist provided some unity. Celano deliberately reinforces the parallels between the son of Zechariah and Elizabeth and the son of the Bernardones, insofar as in both instances the parents had a role in naming their son, so it appears just too likely that Celano invented the story to give a particular theological emphasis to his leading character. Francis was named Francesco from the beginning.[7]

A Wild Youth or Early Holiness?

If questions concerning the name of Francis appear insignificant, given that in the end the name that has come down to us from posterity is likely to be correct, other questions concerning his youth are of a different order of importance. Attempts to write his story in the 1240s had a great impact, not least because Celano appears to contradict himself: if we only had the accounts of the youth of Francis in Celano's two biographies, we might be forgiven for coming to the conclusion that they refer to two different people. In the *First Life,* Celano described a hapless young man who until he was twenty-five led a profligate life, but he does not provide us with much concrete detail. He might only be asserting that children generally tend to imitate the bad habits of their parents, which was perhaps true for Francis too. Celano maintained this position but made the further point that though Francis became a leader in spiritual matters after his conversion, in his early life he exceeded all his peers in his bad behavior, leading a gang of troublemakers in Assisi. He may in later life have given money to the poor, but as a youth he was known to burn through money in a careless fashion. Celano didn't identify precisely Francis's sins in these matters, but for the reader it is clear that Francis gave himself over to his passions and lusts. His later holiness can only be understood in direct contrast with his earlier sinfulness.[8]

If this kind of narrative serves to contrast the later and earlier life of Francis, with exemplary holiness canceling out egregious sin, so a new danger arises. In reading Celano's biographies, it would be tempting to link the earlier unnamed sin with a later named posture of obedience, which is not too far from speculating about Francis's early sexual misadventures, often associated with life in a gang, even if Celano refuses to make the contrast explicit. Indeed, in the recently rediscovered summary of the *Life,* drafted in the 1230s, Celano stressed that despite his persistent sinning as a youth, Francis had held himself back "from those egregious sins" by which the reputation of adults is shamed. This kind of narrative was not intended to suggest that Francis was permanently shaped by youthful indiscretion, nor that he had lost his sexual purity. Such a caution proved to be the hinge on which revisions in the *Second Life* turned, for in this account Francis's youth was rather characterized by magnanimity, largeness of soul, and respectability in his manners, reinforcing the possibility that he was not the son of his parents. But the correction of the image of Francis was finally not far-reaching enough. And one senses the tension especially in the *Legend of the Three Companions:* he might not have answered back to people who were saying despicable things about him, but among the stories of profligacy, he was still described as ready for fun and even mischievous, "gregarious and worldly."[9]

Even Celano wasn't able to sustain the revised picture of Francis in his *Second Life,* and indeed could not, for if the biographer portrayed Francis without the stains of sin, then any presentation of his conversion would be unnecessary or at least relativized in the story, undermining the biography's overall architecture. Consequently, there is a major transformation in Celano's presentation. Francis became a new person, though the memory of Francis as leader of a band of youths remained prominent in the *Second Life.* These apparent alterations, the attempt to retell the story despite the fact that many of these cosmetic changes did not succeed, speaks for the view that in producing a biography of Francis, the *First Life* rather than the second is to be preferred; in persisting with the narrative in which the youthful Francis sought above all money and adventure, though including the more hagiographical account of his life, the biography is built around his conversion from sin to sanctity. In the history of Christianity, there are at least two other major figures whose story follows such an outline: the apostle Paul, who became a follower of Christ after persecuting Christians, and Augustine, who in his *Confessions* described in detail that although he was a seeker after God before his conversion, this was accompanied by a thoroughly worldly lifestyle. We notice something else that was as true for Francis as it was for Augustine: their tumultuous conversion experience was matched historically by several other less significant conversions or turning points, which makes the prototypical conversion from evil to good, from sinner to saint, more questionable. An unambiguous portrayal of Francis's youth is simply not possible, for the elements we need to flesh out the story of that period are too few.[10]

That neither account is entirely adequate could mean that both are. If we are prepared to pay little regard to accounts that trade in stark contrasts—which both are to some degree—we can expect to paint a picture that is more nuanced or differentiated. If we peek under the covers of religiosity, we can see the obvious fact that Francis grew up as a son who followed the norms of his parents and his world. This is indeed the essential backdrop to the negative presentation of Francis in Celano's *First Life.* In the midst of his profligacy, he could also be painted as "a cautious business man." He could be both successfully apprenticed in his father's business (having learned to read at San Giorgio) but also characterize himself later as unlearned, as completely unschooled or untrained, which was a way of styling his early poverty. His education was certainly not exceptional, but he was skilled in elementary grammar and mathematics. He occasionally wrote texts in Latin, showing that he had learned at least the basics of the language, though he never mastered it. With this in mind, we can say that his identification as unschooled is not entirely false but is certainly an exaggeration of his meager educational achievements.[11]

Other features of his early life also demonstrate a fundamental alignment with the lifestyle of his parents. When we learn, for example, that his clothes were made from costly fabric, as was appropriate to his upbringing, it is best not to imagine that this was an instance of his wasteful lifestyle, but it could equally be a sign that he, along with his parents, celebrated their upwardly mobile station in life and were prepared to break through class barriers by showing off their clothes. Possibly the references to his gang refer to nothing more than memories of an extended friendship circle. Whether he was charismatically gifted, able to form around himself a close-knit network of friends, a characteristic that later found expression in the creation of the brotherhood under vastly different conditions, is hard to tell, though later biographers point us in this direction. The later course of his life probably attests to how his charismatic personality emerged after he found clarity in shaping his message, though we can't say precisely. At the same time, in pointing to signs of early sanctity despite his developing mind, his biographers were prepared to acknowledge how difficult it must have been for him to grow up in a world of money and profits, which created a sense of inner tension. It doesn't take much to imagine that a young man could rebel against his father, a universal trope in human experience, but in Assisi this experience may have been even more likely, given the conflicts between the middling sorts and the nobility, which would call into question the very notion of trust in fundamental values. The pursuit of money and riches that we observe in the commercial contracts of Assisi proved to be for Francis not something positive to emulate, for it had certainly shaken the very foundations of traditional order in the town. Many in Assisi felt these rising tensions, but for Francis these provoked a more fundamental crisis leading to his conversion and a new conception of spiritual life, the legacy of which was to last for centuries. In the end, this tension accounts for the varying narratives of his youth in the two accounts by Celano. What was for Francis something inextricably connected within was explained by Celano through two accounts with different narrative functions.[12]

Restlessness

It wasn't only the early biographers who wanted to find a decisive moment around which to narrate Francis's conversion. This was part of his own account too. In his *Testament*, Francis provided a clear cause for his fresh start: "This is how God inspired me, Brother Francis, to embark upon a life of penance. When I was in sin, the sight of lepers nauseated me beyond measure; but then God himself led me into their company, and I had pity on them. When I had once become acquainted with them, what had previously nauseated me became a source of spiritual and physical consolation for me. After that I did not wait long before leaving the world." According to this recollection, it was when he was confronted by some lepers on the margins of society that his conversion began. In more recent scholarship, this story has proved remarkably influential in isolating the very moment of his singular conversion, freeing interpreters from Celano's (and others') hagiographical accounts and allowing them to locate and relate Francis's experience within the great tradition of conversion stories.[13]

But some degree of caution must be exercised here too. An autobiographical interpretation of one's life remains nonetheless an interpretation; looking to find a moment of breakthrough can be an attempt to locate oneself within a received pattern of conversion. Even Francis acknowledged that it would be reductionist to locate his conversion in his encounter with the lepers alone. His withdrawal from the world, as he reported it, was only achieved after a period of great hesitation. An important reflection, but we need to keep in mind as well other fragmentary elements contributing to his conversionary mindset that are evident in the biographical accounts and are arranged in different ways. His meeting with the lepers was no doubt a significant and destabilizing experience, but it was preceded by other psychic tensions emerging from the contrast between assumed norms and other pressing contingencies. This is mirrored in the various accounts of his conversion, and more particularly the various stages of his conversion that the biographies narrate. Celano and others attempted to make a coherent narrative out of several diverse experiences that otherwise stood alongside each other without shape or any sense of causation. It is for this reason that his restlessness rather than his conversion is the guiding category here, especially since Francis at this moment of his life had not arrived at a sense of clarity about his state, which would normally be the precondition for someone who had undergone conversion.

With these narrative tensions in mind, we need to seek out a more comprehensive category that might serve to hold together various dimensions of Francis's life, for example, the pressures he faced, the changes he experienced, and the new approaches concerning the future he adopted. Instead of merely assembling fragmentary moments from complex narratives, we might choose instead to embrace umbrella terms like "feelings of dissociation," "feelings of dissonance," or "feelings of dislocation" to draw them together, for Francis experienced some measure of psychic tension with his environment as well as within his soul. The most basic experience of dislocation for the merchant's son from Assisi was noted when he looked back at the various episodes of his life that together raised the question of whether his life of material security in the middle class was the right one for him, though he might not have had a clear answer. As his biographers narrated the various episodes, they wanted to outline impactful experiences and give them some shape, though the experiences might not have changed him fundamentally. Celano attempted this narratively when he wrote about early changes in Francis's life, but even he makes the disclaimer that these were internal rather than external. Some accounts project knowledge of the future back into an earlier puzzling conversation, for example, an exchange about possible marriage: "People thought that he wished to take to himself a wife, and they asked him, saying: 'Francis, do you wish to get married?' But he answered them, saying: 'I shall take a more noble and more beautiful spouse than you have ever seen; she will surpass all others in beauty and will excel all others in wisdom.'"[14]

Celano added an interpretation of the conversation straightaway. When Francis spoke of a bride, he was referring to life in the order. Even if a true memory lay behind this account, Celano nevertheless suggested a deeper meaning to a phrase that might have been nothing more than the insignificant musings of a young man. For instance, Francis in one story is speaking to a friend of a costly treasure that he had found, which he intended to be understood as the hidden treasure of the Kingdom of God according to Matthew 13:44, but the friend understood that nothing more was intended than material blessing. This is of course intended to highlight how Francis, though living in the world, was already "holy by reason of his holy purpose." Phrases with double meaning like this are simply an attempt to paint his portrait in contrastive tones, reinforcing thereby the account of his conversion. But biographically they may not be the final word, for the earliest accounts were not so fixed. To be converted might have external consequences, but it can work in the other direction too.[15]

In several accounts, there were of course indubitably factual experiences that shook Francis as a well-to-do citizen of Assisi, and these often had early attestation before the meeting with the lepers. One such devastatingly existential crisis was of war, more especially imprisonment, which Francis experienced when he was around twenty years of age, for Assisi had been at war with Perugia for some years. These two cities lay just twenty-five kilometers apart and battled for preeminence in Umbria. In November 1202, in the town of Collestrada, which was close to both cities, Francis was involved in a very significant battle. He was taken as a prisoner of war, and it was only after a year that he was released, presumably at the conclusion of a peace treaty, subsequently revised, between the two cities in November 1203. For twelve months he was a captive of the Perugians.

The reports of his imprisonment can be found in the *Second Life* of Celano and in the *Legend of the Three Companions,* though other early memories of Francis's life made almost no mention of this episode. But in these two texts, the prison years are reported in great detail despite their worldly context. The most important thing to note here is that Francis is reported to have exhibited exemplary behavior. Both Celano and the Three Companions relate how Francis, perhaps surprisingly, reacted with joy, which apparently was extremely irritating to those imprisoned with him. And Celano provides a religious explanation: Francis found joy in the Lord, enabling him to mock and thereby despise his chains. The account describes in concrete detail how Francis ministered to a fellow prisoner whose unbearable arrogance led others imprisoned there to mock and exclude him. Later biographers saw in this incident some similarity with Francis's approach to those who were marginalized. But we should be careful not to overlook the fact that in the report of the Three Companions, not only is the character of the knight criticized but he is also accused of treating another prisoner unjustly, although we can't be sure how. It appears that Francis withdrew from solidarity with the other prisoners in order to take upon himself the role of an outsider. All of this appears in the sources over forty years after the events, with little connection to historical accounts. The sources do, however, recognize that Francis fulfilled a very particular role among the prisoners, in all likelihood because he was the only representative of the bourgeoisie in a prison made to accommodate the nobility, even if it was barely comfortable for them. Despite the Three Companions suggesting that he was imprisoned there because of his courtly manners, it was his poor health that really explains the outcome. His marginal existence beyond the fellowship of the prisoners was to some degree mitigated through the welcome opportunity the ostracized knight provided him to find a friend there among all the strangers. Whether or not the middle-class conditions that had shaped his style of life made things in jail easier for him than for the nobles can only be surmised. Overall references to his happiness in the jail are too vague to draw settled historical conclusions. It is possible that particular moments of torture that he survived led to more general conclusions about his emotional state.[16]

More interesting, however, is what followed his imprisonment. In his *First Life*, Celano relates how after his incarceration Francis experienced a grave and prolonged illness, giving rise to the assumption that its origins can be traced back to his onerous imprisonment. It is possible that it was there that Francis first encountered the sickness from which he suffered until the end of his life. It appears that it was not the time in jail itself but rather the sickness he contracted there that functioned as the tipping point in revising his own view of the world and sense of self. From the perspective of Celano's *First Life*, which highlighted Francis's troublesome youth, his imprisonment represented God's providential intervention, the consequences of which would be positive change and growth in holiness, leading to a fascinating critical question concerning the sources. In this view, it was Francis's sickness (not social conditions or bad company) that led him to see the world around him more pessimistically, perhaps going against the grain of the whole narrative. He lost joy in the fields and vineyards around Assisi, which does suggest something of the reliability of the account as it stands in tension with Francis's later famed nature piety. This defiant rejection of nature as an essential part of his conversion narrative therefore can't be explained as a projection of later habits of life, but rather seems to represent the transmission of reliable memories.[17]

Then Celano took another step to recount Francis's transformed outlook: "From that day on, therefore, he began to despise himself and to hold in some contempt the things he had admired and loved before." Francis despised not just the outer nature but even his own self and—especially noteworthy—the affections of his soul. When we acknowledge the later development of his spirituality, we observe here elements of a penitential frame of mind, borne out in the contrast with his parents' path as merchants. This feeling of dislocation only got worse when his parents didn't change their lifestyle, though Francis does fall again into worldliness. Yet the neatness of this account does raise some critical questions. Perhaps we should assume that the account of his doubt about nature is reliably sourced from his more penitential frame of mind. Then we could say with confidence that Francis's sickness shook him to rethink the direction of his life, which stretched out before him so comfortably, without tying his rejection down to any particular incident. Perhaps Julian of Speyer understands the incident correctly when he writes that Francis began "to think differently about things than he had been accustomed."[18]

If this story of imprisonment reflects a personal crisis in Francis's life, other episodes might better highlight how social crises in Assisi confused him. He experienced how old social assumptions no longer seemed relevant or capable of keeping society together, for example, when he met a poor knight on the side of the road and gave him his clothes, a suggestive parallel with one of the great representatives of piety in the Western church, Martin of Tours, who divided his cloak with a poor man and recognized Christ in him. It is sheer irony that Martin as a knight was supporting a beggar, but now the beggar was really a knight, perfectly capturing the social tensions that Francis felt: acquired wealth stood in contrast with received nobility. And just because the parallel with Martin seems too easy doesn't mean that it is entirely fabricated, for other elements in the story highlight independence of provenance.[19]

A little later something else occurred, demonstrating more clearly still the social tensions within which he lived. According to Celano's *First Life*, Francis wanted to travel to Apulia with a nobleman from Assisi to accrue both money and honor. At first it appears simply to have been an opportunity to prove himself in military service again. At the beginning of the thirteenth century, Walter of Brienne had attempted to protect his wife's inheritance in Apulia with the support of the pope, and Francis had imagined he could make himself useful, perhaps even to make amends for his earlier unsuccessful military adventure against Perugia. However, John of Perugia adds complexity to this account, for he pitches it as an attempt by Francis to achieve a change of social standing: "After giving the matter much thought, he decided to become a knight to obtain this princely power. After having as expensive a wardrobe as possible made for himself, he arranged to join up with a noble count in Apulia, to be knighted by him." This observation concerning Francis's desire for upward mobility is likely to be reliable, not just because John belongs to a relatively early group of independent witnesses but more importantly because he actually knew the name of Count Gentile, who in the writings of Celano went unnamed, though in the account of the Three Companions his name might be capitalized as a given name or written without the initial capital, thus functioning as an adjective. It appears that a very particular memory is in play here that relates to Francis's social ambition, attested to elsewhere in a recurring dream he experienced before setting out. In the dream, the entire bourgeois estate of a merchant had been transformed into a knight's armory.[20]

Of course there are many ways to interpret a dream, but the vision of arms took place exactly at that moment when Celano recalled Francis's break with his former life and began to stress God's role in leading the saint on his journey. In Bonaventure's *Major Life*, reference to the transformation of the Bernardone home is missing, but there is mention of a palace and the inclusion of God saying to Francis: "Go back to your own town. The vision which you saw foretold a spiritual achievement which will be accomplished in you by God's will, not man's." This spiritual interpretation, which biographers since Celano have kept in view, has been narrated alongside another account, even though its relationship with that narrative doesn't always fit naturally with its flow. It appears that enthusiasm for the life of a knight with his weapons held early appeal for Francis, such that he, unlike those citizens of Assisi who fought for equivalence between their civic life and that of the nobility, actually aspired to transcend his bourgeois social standing. This also points to the fact that in relation to his family background, Francis's divergence from his parents' values was not essentially religious. His attempts at social climbing were a sign that the young merchant despised or at least set little store by parental norms. He looked down on his parents through the eyes of those who were opposed by the bourgeois citizens of Assisi.[21]

Such a social conflict exacerbated an existential conflict for the Bernardone household. This was more than about the challenge of war; rather, it concerned the loosening of the bonds that held Francis to a parental home that he felt was increasingly constrictive. And it is exactly this existential dimension of the social experience of dislocation that appears to have provoked (among other things) his conversion. According to the development of the narrative told by his biographers, it was in the jumble of ambitions toward nobility amid middle-class constraints that he experienced what came to be such a profound turning point in his life. He had traveled just one or two days when he arrived in Spoleto, half asleep, according to the Three Companions, and here he experienced God anew, not so much as a vision in a dream but more as a voice that asked him what his business there was. When Francis replied, he was subsequently asked, "Who do you think can best reward you, the Master or the servant?" Even in the way the question was posed, we see how the voice, which Francis interpreted as being the Lord's, is suggesting to the traveler a fundamental mistake in his hierarchy of values. His aspiration to achieve fame, honor, or even preeminence was nothing more than seeking out earthly companionship, whereupon the voice reminded him that all mundane authority is finally subject to another and higher Lord. So God then called on Francis to convert: "Return to your own place and you will be told what to do."[22]

The meaning of this tale, however, is found when we look beyond the mere details of the story, for it combines the admonition to the patriarch Jacob in Genesis 32:10 to leave Mesopotamia to return to his homeland with the instruction from the Lord to the apostle Paul to head to Damascus to discover there what he was expected to do next (Acts 9:6). Adopting such a dialogue format gives us a clue to the narrator's intention—namely, to present Francis's experience as corresponding to Paul's experience, both as types of sudden conversion to which Celano, with his knowledge of Christian history, deliberately draws our attention. This kind of interpretation would have been part of the account even before it was integrated into the stories of Francis's life, for in those works it was largely other moments of his life onto which a more explicit conversion experience was projected. The narrative incorporates a memory that reinforces the notion that Francis's conversion was a long process, achieved through multiple stages. But even in its retelling here it is clear that it is shrouded with legendary associations when God's voice at the conclusion of the dialogue said: "You must interpret your vision in a different sense." This statement presupposes the spiritual interpretation of the vision of the weapons chamber, which is only meaningful when looking back on the whole of Francis's life. The voice he heard in Spoleto combined with the vision of the armory together constitute the most fundamental of turning points arranged providentially by God, overshadowing any other possible reasons that might have shaken Francis from his previous path.[23]

It is surprising nonetheless that in his *First Life* Celano recounted nothing of this experience of Francis at Spoleto, but he did describe how he turned back from his intention to visit Apulia immediately after having the dream of his parents' home turned into an armory. Uniquely in the account of Celano, upon waking Francis did not rejoice in the dream and the prospect of knightly joy—as later the Three Companions would suggest—but instead he had to force himself to complete his plans. And for this turn of events, Celano used an ambiguous turn of phrase. Perhaps most obviously he might have meant that Francis forced himself to get to Apulia, but equally he might have intended to convey the idea that Francis forced himself to repudiate that plan and therefore never set out at all, never actually passed through Spoleto. The voice in Spoleto is not mentioned in the *First Life,* and even in the *Second Life,* which does make mention of the voice, the place where Francis heard it was not named, nor was there any doubt about the action he should take in response: he returned home without delay. And this is exactly the way that Julian of Speyer tells the story: it took increasing effort for Francis to persevere with his travel plans, until finally he gave up on them altogether. His decision to remain would then have been taken before setting out, according to the *First Life* and according to Julian, without any clear intervention from outside, although the Three Companions do refer to the incident in Spoleto. However, they offer a further complicating detail: Francis had fallen ill during his stay there. And John of Perugia offers yet another detail beyond the context of Spoleto that he shares with the Companions: even before Francis heard the voice, he found himself in anguish concerning his itinerary. In both sources, Francis experienced some measure of irritation before hearing the voice. If we bring all these features together, we can surely conclude that Francis had enough reasons to discontinue his journey even without the voice making its demand on him. Falling sick on the way might be the most plausible reason of all, but the incidents narrated are surely fascinating areas to explore, even if they remain unexplained by Celano and John of Perugia. Perhaps it was Francis who couldn't satisfactorily explain his change of plans after his initial enthusiasm.[24]

It seems reasonable to suppose that the explanation must be understood in relation to the broader arc of Francis's biography. At this stage, his experience of imprisonment lay only two years in the past. Warfare and being a prisoner of war can be seen as experiences of upheaval that no doubt contributed to post-traumatic stress, as we have come to understand so well in the twenty-first century. Of course, we have to be wary of projecting back onto the life of Francis a contemporary diagnosis after nine hundred years, but it is not unreasonable to assume that Francis's mood might have swung between the hopes of finally making good on his failed mission to Perugia a few years earlier and the possibility of experiencing failure once again. But on this occasion, his disgrace may have been magnified, especially in the eyes of his father, for if it is true that Francis had bought new clothes for the journey, the irony of the whole situation and the increasing conflict with his father would be abundantly clear. Francis, after all, was a merchant in his family's business and lived in their home, so presuming to wear fine clothes would have been a burden to the business, even if he could purchase them cheaply himself. The episode only served to provoke his father, who underwrote their purchase, signifying their wearer as belonging to an elevated social group. In the light of this, it may be both too simple and yet perfectly acceptable to say—like John of Perugia—that this episode falls into the larger story of Francis's conflict with his father concerning money, which ultimately led Francis to distance himself from the family home. If Francis and his father had already fought about money, then in this account spending it on a horse and clothes for his journey to Apulia provoked further conflict. And it wasn't John of Perugia alone who saw in this interrupted journey to Apulia—or perhaps one never actually undertaken—the first and perhaps most dramatic turning point in the life of the young son of the merchant from Assisi.[25]

It is Julian of Speyer who makes the most of this conversion when he describes Francis no longer as a worldly salesman but as a merchant for the Gospel ("evangelicus negotiator"). Like John of Perugia, Julian wants to show that Francis's understanding of the Gospel went against the grain of his parents' values, just as might have been the case if he had followed through on his plan to become a soldier and knight. But we need to exercise some caution before making too quick a connection between the Gospel and his life choices, for the accounts draw attention to a variety of possibilities, not all easily reconciled with each other, that provoked a crisis for Francis. He might have indulged several types of affections, among which the pull toward a more radically intensive model of piety in contrast with more conventional religion was one. Celano begins with just such an exalted posture of piety, which represented in his telling a complete change of heart, even if this transformation had not yet begun to reform Francis's external patterns of obedience. He began to withdraw from social life and from business dealings in order to experience Christ in his heart. And it was apparently in this period that his friendship blossomed with another young man, about whom we don't know very much except that Francis trusted him with his innermost secrets. But even then there seems to have been a limit to their friendship, for the friend understood Francis's talk of treasure to refer to something material. The friend was also shut out from the ecstatic prayer that Francis adopted in this period, for Francis is said, according to Celano and the Three Companions, to have gone into a grotto alone to undertake some spiritual warfare in prayer before returning completely exhausted. As in other biographical sections of the accounts of Francis's life, it is difficult here to capture precise details, especially their chronology. While Celano brings together the experience of ecstatic prayer with the experience of war, the Three Companions situate other experiences between the two.[26]

These various events form the backdrop to what Francis himself later presented as the most decisive event of all: his encounter with the lepers. Whatever impact the experience of being a prisoner of war had on Francis, and whatever else contributed to his growing identity crisis, this new encounter made his wounds still more tender and clarified his growing awareness of being an outsider, which is perhaps why he later stressed this experience so much. It pointed him to a new appreciation of the radical distance he had come from his former lifestyle and from a commercialized understanding of the world of his upbringing. Nowhere was such an intensive awareness more evident than among the lepers, for their sickness had not just physical but social ramifications as well. Those suffering with the disease and its attending disfigurements were driven from the cities. If they were lucky, they found refuge in special hospices that aimed to care for the sick rather than cure their sickness with medicinal interventions. Awareness of the danger of being infected was high, so most people avoided contact where possible. Even the hospices were located at some distance from the towns; for example, the leprosy hospice for Assisi, San Lazzaro dell'Arce, was more than a kilometer from the city's border. Typical reactions to those suffering from leprosy are recounted by the Three Companions: passersby would pinch their noses to avoid the smell of the festering wounds and would always hand over alms through a third person, thus fulfilling their financial duty to love their neighbor without ever actually coming into direct contact with them. This kind of modest behavior was rational and in line with the best notions of medicine and protection against infection in the thirteenth century, which focused on avoiding further spread.[27]

Against this background, Francis's behavior on one occasion was particularly outrageous. He got off his horse, handed to one leper some alms without the aid of an intermediary, kissed his hand, and received in turn the kiss of peace. This was a practice from the Eucharistic liturgy attested by St. Augustine in which, as a sign of greeting, the lips of fellow believers came close to each other but never touched. Francis's action was spontaneous but not without precedent: he followed the example of Martin of Tours in this, but if true, it was no less extraordinary for that. From the perspective of science, this was clearly risky behavior, but the biographers are united in recounting the story of Francis overcoming his emotional aversion in order to draw this leper back into the world of social relationships although he was under no compulsion to do so. For Francis, on the other hand, it was a step away from the society that he had known, embracing the risk of infection to draw close to those he had previously avoided. If Francis's decision to renounce military adventures and the desire to become a knight is understood as a return to the norms of his previous social standing, then his approach toward the lepers of the town should be seen as a step in a completely new direction. According to this logic, it is no wonder that the biographers normally place the encounter with the lepers after Francis's repudiation of his ambition to become a knight and the aborted trip to Apulia. Of course, whether or not this was the historical sequence we can no longer adjudicate. But nonetheless, whether placed in this narrative order or not, these incidents represent Francis's tense relationship with the values of his family. His striving for knighthood demonstrated his dissatisfaction within the social order of his day. And his turn to the lepers—whether early or late—reflected his repudiation of the glue of civic or noble social values. Francis made himself an outsider. As the Franciscan Anton Rotzetter has so pointedly said, "After he kissed the leper, the lepers became life partners with St. Francis."[28]

We should remind ourselves of how drastic this turn of events really was. As the son of a rich merchant, Francis had every chance to take his place at the center—perhaps even the apex—of society. Yet he tested out possibilities other than those expected roles, and turned toward the opposite, the lowest rung of society, as many an adolescent might do in their own developmental experimentation. But with Francis, if the stories of the encounter with the leper are true, these steps were about not just self-exploration but potentially self-destruction if taken to the extreme. So perhaps the most challenging question in our interpretation should be: were these self-destructive characteristics the equivalent of today's drug addict? For it was not just once that Francis served the lepers; he repeatedly visited them. He might have been expressing his opposition to the norms of his day, or alternatively demonstrating his commitment to new and different sets of duties, in which case serving the interests of the lepers was equivalent to taking a step toward fulfilling traditional works of mercy, as Jesus himself had taught concerning the Last Judgment in Matthew 25:35–36: to those who had escaped condemnation he said: "For I was hungry and you gave me food, I was thirsty and you gave me something to drink, I was a stranger and you welcomed me, I was naked and you gave me clothing, I was sick and you took care of me, I was in prison and you visited me."[29]

However, it is worth noting that this particular motivation for service barely gets a mention in the Franciscan tradition—quite different from his contemporary Elizabeth of Hungary—and therefore does not shape the literary form of the incident with the leper in any significant ways. Celano attempted instead to place the encounter in the realm of the miraculous, for according to his account the leper whom Francis had kissed suddenly and without explanation disappeared from the story, classically a literary indication that this leper was not a real person but an appearance of God. Perhaps this account submits to the rules of hagiography, though it is less clearly aligned with the behavior of Jesus. Either way, both approaches should then be seen not as stories deliberately crafted as theological statements but instead as genuine memories of events experienced, and as occasions to explore not merely the Christian ideal of care for the most vulnerable in society but Francis's growing negative evaluation of his parents' social and economic roles in society.[30]

In contrast to the question of money and wealth, themes in the later story of the Franciscan movement as well as in its origins, we observe how Francis's concern for the lepers took precedence. It was no accident that in his *Testament* Francis put his encounter with the lepers at the very beginning and center of his new religious existence. It was those who came after him who shifted the emphasis. For example, John of Perugia focused on the issue of poverty when he described how Francis shunned a beggar in his shop even before recounting the story of traveling to Apulia. Later Francis second-guessed his decision, asking if he would have shunned the beggar if he had come asking for money not for himself but for some baron or count. John's narrative is so exquisitely shaped, with the concern about poverty a clear focus, that it is hard to see it as a historical report. But it must also be acknowledged that his account does reflect other foundational themes from the early years of Francis's life, not least how his professed values were shaken when he saw their potential application to social forms (like the question concerning the nobility) or in their religious interpretation. John had chiefly projected onto the young Francis the notion that Jesus Christ had met him in the poor.[31]

At this stage of his life, when Francis turned to the poor, we shouldn't think first of his concrete and active obedience to the commandment of Christ but instead his path toward the life of a dropout, with which this merchant's son increasingly flirted, even if this was only occasionally acknowledged by him. As we have seen, Celano's evaluation that Francis had experienced some kind of change in his soul but not in his physical life reflects well the fact that there were yet no visible changes emerging from his early feelings of dislocation, suggesting that in these early years of upheaval, he still had not found a clear alternative to the professed values of his parents. His irritation was most concretely expressed in the way he distanced himself from other youths in the town. Even if he can't be identified as one of their ringleaders, it is easy to imagine him as one of their number who in time withdrew from the crowd. The *Legend of the Three Companions* recounts how once when traveling with friends, he was so gripped by the Spirit of God that he could no longer move and all of a sudden stopped walking. His companions on the road had kept walking, so when they turned around to ask him what the matter was, whether he was arrested by the thought of getting married, he replied that he wanted a more attractive bride than they could ever imagine. The story had been elaborated after the accounts given in the *First* and *Second Life* of Celano. Those reading this at the beginning of the 1240s would immediately have understood such a wife to be Lady Poverty herself, to whom Francis would be bound, according to the title of the allegorical account *The Sacrum Commercium; or, Francis and His Lady Poverty.* It is just as apparent that those friends on the road would have struggled to understand Francis's statement and no doubt had laughed at him because they didn't think he was at all well positioned to find such a beautiful bride. Despite the prophetic intent of the resulting narrative, it remains true that Francis was not always accompanied by his friends and was perhaps even lost in his thoughts even if technically present with them. His way of life became increasingly difficult and irritating for his contemporaries as he began to behave in ways that brought to light deeper feelings of emotional dislocation.[32]

In the midst of this process, he became more and more aware of the fact that his own wealth was not something he should take for granted. Without it being really clear that his earliest ethical motivation was essentially Christian, he began to share his prosperity not just with lepers but with the poor more generally, yet still without redefining the boundaries of his bourgeois existence, according to the accounts of the 1240s. For example, in Celano's *Second Life,* he was identified as "chief lover of the poor" as he gave away his clothes to them. The *Legend of the Three Companions* relates this posture concretely and presumably therefore realistically:

> He was already a benefactor of the poor, but from this time onwards he
> resolved never to refuse alms to anyone who begged in God's name; but
> rather to give more willingly and abundantly than ever before. If a poor
> person begged of him when he was far from home, he would always give him

money, if possible; when he had none, he would give his belt or buckle; or, if he had not even these, he would find a hiding place and, taking off his shirt, give it to the beggar for the love of God.[33]

Looking back, this appears to anticipate Francis's later decision to devote himself to a life of poverty, and of course it is not unrelated. But understood as a discrete phase of his life, not assuming his later sanctity, this could represent nothing more than the intentional fulfillment of familial expectations to provide alms. It was a conventional practice in the Bernardone household to care for those suffering from leprosy, even if the practice was perfunctory rather than heartfelt. The Three Companions might merely be referring to this, even though Francis in this account may have given more than usual. We should take seriously nonetheless that the reference to him giving generously "when he was far from home" alerts the reader to the probable historical nature of this characteristic practice. He made good use of the realm outside the parental home to practice almsgiving beyond what was expected of him. And this he did with aforethought as he took coins to give away, though distributing his clothes was likely to be a more spontaneous and muddle-headed offer. He probably didn't plan to give away a belt or hat or his undershirt, though he did choose not to draw attention to himself by doing this in a concealed location rather than publicly. In all these ways, Francis was testing himself with new commitments and practices out of sight of his worrisome parents, especially his father. We see again how he lacked contentment within his present circumstances but also the wish not to lose the status he had. He was still constrained by the expectations of his family, though pushing at the limits of those expectations in small ways. What Celano describes as a simple contrast between soul and body was actually a symptom of profound uncertainty and confusion of values on the one side, and on the other fear of revealing his feelings to his father.

In this regard, the Three Companions contribute an important element to the discussion, for they draw our attention to incidents that took place while Francis's father was away. He set the table for the entire family, even though only he and his mother were at home, with the explanation that the surplus bread was intended for those in need, which his mother accepted, for she "loved him more than her other children." Unfortunately, however, we have to exercise caution in evaluating this account, for the oldest son fearing his father but being loved and protected by his mother was a standard trope in literature. Indeed, the pattern reached back to the biblical story of Jacob and Esau and has been retold with different characters on numerous occasions, if sometimes stressing the mother's love rather than fear of the father. The question is raised whether the emphasis given here to "those in need" was later written back into the account or belonged to this early phase of Francis's biography, sitting uncomfortably as it did with different trajectories within it. And even if there is some exaggeration in the account we have, it is nonetheless likely that there is a kernel of truth in the story; there does appear to have been conflict between father and son in the Bernardone household, regardless of Francis's status as his mother's favorite son. Acknowledging the myriad changes that have come to pass in families and households over the intervening centuries, recognition of tensions within families between parents and their adolescent children is something that joins their family to many others through time.[34]

Francis's spiritual search took many forms, though his choices risked causing further irritation to this father. Among them, one story is told—with only limited historical corroboration—of Francis himself living a life of poverty that was provoked, according to the biographies, by a journey to Rome intended as a pilgrimage. This was in a period before pilgrimages to Rome were taken up with new enthusiasm among the masses across Europe with the proclamation of a Jubilee in 1300; a plenary indulgence was promised to any pilgrim who visited the seven station churches. But even at the beginning of the thirteenth century, Rome was a spiritual destination, given that both Peter and Paul were buried there. Other inhabitants of Assisi made the trek to Rome too, for example, Ortulana Offreduccio, the mother of Francis's later spiritual sister Clare, for the Eternal City was only two hundred kilometers away. Thus that Francis chose to visit Rome is not at all surprising, and he had the added motivation of making good his failed military adventure in Apulia, not to pursue war this time but to visit the graves of the apostles, now housed within magnificent churches built in the time of the Emperor Constantine: St. Paul outside the Walls, and St. Peter's Basilica in the Vatican, which predates the Renaissance cathedral of St. Peter's that we know today. To draw near the bones of the apostles in veneration was in effect to draw near to the presence of God himself as well as to the origins of Christianity, though there is much modern scholarship investigating the true resting place of the apostles' remains. Because both Peter and Paul died as martyrs, it was assumed that their obedience to Christ was perfect, making the glory of Christ present to pilgrims. When understood in the context of a widely held form of medieval spirituality, the piety of representation, even their bones were considered material representations of the presence of Christ and consequently Jesus Christ was venerated through them. This would have provided the spiritual meaning of Francis's visit to Rome, if indeed it happened.[35]

If he did visit Rome, it was here that Francis could undertake a probationary life of poverty. Yet even here it was irritation rather than resolution that propelled his choices. He saw how little people gave to the churches as their offering, so he determined to give generously, perhaps even recklessly, by leaving behind on an altar a pile of coins. Upon leaving the cathedral, he confronted a throng of beggars and decided, again spontaneously, to take off his own clothes and put on beggarly rags instead. In this scene, it is possible that different accounts have been confused, as it is highly unlikely that Francis would have worn his normal costly clothes if he were undertaking a pilgrimage, but instead would have clothed himself in a penitential robe or hair shirt. In fact, he may have worn a hair shirt underneath his precious clothes, another indication that he wanted to hide a growing antipathy toward his parents' lifestyle, even if that transition was not yet visibly complete. On a trip to Rome, however, there would have been no reason to hide his penitential robe. Or perhaps it was the case that his penitential robe was still opulent compared with the rags he saw on the beggars, such that the Three Companions wove into the account of his visit to Rome events from his life in Assisi. In each of these scenarios, we are still forced to ask the question of how believable the entire episode is. If Francis did indeed take the clothes of a poor beggar, he almost certainly then spent time on the steps of St. Peter's living as a beggar himself, with the whole episode narrated as a discrete experience, for we are then told by the Three Companions that he returned the rags to the beggar and put his own robe back on in readiness for the return journey to Assisi. This whole encounter can only be seen as realistic if the clothing swap was something premeditated and not spontaneous, emphasizing even more the probationary character of this decision, for the Three Companions tell us that the whole point of the journey to Rome was to find a town away from Assisi to change clothes and thereby to change roles. This corresponds with the comment by Celano in his *Second Life* that Francis had long wanted to live among the poor if only this would not disgrace him in the sight of his friends.[36]

This whole story, which in its several elements appears to ring true, reinforces the claim that Francis in this phase of his life was deeply shaken by the lifestyle handed on to him by his parents, so sought out contrasting patterns or models for a more satisfying life. In a sense, we can look back from his later life and see here a preview of his commitment to a life of poverty. Perhaps this really was Francis testing himself as well, flirting with a life of poverty to see if it suited him. And, more fundamentally, we see here Francis adopting a new mode of living yet doing so hesitantly for fear of disappointing and breaking with his family. They would never know from a distance that their son was experimenting with self-denial while at home he continued to conform to their social expectations. It would be extraordinarily difficult to maintain this kind of psychic tension in the long haul. He swung between extremes, overdoing it by kissing the leper and by being abundantly generous, exceeding his parents' own commitments to giving alms, and when in Rome he even left behind his station in life to explore a new identity. In sum, we are left with the impression that this young man's most basic values had been shaken beyond repair, with the suspicion that the trigger for all this reevaluation had been pulled when he first experienced warfare and imprisonment as a soldier.

Thrown Down at His Feet: Rupture with His Father

All of these experiences happened before Francis was twenty. As a young man, he was still conflicted between life within his family's sphere of influence and his possible rejection of their values, all the while knowing that there was something just not right with his parents' attitudes. And in growing up, he came to understand, like many young adults, that he needed to distance himself from the values his parents had passed on to him, without clearly discerning an alternative path. But at least this was clear: what might have remained merely a crisis of adolescence in his case had a religious dimension that was to have an impact reaching far beyond his own life.

In all the accounts, as overlapping or filtered as they may be, the tension between Francis and his family emerges effortlessly, and it is just such spontaneity that distinguishes him and his behavior from other patrons in Assisi who behaved like him. In the Middle Ages, of course, lepers and the poor were cared for. That lepers gained their livelihood through begging and the fact that lepers' hospitals existed not only acknowledged their social exclusion, but from a different perspective were also strategies for their integration. In both instances, the healthy and the rich were offered the chance to support the marginalized and thereby to do good works according to Christian principles. But for Francis this kind of piety effectively objectified the recipients. The system of almsgiving in the medieval period certainly provided a measure of integration for those who were poor and rejected, as both the donor and the recipient belonged to the same communication network. Objects of piety the poor and afflicted certainly were, but subjects of the common life they were not. And it was just this hurdle that Francis attempted to surmount, demonstrating his ambivalence toward his social background. One way of leaving behind his bourgeois ways—his pursuit of the life of a knight, with its upward social mobility—had been unsuccessful, but now he sought another strategy to distance himself from that pattern of life through downward social mobility, by serving the poor, before he renounced middle-class norms entirely.

That Francis the social dropout would choose a religious exit could not have been easily anticipated. The pathways his biographers described may have been in part their own pious construction. It is uncontested that before he was known to offer the greeting of peace to others, he was first greeted by a leper with a kiss. His subsequent practice of begging took shape when visiting Rome, though later accounts are not clear in their details. Looking back on his life, the biographical fragments cannot easily be distinguished from the established patterns of writing in such biographies. This is also true of one of the most dramatic of Francis's early religious gestures, his connection with the small church of San Damiano, just a couple of minutes' walk south of Assisi in the valley, although this church is easily missed today when streams of tourists head directly up the hill to the grave of Francis and the frescoes of Giotto. The church's spirit of simplicity, which is hard to imagine in contrast with Assisi itself, is striking. It was to play an extraordinarily important role in Francis's later life, but at the beginning his connection with this church appeared to be an expression of spontaneous and exaggerated piety. We read in Celano's *First Life* that as Francis was setting out on a normal business trip, the expectation was that he should first cross himself. As was typical in accounts of the saints, we note how his life as a merchant was not without signs of piety, though such a pious life was radically different from its later expression. This merchant lived his life under the sign of the cross, though at this stage it didn't fundamentally change his heart but was rather a nod to the overall framework of his life and the source of his protection. Indeed, on this business trip he experienced the providence of the Lord when in Foligno, some fourteen kilometers from Assisi, he sold costly scarlet fabric and even his horse when a good deal presented itself. The deal done, he had to carry quite a sum of money back with him to Assisi, which caused him to wonder "with a religious mind what he should do with the money." Upon reaching San Damiano, we learn from Celano that Francis "proposed" to do something in particular with his profit, a word that we have met before and is likely to have been carefully chosen by the biographers to position his decisions within a greater narrative arc. At this stage, though, there doesn't really appear much that is premeditated in his life; instead, his encounters give the impression of spontaneous acts without much underlying structure.[37]

Yet despite this, there may be one area of his life that naturally expresses intentionality, for Francis didn't merely demonstrate his love of neighbor but also his love of the church, and one church building in particular. Serving the sick and the poor can find its origin in several different kinds of motivation, Christian or not, but being committed to loving and serving a particular church, San Damiano, does point to a sustained pattern in Francis's life. Recognizing the dilapidated state of the building and the needs of the poor priest (whose name was possibly Peter), Francis insisted on giving him his money. According to Celano, Francis wanted to hand over to the priest all that he had. This probably lies closer to the truth than the account by John of Perugia, which is otherwise similar to Celano's. For John, the money was not to be seen as a gift; rather it was given to the priest for safekeeping, stressing Francis's foresight. But this barely makes sense, for Francis as a merchant was always receiving money and he wouldn't just deposit it anywhere. This detail only makes sense if someone like John of Perugia already knew with hindsight that Francis was soon to underwrite repairs to the church. The spontaneity of Celano's account, so emphatically asserted and fitting in its biographical context, is robbed of its meaning in John's story. As he had kissed the leper, so Francis here kissed the hands of the priest, creating an important parallel in the later narrative, for the hands of the priest laid claim to an elevated sanctity. In the Eucharist, the church completed its sacrifice of Christ, with the priest's hands touching Christ's body, just as Francis, in touching the lepers, the least of the brothers, touched Christ himself. No one had permission to come so close to Christ as the priest, whose very hands handled him.[38]

According to Celano, Francis presented a twofold concern to the priest: he wanted to give him all his money, and he wanted to find a dwelling in San Damiano, which might nudge us to see in this encounter a central moment in Francis's life. His conflicted existence, in which his sense of distance from the reality around him was often only momentarily felt and mainly kept hidden, now came to a crossroads, although the choice before him still lacked clear definition. San Damiano was not a monastery and Francis was not a priest. And this new turn in his life was not expected, for the priest resisted the twofold request, and as Celano wrote, this was not least because he knew Francis as the wealthy merchant's son and knew of his prodigal lifestyle. Such a quick about-face on Francis's part just isn't plausible. The priest stood his ground in refusing to take the money, though his reason for doing so was shocking: he feared the Bernardone family. However, he was prepared to give Francis lodging. At this juncture, Francis threw the money onto the windowsill (according to Celano) and despised it as dust.[39]

Now for the first time we see, if we can trust this account, Francis's clear hatred of his social background explained through religious action and his unambiguous decision to distance himself from his parents. With one hesitation: the connection of this account to San Damiano, given emphasis in the narrative because for later Franciscans it was a place of great sanctity, proved significant also because it was here that Clare and her sisters would in time make their base. Here some verses of the famous *Canticle of Brother Sun* would be composed. That this was the site where Francis experienced such a significant turning point in this life could explain its place in the later story, but the opposite could also be true: this early encounter might have had layers of meaning applied to it later. Celano, and in part John of Perugia and Julian of Speyer, tell the story with deliberate allusion to Francis's holy pursuit of poverty beginning at that moment: "He sold all that he had and offered the money gained thereby to a certain poor priest. But the priest refused to take the money because of his fear of Francis's parents; at this, Francis immediately threw the money down at the priest's feet since he considered it to be so much dirt."[40]

It was in this way that Celano drafted his version of the life of Francis for the liturgical use of the brothers in the chancel. Of particular note in this quotation is what is included and what is left out. Significantly, Francis is said to have thrown his money onto the ground, not the windowsill. Of course, this might be explained by Celano needing to write with a rhythm that was useful in the liturgy, but this aside, though the architectural niche is still pointed out as a notably visible point of reference for his biography in San Damiano, in Celano's account its absence means that it still hadn't received the sanctified meaning fitting for the veneration of a saint. Other things are missing too, for example, the commission of Christ that appears shortly after, or any thought of what else the money could have been used for. By including, however, the words of Jesus from Matthew 19:21 exhorting the rich man to "sell your possessions, and give money to the poor," Celano adds a further theological reflection, suggesting the value of the redemption of his money in order to aid the poor. This episode was to play a large role in Francis's later ministry. Clearly Celano here is superimposing onto the episode in San Damiano an interpretative layer of meaning, pointing to Francis's later life of poverty. This approach therefore gives support to the commitment of later Franciscans to mendicancy, though it doesn't go far enough to establish the veneration of Francis himself. Indeed, one looks in vain for a passage in the biographies of Francis that has been as intensively shaped as this one. What in Celano's *First Life* is presented as an entirely spontaneous act of Francis is reshaped in the early 1240s to present him in a completely different light.

However, the first unambiguous account of San Damiano as the location for an encounter with Christ can be found in the *Legend of the Three Companions*. Serving as both a commission from Jesus Christ and at the same time an origin story that is paramount in forming his holy memory in the later Franciscan tradition, it was the crucifix of San Damiano, an impressive example of twelfth-century Umbrian painting under the influence of Syrian art (moved in around 1260 to the church of Santa Chiara in Assisi), that focused his aspirations. In this account, it is not after a business trip to Foligno that Francis entered this small church, but after one of the many conversations he had with irritated friends from Assisi. As he was walking near the church, the Spirit of God intervened to encourage him to go in to pray. So far this sequence of events is nothing out of the ordinary in middle-class piety, as we have seen already when Francis crossed himself, for everyday prayer was an established Christian practice. But what happened next according to the account of the Three Companions is a marked escalation of everyday norms. When Francis prayed before this crucifix, now made famous through mass tourism, the crucified one began to speak: "Francis, do you not see that my house is falling into ruin? Go, and repair it for me." And Francis immediately agreed, even if this decision, as the Companions note, may not have been entirely understood by him, for he interpreted the command to be a literal call to repair the fabric of the building in San Damiano, not a spiritual exhortation to repair the church of Jesus Christ. This kind of confusion recurs in the story of Francis, for example, when he met Pope Innocent III and oscillated in his understanding of repair of the entire church of Christ compared with repair of the Lateran Basilica.[41]

The encounter with the crucifix likely reflects hagiography rather than pure historical reportage, especially since Francis himself never mentioned this encounter in his own *Testament,* but it connects a great moment of revelation with a later event, the foundation of the Franciscan community. But there is no reason to assume, on the other hand, that the Three Companions invented the whole thing. It only took around fifteen years from the death of Francis for the memory of the crucifix to become so embedded in the narrative that those biographers began to appeal to an early experience of Christ's leading that would go on to shape the entirety of Francis's life, with the addition of ever more intensive attributes along the way. That Francis spoke to a crucifix is significant in the resulting literary form, for typical of the age was the acknowledgment of the wounds of Christ, which invited Francis to an identification with him. Celano writes deliberately in the *Second Life* of the compassion Francis felt for the one who had been crucified, and by extension compassion for all Christians who lose themselves in the Savior to the point of identification. His compassion was not just for saints. The condescension of the Son of God to human beings makes possible our being raised to God himself through the wounds and the suffering of the Savior. But in this account, Celano intensified the impact of the crucifix of San Damiano by pointing further than the importance of the imitation of Christ to the miraculous occasion of the stigmatization of Francis, which we will treat later. Celano asked in the appendix: "Who would doubt that Francis, returning now to his native city, appeared crucified, when, though he had not yet outwardly completely renounced the world, Christ had spoken to him from the wood of the cross in a new and unheard of miracle?" Seen from this angle, Francis's life was made to appear as conforming to Christ in such a way that he might be described as an *alter Christus,* another Christ, from this moment on.[42]

This early incident in the life of Francis was, of course, interpreted through the lens of later events. And so Celano in his *Treatise on the Miracles,* the account of the miracles Francis experienced as well as the miracles he himself performed, draws together the speaking crucifix with his stigmatization to illustrate his point. The account of the talking crucifix in San Damiano played such an important part in the biography of Francis because it illuminated the fact that Christ gave meaning to his life from the beginning, and perhaps even that his prayer on that occasion was motivated not just by the poverty of the church but by his feeling for the passion of Christ as well. But there is one further feature that must be examined, for directly after the description of the speaking crucifix, we are told that Francis did not leave behind a large sum of money for the priest in San Damiano, but only enough money for a lamp and some oil. Given that this was a standard expression of Christian charity in the medieval world, like crossing oneself or simple prayers, we might judge this to be a realistic rendering of events, but it does create a difficulty in the narrative, for such a typical and in no way exorbitant gift would be unlikely to lead to Francis's father persecuting him, which is related later in Celano's *Second Life.* The attempt to minimize in this portion of the story Francis's turn to Christ makes the break with his family, or indeed any turn against his father, less plausible. Moreover, the logic that Francis began working to renovate church buildings before he experienced the ultimate breakdown in his relationship with his father doesn't appear conclusive.[43]

To investigate further what actually happened appears fruitless. One could interpret the episode with the crucifix of San Damiano that exhorted Francis to repair the chapel as the construct of his biographers, who took ambiguous stirrings of Francis and distilled from them clear instructions from the Lord Jesus Christ. Or perhaps we can scent behind the hagiographic accounts other historical leads. In an age when many feared succumbing to any number of heresies, the commission of Christ to Francis along with his positive response spoke of the origins of this new movement as one aligned with the church, not at odds with its teaching, an approach to Francis's biography that was central to the concerns of Celano and others. Much here appears to point us to the fact that the narrative of the crucifix—as it has come down to us—is a fabrication.

However, this is a dangerous tightrope to walk, for suggesting that this kind of historical event is unlikely to have happened easily plays into the mindset of skeptical moderns who are already predisposed to reject as suspicious any account of miracles. And for this reason, it is worthwhile to linger just a little longer, to imagine what such a miracle meant for the contemporaries of Francis, and how it might have been used in a biographical account of his life. We could assert that any miraculous episode was fabricated, but that still would not mean that for his contemporaries it was implausible. It wouldn't make sense to invent a story that was from the outset impossible for its earliest readers to accept! And this wouldn't apply merely to this instance but would equally be true for other accounts of healing and miracles. For the earliest followers of Francis, all these stories were true, and they could be regarded as true because they fit well into a premodern worldview. Simply to write them off or to define them in acceptably modern ways doesn't help us to get to know Francis—instead it forces him to lie on a Procrustean bed of our own making.

The account of the crucifix in San Damiano must not, then, be understood in reductionist terms, merely as a constituent element in a chronologically comprehensible account of the external events of the life of Francis; it may be important for purposes both chronological and personal. The call of Christ and the pursuant events leading to Francis's break with his father together form the ultimate turning point in his life, which Celano dates as exactly twenty years before Francis's death on October 3, 1226. His decision to become a follower of Christ and to dedicate himself to an apostolic lifestyle must then have taken place around 1206. There aren't many other dates to glean from Celano's *Life,* and in any case dates aren't the most important thing about a biography, which is much more than a string of events. As questionable as the dialogue with the crucifix might appear from a modern perspective, the narrative of the San Damiano crucifix isn't simply an invention. It helps us to understand Francis from a spiritual perspective. It can't be entirely discounted, and perhaps it should be expected that Francis experienced the presence of Christ while looking at his face on the cross, not necessarily as he stood in the church, as the Three Companions and others present it, but at some other opportunity. Francis lived in a world where representations of God and of holiness led to encounters with the presence of the Lord in a multitude of places, not just in sacramental actions. A picture wasn't simply the work of a painter but played an important role in the execution of a believer's cultic responsibilities, a medium between God and humankind, a place of presence, a subject of pious performance. In a society where icons of saints were themselves actors in the liturgical drama, of course a crucifix could speak. This wasn't the result of extravagant imagination or pious deception—it was only to be expected in a God-entranced world. In Francis's spiritual development, his experience of the divine presence grew more and more intense. The representation of Christ on the cross became a gateway into a closer experience of Christ himself.

Thus the narrative of the speaking crucifix has an essential place in the story of Francis's life, although the prayer often attached to it is less secure in the tradition. Relatively late manuscripts suggest that Francis spoke before the crucifix when he received his divine commission. It has come down to us in both Latin and Italian, and reads: "Most high, glorious God, enlighten the darkness of my heart and give me, Lord, a correct faith, a certain hope, a perfect charity, sense and knowledge, so that I may carry out Your holy and true command." Unfortunately, locating the time and place of this prayer's origin presents so many challenges that it is difficult to say unequivocally that it derives from Francis's encounter with the crucifix of San Damiano. Occasionally, it has even been argued that it doesn't derive from Francis at all. We seem to come no closer to that moment of commissioning. However, we can't rule out the possibility that Francis's encounter with the crucifix was an encounter with Christ, which in time contributed to his conversion and the path his later life was to take. Though this is plausible, and his earliest biographers clearly want us to make precisely this connection, the next steps Francis took might have been shaped by other factors. His life trajectory took shape slowly, and it was clarified by other, even more surprising interventions.[44]

It must suffice to say that the events in San Damiano are a possible historical explanation of how Francis came to leave the old pattern of his life behind. But we must remember that the visit to this church was coupled with his intention to leave there a significant donation, which ran up against the suspicions of the priest, at which point Francis threw away the money, a not insignificant sum, perhaps as much as a day's earnings in a sizeable business, and included as well the gift of his horse. It is not too hard to imagine that it might soon have dawned on Francis that his spontaneous gift, well beyond the expectations of conventional piety, might have won no enthusiasm from this father. Seen from this perspective, the events of San

Damiano did indeed constitute a turning point in Francis's life, for his game of hide-and-seek was now undeniably finished. Though he might have tried to obscure his earlier losses of clothing, it was no longer possible to hide such a significant loss. The priest's fear was likely a mirror of Francis's own fear of his father. Perhaps the penny had now dropped that giving away a generous portion of daily earnings, which belonged in the end to his father, would be sheer wastefulness in his eyes. With this background in mind, Francis's intention to move into the residence of the priest can hardly be interpreted as a deliberate decision to pursue an ascetic lifestyle. More likely, Francis sought somewhere to hide as he anticipated his father's reaction. It was just at this moment that Francis heard his father was looking for him, so he hid himself in a cave, which in the report of Celano was on the grounds of San Damiano. Other accounts describe the cave as hard to find, stating that only one person knew the whereabouts, so they don't fit easily with Bonaventure's and Celano's reports. And the person who was alleged to know was, surprisingly, not the priest of San Damiano but someone who belonged to Francis's father's household, perhaps a servant, to whom Francis had grown especially close.[45]

Perhaps Francis did indeed take refuge in the cave directly after meeting the priest, but more certain is the imminent and decisive conflict with his father. The rupture in their relationship, not planned but perhaps inevitable, had grown intermittently, but now Francis was in a position to confront, even celebrate, the distance that had emerged between them. It was a major breakthrough and resolution of the feelings of dislocation that he had wrestled with in the midst of his middle-class environment over the three years since the end of 1203. At the beginning of the story of the saint from Umbria lies a sharp conflict between generations, a break with his past, though this break wasn't all it would take for him to start out on a new path. His biographers have recognized the need to provide further explanation. The device of the talking crucifix certainly illustrates a challenge to his previous lifestyle, but we can sense that beyond this lay a son's conflict with his father, demonstrating delayed adolescent characteristics that surely complemented any decision to dedicate his life to Christ that the crucifix provoked.

In the descriptions of the biographers, Francis's father, naturally, doesn't come off well. He is presented as a brutal persecutor of his son. But if we pause to reflect on the details, we may develop a little more sympathy for his situation. The sum of money that his son threw carelessly onto the windowsill was not insubstantial, and the son must have appeared to his father as a ne'er-do-well, given all that his father had done for him, despite his lack of sympathy with Francis's wishes. Perhaps it was his father who had redeemed Francis from imprisonment in Perugia in 1203. Even if this can't be determined, we can see in Pietro Bernardone a classic representative of the merchant class who was grooming his son to take over his business. We can perhaps imagine the younger man's efforts to comply, standing behind the counter of his father's business, undertaking at least some business trips on his father's behalf, though frequently shorter than those his father undertook. The reports don't make clear whether or when Francis's father became aware that Francis had been profligate in giving money away. But now that the point had been reached where it was no longer possible to keep his generosity hidden, Francis reacted in a way that was anything but sensible by hiding himself. Like an adolescent boy, or perhaps even a younger child, when confronted with the consequences of his actions, Francis made matters worse.

Of course Francis's father began looking for his son, whom he thought had failed to return from a business trip. His father might have assumed that Francis had fallen prey to robbers—though this is not explicitly recounted in the earliest biographies. Then, to his amazement and horror, he heard what had happened when Francis stopped in San Damiano. He disapproved not because of Francis's desire to pursue an ascetic Christian life, as Clare's family was later to do when she entered the order, or as Celano and others might suggest. Francis's refuge in the church didn't anger his father—or if it did, it wasn't the sole provocation—he was incensed by the inexplicable loss of the money. And this we can surmise because property and money were ongoing causes of conflict in their relationship. In John of Perugia's hagiographic intensification of this incident, we learn that Francis's father loved his son only according to the flesh ("carnaliter"), which adds a moral and external dimension to the conflict. The Three Companions highlight the father's deep love for his son without making reference to this dimension. There is still today no real reason to doubt the propriety and in the best sense the normalcy of Pietro Bernardone's love for his son, a love that, when tested by Francis (as the Three Companions recognize), did not withstand the test, erupting later in full-blown hatred toward his son, for "whenever they met, he cursed Francis."[46]

Francis's father set out to fetch his son in San Damiano, but the biographers are not clear about whether he was able to find him. No reference is made to the potential high point of the narrative when Francis was flushed out of his hiding place. Rather, Francis just emerged at some point—perhaps after about a month. His eventual appearance would have been dramatic, almost horrific. In speaking of the cave, Celano suggests that in those four weeks, Francis "hardly dared leave it to provide for his human needs." Around the clock, Francis found himself in an airless small space, without human contact, without the wherewithal to bathe. One of the rich sons of the city had gradually been transformed into a wretched and filthy figure. What had been a trial case in Rome was now reality. Long before he interpreted his poverty theologically, Francis, still legally the son and heir of his father's fortune, had freely become a beggar.[47]

How deeply Francis's life had changed was noted by other citizens of Assisi. When Francis left his voluntary imprisonment, he was roundly mocked. The hagiographies color this incident by the light of Christ's leading and the rejection of a sinful world. Praying, Francis left his hiding place gripped by joy, as Celano and others present it. Christ's power in this incident appears much less concrete and explicit than in the account of the talking crucifix, but it isn't difficult to imagine its impact on Francis after so many weeks of uncertainty. According to Celano, he lost all fear of those who persecuted him. And this assurance overcame him spontaneously, following a pattern established in his life before this incident too. Indeed, his transformation paralleled the experience of the prodigal son described in the parable of Luke 15, whose inheritance had been granted, then squandered, and who then returned home impoverished. The various biographies of Francis don't make this similarity explicit, but the story is so well known that we can't help but see some likeness between the two, with one difference. In the parable, the son returns humbled to be reunited with his father, but in the case of Francis the break with his father was now complete, though this was not apparent yet to the denizens of Assisi as he took his first trembling steps back in his hometown. They did see a transformation, though, for he had left the town on horseback wearing the fine clothes of a wealthy merchant and came home from his hiding place a dirty figure and emaciated to boot, according to Celano, which is no great wonder after he had endured such pitiable conditions. Four weeks had passed, changing his appearance dramatically, and this in a society where clothes marked your social status. Without others being able to understand his reasons, he had given up the accoutrements his class and his pride required. This is how others in the town saw him, perhaps having heard the rumor as well that he had wasted a great deal of money. No one really knew where he had been, although it was now unlikely that he had fallen into the hands of robbers. Francis had now achieved what he had so long yearned for: he was stripped of any middle-class emotional connections. But of course the change was not an expression of upward mobility like joining the knighthood, as he had once desired, but heading in the opposite direction toward social ignominy. He was now finally one of those toward whom he had formerly turned, an outcast beyond all the norms of urban society. In these circles, it was clear how unusual his turn toward people on the margins (and beyond) was. The prodigal son was not welcomed in, but his self-initiated exclusion was confirmed: "When those who knew him saw this, they compared what he was now with what he had been; and they began to revile him miserably. Shouting out that he was mad and demented, they threw the mud of the streets and stones at him."[48]

He now qualified as mad, a description that had already been applied to him during his imprisonment in Perugia. Francis was clearly walking a social tightrope. Those who push back against the norms of their upbringing like Francis risk losing their footing, especially when the reasons for his break with the past were not yet clear to those around him in Assisi—and perhaps they were not even clear to him. This outcast had no place in society. Indeed, he had left normality so far behind that he appeared now to be nothing more than a fool. And this judgment wasn't as much an explanation as it was a provocation to find a new way of fitting in. To define oneself over and against normal expectations as a kind of existential protest was to create for oneself a new kind of normal, to which Francis's biographers lent support when they pulled together the various pieces of his life in differing ways. Of course, we could read these biographies like a set piece for the life of any saint, but we could also read them as a pathological account of an increasingly rootless young man trying desperately to break free from his patrimony. As in any developmental process, the outcomes at the time were not clear. No one could guess on his return to Assisi whether Francis's shocking transformation was merely the result of temporary enthusiasm or instead the beginning of something lasting—and ignominious to the townsfolk.[49]

Of course, entering Assisi in this way would cause a splash that rippled outward to grab the attention of his father, who promptly seized his son. According to his biographers, this incident was menacing, like a wolf attacking a sheep. Indeed, the Three Companions took over the language used by Celano word for word. The father hid his son, who had just emerged from his own dank hiding place, in a dark cellar, where he tried to bend his will through beatings and chains. However, we shouldn't measure the behavior of Francis's father against the assumptions of modern pedagogy, or even just modern assumptions of how to manage someone who is sick, as Francis was viewed by many. His father believed the punishment was commensurate with the offense. In fact, we could perhaps go so far as to suggest that those blows were instead a sign that he had not yet given up on his son. Francis was not yet irretrievably lost to his madness; there was still the possibility—according to his father—to restore his son to middle-class life through punishment that maybe should have been given to Francis years earlier. Beatings like this employed as an educational strategy have not been unknown to modernity either, so it should be no surprise that a merchant in Assisi in the thirteenth century might suppose that such blows could be beneficial. We might take umbrage against the rage and lack of understanding expressed by Francis's father—not inappropriately—but we can also pause to observe a father who in his despair uses all in his power to restore his son to the life prepared for him, a course of action necessitated by Francis's evident determination to pursue a different course, which Celano makes clear. In fact, the treatment meted out by his father just confirmed Francis in his own resolve to aspire to a life of sanctity as soon and as quickly as he could. Even if Francis had not wanted to pursue this kind of life, his father would still have intervened to direct him back to the middle-class way, as his goal was not merely to keep Francis from the ascetic path, as his biographers suggest, which was in any case not clearly formed in Francis's mind. His son's rebellion was met with the father's oppression, resulting in a game of power and resistance which, though obscured by the biographers, was effectively a battle concerning love and its loss, with the issue of money adding its own menace.[50]

Naturally, money provides further insight to explain the conflict, for it gives us the key to understand how Celano's account of Francis's early religious aspiration could hold together various conflicting dimensions. We have learned that Francis spontaneously and dismissively hurled some coins onto a windowsill, money that, in his *First Life,* Celano reports was intended to provide for the poor and for reconstruction of the church building, which of course made sense given the later trajectory of Francis's life. But in our own challenging attempts to create a narrative around these incidents, we have to acknowledge that Francis's behavior in this period of his life was not characterized by intentionality or a sense of purpose. The mention of a possible use for the money points to the fact that Francis had later retrieved the coins and given further thought to their use.[51]

It appears that it was his mother who engineered an opportunity to do just this. With her husband away, she spoke again to Francis, intending, according to the reports, to mediate the generational conflict that had played out so vehemently between her husband and their son, though her efforts were in vain. After this fruitless undertaking, she let her son out of the cellar. Whether she was "moved by motherly compassion for him," or perhaps motivated by the prospect of Francis retrieving the money for his father to foster their reconciliation, we will never know. In either case, it is fitting that upon his release, Francis rushed to San Damiano and then returned just as quickly (according to Celano) to Assisi, because his father had come home and was raging through the town in search of his son. Pietro Bernardone was threatening to have Francis exiled from the territory of Assisi, which is essential background for understanding the resulting trial before the bishop, which the Three Companions narrate in more detail than Celano.[52]

In the presence of the consuls of the city, those regents who since 1198 had been elected by the people's assembly to exercise executive and judicial office, Francis's father began proceedings against his son, aligning well with the view that he wanted him gone. The development of these branches of government was of course part of the general trend toward the dominance of middle-class norms in cities, marginalizing the traditional authority of the nobility. However, Francis was not prepared to obey the summons of the consuls, because he declared "by divine grace he had obtained freedom." Even if these were not precisely his words, this quotation functions as an accurate summary of his emotional posture at this stage of his life. He had found courage to deal with the conflict with his father and, as we shall soon see, to renounce all connections binding him to middle-class ways. In this sense, he had indeed been liberated, freed from all that caused him hardship, all that had effectively ripped him in two through such powerful experiences of dislocation. He had clearly repudiated his parents' expectations, which was itself a kind of freedom. The consuls now had to interpret his spiritual or theological pronouncement in judicial form, and they did so by assuming that his stay in San Damiano effectively rendered him a cleric rather than a layman. Their ruling made clear something that in Francis's mind may have been confused, contributing to a positive vision of his future. The church offered a place in its monastic orders for those who would not or could not live in the bourgeois world around them.[53]

The sifting of Francis's ambitions was further clarified when his case was referred to Guido I, the bishop of Assisi. The sequence of events is both legally and socially straightforward. On the legal side, the consuls declared their secular incompetence to resolve Francis's case, because he was regarded as a cleric, and so referred their question to a spiritual jurisdiction, which Guido presided over. Francis accepted their decision, as apparently his father did also—indeed, he had to. The bishop's jurisdiction meant that it would not be representatives of the middle class who would determine the case, but instead a nobleman, a member of the ruling elite, someone who would not necessarily be sympathetic to Pietro Bernardone and the practices of the mercantile class. The conflict between father and son was almost immediately resolved—if we follow the account of the Three Companions—in a recognizably Solomonic fashion. The bishop affirmed the rights of Pietro when he demanded that Francis return the money— which he had handled so carelessly—to his father. And he affirmed the rights of Francis when he agreed that though the coins must be returned, Francis's attitude toward money was valid. Pietro may well have acquired the money in an unjust manner and may not have intended to use it in a way that honored God. Guido ruled in favor of the father in regard to the question of possessions, but it seems that in the moral or religious sphere he took the side of the young rebel, giving the impression that Francis's protest against riches was not the singular protest of Francis alone but aligned with that of the church itself, in whose fellowship Francis had finally found his place.[54]

From a contemporary perspective, this impression is of course irritating. The church in Francis's day was not poor, and many had long protested against its wealth. Even Guido played along with the power games of the church in his age. The challenge of reconciling the church's commitment to serve the poor with its own great prosperity was evident, and even the monastic orders, which had been a refuge for those aspiring to a life of poverty in the church, had succumbed to the allure of money and possessions. But Guido was a man whom Francis saw not merely as a successful mediator between him and his father but as someone who could serve as his patron in the fight against riches, someone who could help him to live in freedom and leave behind the conflict with his father, which literally had resulted in chains. Under the care and protection of a mighty bishop in a wealthy church, Francis had experienced something that truly changed his perception of his world. Further, this emotional resolution explains Francis's very deep trust in the officeholders of the church, helping his biographers to explain the puzzle of how Francis, a poor man, could make peace with such a power-hungry world ruler like Pope Innocent III. This kind of relationship was a corollary of his early experience of the church, whose office bearers took his side in this matter. At a minimum we can see his mixed feelings when he critiqued the wealth of his middle-class society yet accepted the riches and power of the church, though such tensions commonly attend the lot of humankind. Putting together all the pieces of his life, it would be easier to smooth out the inconsistencies and present a saintly picture, as his earliest biographers did, but we can easily fall into the opposite temptation: to present Francis as a rebel against the structures of the church. This he was not. This he did not want to be.

He wanted to be free, free from the constraints of his family's wealth. So after the conclusion of the trial—of perhaps more accurately after the bishop's mediation—a key scene in his life played out. He not only gave the money back to his father but gave to him as well all his clothes. The spontaneous Francis of the preceding years was back, fitting well into the narrative of Celano. Francis undressed himself publicly, though we don't know exactly if this took place before the court or just in the presence of his father and the bishop. Though the Three Companions tell us that he retired to a private room in the bishop's palace to leave his clothes and money and returned wearing the robes of a penitent—so not naked—this is likely not the case. They might have felt some sense of shame on Francis's behalf as they narrated the events of that day, but we must remember that Francis had put all such shame behind him when just a few weeks earlier he had wandered through Assisi in filthy rags. Now he appeared before the world and its representatives fully naked. Freed from all worldly attachments, he surrendered himself to his heavenly Father: "Hitherto I have called Pietro Bernardone my father; but because I am resolved to serve God I return to him the money on account of which he was so perturbed, and also the clothes I wore which are his; and from now on I will say 'Our Father who art in heaven,' and not Father Peter Bernardone."[55]

Just one thing here reflects later tradition: the claim to serve God, which biographers never tire of repeating again and again in this part of the story, even if Francis's intentions of service were not yet fully formed. Indeed, the words of the Lord's Prayer embedded here point us to another context, the words of Jesus in the Sermon on the Mount, which remind us that birds and plants don't concern themselves with their daily needs because their heavenly Father provides for them (Matthew 6:25–34). It was exactly in this sense that the bishop had encouraged Francis to return his father's money and not to worry about his own needs, for God would amply supply all things needful. His repudiation of his father was nonetheless unambiguous. We don't see here the common interpretation suggested by Celano that Francis in this act affirmed his commitment to be naked to follow someone who was naked, though it does to some degree explain Francis's approach to the life of discipleship. But we can see how this whole scene might deepen his feeling that in the church and under its bishop he could find a refuge for his life. The bishop gave Francis his own cloak and thereby communicated symbolically that the shame he might feel in the bourgeois world had no place in the church.[56]

This whole incident is a typical example of medieval symbolic communication. To express oneself adequately or to take one's place in the feudal world, more was required than merely vocalizing or gesturing, for particular actions could create meaning and convey communication as performative acts in the Middle Ages. In the story of Francis, things are not merely verbalized but demonstrated as well. Traditionally, scholars wrote of prophetic signs, which Old Testament prophets might have enacted. Francis followed their lead by sharing his own views through staging incidents that reflected his own principles, whether consciously or not. We don't have to look further than his departure from Assisi as a rich merchant and his return as someone poor and unkempt just a few weeks later. The change in his status could thus be plainly seen. The high point of these performative acts was when Francis undressed before the bishop, who subsequently bestowed his protection on Francis.

Francis had grown in his assurance, but still not everything had been clarified. Despite events like the talking crucifix or the scene before the bishop, and despite his confidence to lean into the split with his father and live outside the values of his society, he was still in search of a new pattern for life. This was exactly how Celano in his *First Life* and Bonaventure in his *Major Life* presented it, while the Three Companions, and Celano in his *Second Life*, turned immediately after the separation from his father to Francis's task of rebuilding the churches. In Celano's first account, the emphasis lay on Francis's discipleship. Here, after removing his clothes, he does not find new ones but wanders through the region "clad only in scanty garments." From a hagiographical perspective, Celano's later account of Francis falling prey to robbers and introducing himself to them as "the herald of the great King" is particularly striking. Stories of a mix-up like this were prominent in the early biographies, leading to a wrong worldly and peremptory interpretation of Francis's proclamation. Of course it would be unreasonable to imagine that the robbers would instantly recognize that the king whom Francis spoke of was God himself, and not some earthly monarch who had sent him, especially difficult to believe given that he appeared in such a poor estate.[57]

If we accept as reasonable that in this period Francis was still on some vague quest for meaning, it is all the more interesting that in the course of his wanderings he stumbled into a monastery near Gubbio, presumably the Benedictine Abbey of San Verecondo. His experience here was shocking, according to Celano: Francis approached wearing a simple shirt but received neither better clothes nor any food and was soon driven on by force of necessity. The decisive element in this account, alongside his frustration regarding the monks in this established order, was that Francis clearly was not seeking a religious home as traditionally defined by the life of the ascetic. Otherwise he would not have stood begging near the kitchen but tried to find the entry gate to locate the master of novices. The story would then have focused on the challenge of joining the order of his own free will and not because of his failure as a beggar. So Francis continued to roam, and ended up again with a group he knew well: he began to live among a community of lepers, whom he could no longer care for financially, though he could offer them his loving attention as he cleaned and soothed their wounds. As Celano writes, "He yet remained in the world," but this as an outcast from the world and a follower of Christ. But this at least was clear: the break with his past was complete, unambiguously and irreparably.[58]

CHAPTER 3

Renewal

"Francis, Go, Repair My House!"

HE REPORTS OF THE SPEAKING CRUCIFIX OF SAN Damiano do not precisely overlap with each other, but at least the heading applied by Celano in his *Second Life* captures some common ground: Francis was to reestablish the house of Christ. And he did it promptly, even if the command was not entirely clear. Francis in his restlessness was in search of a new goal, a new task, so he ran without tiring to the lepers and to the poor, though he wasn't about to throw away his life. Gradually, he began to sense his calling, which was expressed in the concrete commitment to rebuild the dilapidated churches around Assisi.

If Francis's vocation can be traced back to the call of the crucifix of San Damiano, then his fledgling attempts to obey Christ's command are grounded in a misunderstanding, for the crucified one—as all the biographers agree—was referring not to buildings but to the entire institution of the church, both the fellowship of believers and those holding office in the church. This, then, helps us understand why Francis did not immediately establish his fraternity upon hearing Christ's call. Further to this line of reasoning, Francis remained in error until he could see his way clear to understand things as Christ did.

However, even if these reflections are valid and the call of Christ was not clear, there yet remains the question as to what motivated Francis to take the precise path he did. Perhaps it can be understood as only a small change to previous patterns of behavior. He had readily served those who found their place in society difficult, and this was not so different to his response to the request of the priest whom he had met in San Damiano. And even if we don't follow the details of the early biographers exactly, where Francis disclosed concrete plans to the priest, at least we can say that Francis trusted the cleric. In any case, we can say that it was the actions of this very priest, who also perhaps hid Francis from his father, who gave impetus to this turning point in Francis's life. And it is not too difficult to imagine that his concern for the building in San Damiano emerged directly from his appreciation of the priest himself: Francis may well have been shocked by the state of the church in which this priest served, recognizing how inadequate it was not only for the priest but for priestly service more generally. Whether the narrative as related here is true—that Francis's respect for the clergy stemmed from the way Bishop Guido protected him—or whether this respect had deeper roots, evidenced by the way Francis kissed the hands of the priest when he first met him, it is equally plausible that he wanted to build—or rebuild—the house of God to provide a suitable space for the ministry of this priest, and in doing so to serve the house of the Lord with growing conviction.[1]

There is, however, something more surprising concerning the activity of rebuilding the church. The Three Companions relate the story more thoroughly than Celano and in greater detail: Francis had begun to collect stone and presumably money for construction in Assisi. Weeks or perhaps months after he had left Assisi naked, he had apparently returned, and it appeared at first blush that his behavior was just as mad as before—since he'd left his hideout many had attributed madness to him. In the public squares and along the lanes of the city he had begun to praise God, and the Three Companions tell us that he sang "in great fervor of spirit." Phrasing like this has biblical precedent, of course, as well as exquisite ambiguity, meaning either that he was filled with the Spirit or literally drunk. The book of the Acts of the Apostles recounts how through the power of the Holy Spirit the disciples on the day of Pentecost began all of a sudden to speak in tongues, in languages they had never learned. However, not everyone present was persuaded, and in fact some "sneered and said, 'They are filled with new wine'" (Acts 2:13). In the description of Francis's appearance, we see mirrored the experience of the apostles, just as in later accounts the Franciscan movement would find a parallel in apostolic patterns.[2]

Francis began to preach like an apostle too, or perhaps like more than just an apostle. He added to his praise, as the Three Companions relate, an appeal for a donation of stones to aid his construction effort: "Whoever gives me one stone will have one reward; two stones, two rewards; three stones a treble reward." His appeal sounded like extraordinary presumptuousness, for Francis connected—as Jesus had once done—eternal salvation with one's behavior toward him here on earth. Indeed, he promised like the Savior a multiplied reward in heaven in consequence of obedience here (Luke 18:30). But his words might have been understood in a much more religiously conventional way too, which Francis had learned as the son of a merchant: doing good on earth in trust of a heavenly reward, for example, giving alms to a leper or to someone who was poor. But equally that gift might be applied to a building project, which had long been part of the system of indulgences. His nonconformist appearance and actions may have been absorbed into a much more traditional model of piety. In other words, his initiative in church building and the pattern of piety that it so radically represented could be reconciled with the more acceptable middle-class piety in which he had grown up, or, more important, with the kind of piety that Bishop Guido espoused. Without renouncing completely his new status as an outsider, Francis took a step back toward the world from which he had emerged, creating links with conventional society even as he looked for an alternative to conventional forms. This turned out to be his choice regarding housing too. Francis did not live alone, squatting in one of the churches he was restoring, but chiefly, though often temporarily, enjoyed the hospitality of rich—and frequently noble—members of Assisi society. His life was still not settled, but he did find moments of connection and peace in regular society from time to time.[3]

If this analysis is correct, with Francis making deliberate connections with traditional forms of piety without being overtaken by them, the meaning of Francis's efforts in church reconstruction can't be overestimated. They were his limited attempts at reincorporation in the church and society of his day, and they distinguished him from other preachers of his time whose heretical views and existence outside the authority of the church were sustained. The dividing line between heterodoxy and sanctity was just as small as that between holiness and madness. Francis walked a tightrope in both instances and could easily have fallen on either side at any moment—indeed, many of his contemporaries thought he had. Being remembered as a saint was not inevitable, for the Christian tradition might have despised him as a heretic or forgotten him as a madman. But his status as a conformist saint wasn't ascribed merely by others' presentations of him. His own initiative and pattern of piety were demonstrated in an especially important incident in 1206, when he sought to define his role definitively in the religious life of the Middle Ages by taking on the recognizable garb of a hermit, which severed his responsibilities from any particular community but gave some religious validation to his perambulations and status as an outsider. As hermit, he would have to live outside middle-class society, which, in consequence of his radical ascetic lifestyle, functioned to define himself over and against society, thus being called back into its orbit of meaning. The heretic or the lunatic had removed himself from society once and for all, but the hermit remained connected to it, perhaps even its counter-image.[4]

Francis, until just a few months earlier, had shared the assumptions of upward mobility that characterized the merchant class, but in pursuing the path of a hermit he was aligning himself—but now in a paradoxical way—with those same family norms, creating for him a very real tension. It was in this dialectic that he no longer faced abject rejection from society, as he had done immediately after leaving his hiding place, but rather a divided reaction, as the apostles had on the day of Pentecost. Of course, many citizens laughed him to scorn, but still others were moved by his appearance and recognized in his drunken demeanor the intoxication of divine love. His appeal for contributions must have been in part successful, for very soon he was able to drag stones to San Damiano to commence the necessary repairs. Those who looked on his cause sympathetically must have provided not just stones but money as well to acquire other building materials. The reports provide the name of a priest, Silvester, from whom Francis bought the stones for San Damiano's reconstruction at a reasonable price. In any case, Francis seems to have quickly got enough together to return the church to good order and was apparently so fulfilled by the achievement that he went on to complete the repairs on two other holy places as well. First, he began work on the church named (in Bonaventure's *Major Life*) St. Pietro, which probably referred to the sanctuary of St. Pietro della Spina near Assisi, which is no longer standing. It is worth noting that this church probably fell into disrepair again not much later, failing to maintain its connection to the work of Francis. It wasn't just the physical contributions of Francis that preserved his memory; often it was the relationship between the church and the later Franciscan movement that was more important, or, in the case of the church of San Damiano, its relationship with the sisters of Clare.

Construction work was not in itself regarded as valuable—Francis did not mention it in his *Testament.* But this does not mean that we should doubt the veracity of the claim that Francis did indeed devote the years from 1206 until the beginning of 1208 or 1209 to the task of renovating churches, which is confirmed in the early account of Celano. Though the building projects are mentioned rarely, this might suggest that they were included in later accounts only when they could be connected to Francis's call by the crucifix, thereby gaining in importance. Work on renovating churches received symbolic significance when his biographers later associated Francis with a vocation to restore the Catholic Church in its entirety. The ambiguity of the speaking crucifix's demand made of the construction work meaningful sign acts, without which the later Franciscan ideal of using buildings noted for their impoverished appeal would have a very loose foundation in the life of Francis himself.[5]

Alongside the building projects of San Damiano and San Pietro belongs another church, which was to maintain its profile in later history: the small Chapel of Portiuncula, a Marian shrine near Assisi. As the place that for an extended period was the center of the brotherhood, and where twenty years after the break with his father, Francis died, the Portiuncula became a place of great renown, and is today one of the most moving places of Christian devotion. Visited by hordes of pilgrims, this small chapel was covered over in the sixteenth and seventeenth centuries by an enormous church dedicated to Mary, making of the chapel a tiny church within a church, a place of remembrance that calls to mind the tension between the modest beginnings of the *poverello* and his later worldwide veneration. That Francis would choose this location for his lasting rest is striking, for we might have expected him to be buried in San Damiano, where he had previously found protection and enjoyed an ongoing good relationship, and where a little later Clare also decided to move with her companions. Perhaps the location of the Portiuncula in the valley spoke of its significance for communication and transportation, unlike San Damiano, which was halfway up the hill to Assisi, but no doubt its spiritual powers of attraction and his hope for Mary's protection played a role. Francis had lost a home in his father's family, but he now found one in the mother of Jesus. Things were beginning to become clear.[6]

Repentance Is Needed

During this period, Francis lived off the support of the priest of San Damiano. He might also have found some extra food, as he learned to do while he was living and traveling alone. Working to rebuild the churches brought him near to civilization again, and the appeal for donations for the building works may have proved an easy path to ask for and receive some alms for himself as well. He had begun to beg. Later, such begging became synonymous with the Franciscans; they, together with the Dominicans and the Augustinians, were known as the "begging orders," or the mendicants. With this later appellation, it is no wonder that hagiographers—like the Three Companions—have stressed the role of begging in their description of this phase of Francis's life: "You should go, bowl in hand, from door to door, and driven by hunger, collect the various morsels you may be given. It is only thus that you can live voluntarily for love of him." It is of course possible—indeed, probable—that Francis himself lived as a beggar as an example of a more dramatic form of his status as social outsider. But these accounts certainly bear the marks of the later lifestyle of the brothers as beggars, and therefore idealize this practice in memorializing the early life of Francis. Perhaps we shouldn't take the description of the mixture of the various kinds of food in the bowl literally, and we should ponder the fact that for Francis begging wasn't voluntary. Of course, he had chosen without external coercion to give up all his possessions and to cast them symbolically at the feet of his father, renouncing thereby his inheritance. But now he really did find himself in dire need, and taught others who had fallen into poverty through no fault of their own how to manage. This pointer to a voluntary choice contains an appeal to others who would endorse his lifestyle to give up their own riches. The depiction of begging in the account of the Three Companions, among others, reflects how at the time of their writing begging had indeed become an ideal of the brotherhood, which in turn demonstrated their trust in God himself.[7]

Despite the interpretative layers, the historical core remains that Francis, having impulsively given up everything that life as a merchant offered, had to learn slowly the difficult lesson of how to work for his own keep, with very few options at his disposal. To renounce his rich heritage was necessarily a path to poverty. Poverty in turn was the obvious reality for a person whose goal was to proclaim repentance and the Kingdom of God. In this context, begging was not merely about the process of finding food. He could have sought out other sources of provision, not least the priest of San Damiano. No, begging was for Francis a way of confronting his own past. He might have found a place in nature outside of the constraints of society to forage for food, but instead he returned to the life of the cities, where he was excluded and reviled. This is the sense of the word *ostiatim*, which stressed how he went from door to door. That he did this is emphasized not just by the Companions; Francis himself noted as much by using the formulation in his *Testament* when he looked back on his life. Hidden in this term is a slice of his lived experience. He really did go from house to house begging for food in Assisi, and for those who knew him as the merchant's son, he really did portray dramatically the consequences of his new existence as a beggar. The resulting confrontation, presented in the account of the Three Companions, shows how frightened Francis was on one occasion while begging. Apparently he was too timid to reveal himself as a beggar to a group of people playing happily, likely because he anticipated their mockery. This memory is probably authentic because we are told Francis immediately changed his mind and returned to the group, confessing before them that he was a sinner and had not trusted himself to ask them for alms. And though on this particular occasion he had wanted to ask for donations for San Damiano, the basic issue remained unchanged that he was ashamed to beg, reminding us that at this stage of his life, unlike later in his order, begging had not yet become an ideal. The path he was taking was in several respects more humiliating than merely roaming around because he sensed the contempt of former friends, relatives, and neighbors. Assisi had grown to be a city of around ten thousand citizens, but it was still easy enough to get a sense of the whole town, for most people knew each other. And naturally everyone knew the wayward son of the Bernardone family.[8]

With his return as a beggar, Francis's conflict with his father blew up again. Seen sympathetically from his father's perspective, we might recognize how painful it was for him that old wounds had been reopened, as the Three Companions suggest. Because of the father's love for his son, he felt great shame, a rare description of the emotional relationship between the two. The father was deeply impacted by Francis's behavior, and his own honor was no doubt called into question as well. His love consequently turned to aggression, resulting in the bond between father and son being irrevocably torn. Pietro showered Francis with curses, whereupon Francis turned to another poor man nearby—according to John of Perugia his name was Albert—and asked him to bless him and to become for him his father. If there was any doubt previously, now it was clear that Francis had changed his social status. He was no longer the son of a rich merchant, someone who could return to his previous life if he so willed. Now instead he belonged completely to an underclass, to the poor of the town. Someone else was ready to claim his inheritance, his brother Angelo, who took the side of their father and who mocked and despised Francis. As Francis begged out in the cold, Angelo asked someone from the town to approach Francis to buy a drop of his sweat. As much as Francis's composed and pious reaction might suggest that this was not a literal account of a historical moment, it nonetheless points us in summary form to the emotional distance that had resulted between members of the family, including his mother, who from now on plays no part in the story.[9]

Throughout these conflicts, Francis was becoming more certain of his path. With his growing confidence emerged not just a clear rejection of the old ways but a new and distinct commitment to Christian discipleship. From the break with his family came a new momentum with Christ. He attributed this transition in his *Testament* directly back to God: "When God gave me some friars, there was no one to tell me what I should do; but the Most High himself made it clear to me that I must live the life of the Gospel." Yet anyone who now expected this call of God suddenly to break into his everyday life was mistaken. It was neither a dream nor a vision, not even a talking crucifix, that ultimately formed his life in a new way. His transformation grew from within usual liturgical praxis and from engagement with the proclamation of the Gospel. According to Celano, Francis frequently attended Mass in the Portiuncula after he had begun living there. He heard, perhaps on February 24, 1208 or 1209, on the Feast of St. Matthias or in a votive Mass shortly after Easter, a reading from the Gospel that deeply moved him. We can't isolate the date more accurately despite notable attempts in the research, nor should we have to, for the most important thing is not the date but the precise course of events, recounted by both Celano and the Three Companions. The text that animated him was the speech by Jesus as he sent out the disciples, beginning in Matthew 10:9: "Take no gold, or silver, or copper in your belts, no bag for your journey, or two tunics, or sandals, or a staff; for laborers deserve their food." Francis was touched by this passage of Scripture and asked the priest for further exposition. It doesn't take too much effort to work out what was going on here. Francis heard in the words of the Gospel reading, together with the commission to repent and to preach the Kingdom, a call so similar to the path he had already taken up, renouncing riches and forgoing fine clothes for ones reflecting a life of poverty. What he had perhaps intuitively lived out now took the form of a deliberate commission from Christ. Until now, Francis had earned nothing but contempt, or at least pity, for his behavior, but in this instant he experienced the most profound confirmation of his decision, which was magnified by the priest. In this confrontation with the biblical text he won a level of clarity, such that the uncertain path he had previously traveled was now a journey following in the "life and footsteps of the Apostles," preaching the apostolic message and at the same time living the apostolic life.[10]

This of course meant that he had to consider how he would give Christian shape to his new life, which up to this point was essentially the repudiation of his parents' way. His task in rebuilding churches, to which he had so long devoted himself, was apparently not exactly what Christ had commissioned his apostles to do. If one believes Celano, the priest of the Portiuncula had drawn into his explanation of the dominical commission from Matthew's Gospel some of the interpretative features of the same speech from Luke and Mark: the proclamation of "the kingdom of God and penance." This was distinctly different from renovating ruined churches. And it was different from what Francis had long done, withdrawing shyly from other people. But the rejection of the social life of a merchant would and should not necessarily entail distancing himself from all human contact, as he had long thought. A sermon is nothing less than engagement with others. Suddenly something became clear: by renouncing the past he could pivot to an apostolic life. In wandering and searching Francis had found his destination. Characteristically, this was then expressed in a new way of being clothed. The garments of a hermit no longer fit with his new way of life, nor did they fit with the word of the Gospel that Francis had heard. As Celano recounts, Francis now took off his shoes, put aside his staff, and denied himself a second tunic. What he kept was rough and ready, and in only a few instances did he go beyond the biblical instruction: for example, instead of a belt he wore a cord, and he "designed for himself a tunic that bore a likeness to the cross." However, being clothed like this wasn't exactly according to the rules of later Franciscans. In the *Rule* officially recognized by the pope in 1223, we read how the brothers could take only one tunic, though they could potentially take a second and wear shoes if necessary, and attaching a hood was permissible even if this was different from Francis's own tunic, though later representations of Francis show him wearing one. With a hood attached to the tunic, its shape no longer resembled the cross, which presumably corresponded with the Greek letter tau, as the habit of Francis (whether original or not) now preserved in the church where he is buried shows.[11]

That this tau shape did indeed mean much to Francis is evident in one of the few manuscripts in his own hand that are preserved. It was likely that, in the last years of his life, as he withdrew to the mountain of La Verna, he wrote a song of praise for Leo, his companion. The verso of the fragment contains a double blessing, for Francis added to the so-called Aaronic Blessing of Numbers 6:24-26 another blessing for Leo, in the middle of which he drew the letter tau. The meaning of this sign can be traced back to the preaching of the prophet Ezekiel, where we read how all those signed on their forehead with this letter should escape judgment (Ezekiel 9:6), which was taken up later by John in Revelation 7:2-4. And both these speak of that eschatological seal by which the saints of Christ might be recognized and gathered together, a seal that became in later Christian tradition the sign of the cross. With this in mind, Celano's description of Francis's garment being shaped like the cross is perfectly consistent with the assumption of a tau-like shape. For medieval Christians, these were effectively one and the same thing, insofar as they believed that the New Testament revealed the hidden intent of the Old. And in both instances the shape of the cross provided protection by warding off demonic forces: "By means of it he might beat off all temptations of the devil." The cross was also a symbol and expression of an ascetic lifestyle, for living under the sign of the cross meant rejection of a life of luxury, and for this son of a rich merchant there was now no turning back.[12]

Despite the norms of the later Franciscan order, we can assume that Francis's robe was just like Celano and the Companions described it, achieving a distinct goal. He had begun life as the son of a merchant who wore costly clothes to test the limits of social propriety. In Rome he had worn the garments of a beggar, then appeared before the bishop naked, after which his clothes were most pitiable, and finally he took the robes of a hermit. In each stage of his life, the clothes he wore were visible symbols of his spiritual journey. Now he wore the clothes representative of apostolic commission—indeed, clothes representing the cross of Christ itself, which were contemptible in the eyes of many, such that Jacques de Vitry (d. 1240) could describe the Franciscans in the famous formula "Naked, [they] follow the naked Christ." A new direction was signaled by new garments. For Celano, this meant that the inner and outer worlds, spirit and body, had become one. And for Francis, this meant that the dissociative experiences of his early life were more or less behind him, allowing him to manage successfully the emotional contradictions of his life without losing his footing. His security lay firmly in Christ.[13]

So Francis followed the call of Christ. Just as Christ commenced his public ministry with the call to repentance (Matthew 4:17), so Francis did too: "He began to preach penance to all with great fervor of spirit and joy of mind," for the priest had explained the commissioning sermon with the help of its parallel passages in the Bible. This was the call of Jesus to the apostles, which offered the near-perfect transformation of the life he had led up to now. His charge against contemporary society morphed into a call that others should follow his own example to place all of one's life under the cross. Just as Francis was growing increasingly committed to traditional forms of piety, so he was also making clear with this call to others that the radical nature of Jesus did not permit a Christian to become overly comfortable with middle-class existence. He preached penance, not meaning primarily participation in the sacrament but rather a spiritual turnaround that would make a difference to the way a person lived. He was effectively saying that the kind of Christianity that he had encountered and experienced in Assisi was heading in the wrong direction and therefore needed to be better aligned with the values represented by the passion of Christ. Already for a long time Francis had been impressing upon his brothers how the commandments of the Lord had been forgotten.[14]

Francis's life of poverty was no longer to be understood as a knee-jerk reaction to the wealth around him, but instead and more significantly became the external expression of an internal attitude toward Christ—or, perhaps better put, a response to Christ drawing close to him. Such repentance wouldn't necessarily lead to life on the margins of society, nor to the abyss of social exclusion or oblivion, but because the call of Christ was to be applied to all who heard, the call would lead to social transformation, not just the reform of structures but also a deeper change of heart.

To interpret this reality, Celano used the unusual phrase "gaudium mentis," or "sensual delight," which well captured the deep conviction out of which this preacher of Christ spoke. If the preceding observations are correct, then it was exactly this frame of soul that explained Francis's experience in the weeks following that day in 1208 or 1209 when he first heard the apostolic Gospel. He found a profound clarity after a long period of uncertainty. And this attitude can be found elsewhere too. Like Jesus in Luke 4:1, Francis spoke in the power of the Holy Spirit, according to the report of the Three Companions. Like Jesus, those who heard Francis no longer mocked him, nor did they pity him; his words "went straight to the hearts of his listeners rousing them to vehement astonishment." Celano summarized their response with this remarkable assessment: "He seemed completely different from what he had been." It wasn't that Celano acknowledged this change alone: he had already noted all the developmental steps from Francis's life as the merchant's son to his life as a beggar. Francis was not an entirely different man because he had become the complete opposite of what he was before, as might be expected in a conversion narrative, but rather because clarity had replaced all of his confusion. Francis was a new man. And this was bound to have consequences.[15]

Francis's Friends: Beginnings of the Brotherhood

This new Francis was an enthusiastic enthusiast, a charismatic in the truest sense of the word. The power of his preaching was not only reported in his biographies but can be seen in the fact of the following he amassed. From now on, he gathered brothers around himself. He became an exemplary leader, demonstrating gifts that his earliest biographers presented in a negative light, though perhaps for the first time these characteristics were expressed in their clearest light: now Francis finally knew what he stood for, or wanted to stand for. It is simply undeniable how powerful the impact had been when he heard the Gospel in the commission of Christ to the disciples, as a consequence of which we acknowledge his leadership in gathering together the brotherhood from 1208 or 1209. His legacy really began in that very moment when with confidence he formed a circle around himself, reflecting the profound transformation he had undergone, so complete that it not only led to a new order but spilled beyond the order as well, spreading through all Christendom, and provoking the question of how the church related to money and riches.

Of course, it wasn't that all of Christendom immediately followed Francis, but there was at least a band of brothers who became the core of the later Franciscan movement. And we know quite a lot about those first followers, though of course the tradition that emerged from the ministry of Francis was not always clear or unambiguous. But at the beginning at least it was clear. We read that "Brother Bernard was the first brother whom the Lord gave to me," part of a document that Francis dictated to a brother that is generally regarded as reliable. Here we have in Francis's own words a note about the beginning of his community, though some might still contest its accuracy.[16]

We do have some information about this Bernard from the biographies and from other sources. He is known as Bernard of Quintavalle, a trained lawyer, who died sometime between 1241 and 1246. What is most notable about his decision to follow Francis was his background: unlike Francis, he was born into a noble family, thereby bridging the social divide that existed in Assisi at the time. From the beginning of the movement until 1210, when a new peace treaty was signed, certain social dynamics were assumed. As Francis had highlighted the needs of lepers around him, perhaps exaggerating his responsibility in the eyes of his family by giving them money or taking them into his arms, so also Bernard exercised some measure of paternalistic care for the poor, as befitted his class, and he even gave food and accommodation to Francis for a time as well. Of all the things that others noticed in the life of Francis, Bernard in this period was particularly impressed by his ecstatic life of prayer, for he would stay up all night to praise God and the Virgin Mary. If Celano's account is true, then it was not Francis's life as a hermit or vagrant that made an impression on Bernard, but rather his practice of piety that was notable, far exceeding the standards of his day. And indeed this was characteristic of his piety right from the beginning of his spiritual quest, even before the break with his father, when he took refuge in the cave.[17]

Francis's life as an outsider had certainly been the cause of Bernard's initial sympathy for him and his offer to him of lodging, but this was not enough in itself for Bernard to become a companion or follower. It was Francis's praying and his preaching of repentance that made the difference in

Bernard's life, categories that were both familiar and trusted yet functioned as something distinctly new as well, with their power to cross social divides. Bernard as a nobleman had no middle-class values to turn from. But following Christ in such a radical way was both motivation and challenge to leave behind the path assigned to him in order to join with Francis to "purchase the Kingdom of heaven," as Celano puts it. As the accounts suggest, Francis did not expressly call Bernard to follow him, but it was Bernard who, with some companions, approached Francis to form a friendship, saying, "We want to be with you from now on and do whatever you do." One of Bernard's friends was Peter of Catania, also a nobleman, who brought a degree of erudition to the order. According to his mention in Jordan of Giano (who died around 1262), Peter was master of both Roman civil law and ecclesiastical or canon law. Jordan relates a brief episode in which it was made clear how this community stood at cross-purposes with the values of wider society. Francis addressed Peter as "Lord," or "Dominus," because of his education and background. In the middle of a community of equals, such a greeting was a surprising reminder of the kind of social divide that the brothers were trying to leave behind, even if Francis could have claimed preeminence within the community.[18]

We may speak of Bernard as the first of Francis's followers, as Francis himself recalled, but truth be told there were several men who joined his band—as the evidence suggests—among whom Bernard was just one, though perhaps his status singled him out. More problematic, Celano includes in his *First Life* the note that before Bernard joined Francis, there had been another man, of pious and simple spirit, who followed Francis. If we acknowledge the principle that the most interesting clues for understanding Francis's life come when the details work against the grain of the hagiographic narrative, then we are prompted to ask significant questions, though still no resoundingly plausible overall picture might emerge. If the man had died early, then why wouldn't Celano have mentioned that here? That the man had later fallen out with Francis and had therefore been forgotten is just as implausible, for then Celano would have no reason to describe him so positively. The further speculation, that this figure had later been expunged from the memory of the order, has no real grounding in the account. However, before we read too much into this person, we will have to remain content that the bare enumeration of followers as first, second, and so on must be seen as a later attempt to create some order within the young and slowly growing movement. Francis himself was not averse to just such a rhetorical strategy.[19]

Francis's portrayal of Bernard as the "primus frater," the "first brother," might be better understood not that Bernard chronologically occupied the first place, but rather that he held a particularly important role in relation to Francis, which Bernard did indeed quickly assume. One of the most interesting discoveries to emerge from investigations of the hagiographic reports of the origins of the movement is how its early impetus may well have had more to do with Bernard than the previous emphasis on the founder, Francis himself, had allowed. Reports collected from the early 1240s are unanimous in their account of Bernard coming to make the decision to sell all his possessions after a conversation with Francis. John of Perugia's earlier cited address to Francis goes on to say, "Tell us, therefore, what we should do with our possessions." Bernard clearly respected Francis's authority, whose leadership and preeminence in the community were paramount. When we put the accounts side by side, they don't always make sense, as we shall soon see when we pay particular attention to the description in Celano's *First Life.*[20]

In this account, Bernard sold all his possessions after witnessing the powerful example of Francis's prayers, and in doing so was merely obeying the instructions of Christ to the rich young ruler in Matthew 19:21, who had asked Jesus what good deed he had to do to inherit eternal life, to which Jesus replied: "If you wish to be perfect, go, sell your possessions, and give the money to the poor, and you will have treasure in heaven; then come, follow me." This verse, which became a guiding text for Franciscan spirituality, and which proved to be a motto for these rich young men leaving their parental homes in Assisi, provided the earliest motivation for their decision, even before Francis taught its merits to Bernard, for Celano adds that Bernard's "conversion to God was a model to others in the manner of selling one's possessions and giving them to the poor." Plainly and simply, this sentence is extraordinary, first of all because here we see how Bernard and not Francis was declared the primary example for other conversions, and second because Francis had not behaved like Bernard in selling his possessions. He didn't sell them to give to the poor but threw his money at his father's feet and thereby reneged on the possibility of using it for the help of the poor. Of course, it is likely that conditions for Bernard were somewhat more congenial than they had been for Francis. In this account what is stressed is that Bernard appears fully in control of his household, whereas

Francis was still in a humiliating relationship of dependence on his father, in which possessions are described as his, although they could be used only with his father's permission.[21]

We can see still more in this story of the relationship between the rich young ruler and Bernard, for it appears that he brought to the movement an element of structure, with more attention to consequences, than had been the case with Francis's spontaneity. With this in mind, later stories regarding his relationship to Francis, whose authority was again affirmed, can be seen in a new light. According to the Companions, Bernard did not immediately sell his possessions and distribute the money, but he did invite Francis into his own home—this much is in agreement with Celano—and asked him a question, which effectively contained within it the answer, much in the mold of the exchange of the rich young ruler with Jesus: "If a man receives from God few or many possessions and, having enjoyed them for a number of years, now no longer wishes to retain them, what would be the best thing for him to do?" Even the assumption that one's possessions are from God shows that Bernard had already begun to feel some distance from his wealth, and his question regarding a better use suggests that he is already contemplating disposing of it for a noble cause. If we follow the account of the Three Companions, we are no closer to finding clarity. How precisely to renounce one's wealth was already hinted at in Bernard's very question, but the authority to make the final call was passed to Francis in the narrative anyway.[22]

The Companions' narrative is surprising in another sense, given that they were sufficiently aware of the literary structure of the tale that even at this juncture in the development of the early Franciscan movement they did not present Francis as the sole interpretative authority. Indeed, authority was shifted toward an oracle, such that the next morning when the friends—Francis, Bernard, and Peter of Catania—went to church at San Nicolò in the heart of Assisi, they heard that very same reading from Matthew 19:21, containing the instruction to sell everything to give to the poor. Whether it was read by Francis himself or a priest, we simply don't know, but what we do know is that this was the second time that a Bible reading had unexpectedly yet powerfully brought clarity to Francis. He sought further confirmation by opening the Bible twice more and on both occasions landed on the same text. This experience led him to declare out loud, "O Brothers, this is our life and rule and the life and rule of all those who may wish to join us. Go, therefore, and act on what you have heard." This declaration alone, which John of Perugia also included, gives reason to believe that this report has more to do with the origin story of the Franciscan community than it does with the actual memory of historical events that Francis experienced that day. Such skepticism is underlined when we note that Celano does not place an oracle at this point of his story but rather in another location in the *First Life*. In his retelling, it was in Francis's last years, just before he recounts his vision of a crucified seraph pointing to Christ, that Francis opened the Bible three times and landed on each occasion on a passage testifying to the passion of Christ. Of course we can't rule out the possibility that such a clarifying oracle did indeed take place, or perhaps even happened more than once, but the parallel with three openings of the Bible suggests that this narrative was handed down to us in several variants, in which case the version given by Celano is likely to be the earlier one as it is the more difficult one. In its context, Celano made great efforts to highlight the correspondence between the life of Francis and the sufferings of Christ.[23]

If this early account leaves us with the impression of literary shaping, we can conclude that for the Three Companions and for John of Perugia as well, the placement of the story of the Bible oracle functioned as a confirmation of the beginning of the community. According to older narratives, the community, first established sometime after the death of Francis, was initiated by divine intervention. Celano's report, on the other hand, appears to be closer to the actual events and is perhaps a mixture of old and new. Presumably Bernard had indeed begun to sell his possessions to give to the poor in light of his fascination with Francis, without waiting for Francis's precise instructions, for it was Francis's very own life which reflected the position of the poor as the spiritual center of life in Assisi. The explanation given by Matthew 19 would only then need to come later, not requiring the intervention of an oracle as the Companions portrayed it but emerging from a deep engagement with the texts of the evangelists, whether or not priestly advice or explanation was forthcoming, like with the commissioning sermon.

As is so often the case with the story of Francis, the biographies don't provide all the clarity we may seek. Combined, these observations don't permit of great certainty in retelling the early story of the Franciscan movement apart from what has come down to us. But they do help us to ask fresh questions and to place the emphasis on new accents. The traditional account, concentrating on Francis's agency, is without doubt substantial, for the movement did coalesce around his person and he may also have given the movement impetus through his preaching of repentance. Even from Celano's earlier *Life*, it is certainly true that Bernard's life turned around under the influence of the fascinating personality of Francis of Assisi. But the development of the community from its beginnings to its ultimate form was profoundly shaped by Bernard himself, as the biographies all communicate. Remarkably, this fits well with what has previously been attributed to Francis. His penchant for spontaneity was at odds with the later need for structure, such that it was for him and his movement a matter of great luck that he found in Bernard such a congenial partner who contributed much to the expression of his ideals.

Bernard, so organized compared with Francis's spontaneity, was responsible for the finances of the fellowship in its early days. The Franciscan ideal, exemplified in its later history, was a community ideal. Francis did not see himself as a kind of authority figure, towering above all others while exercising a determining influence. Rather, he pulled people along through the power of a charismatic personality that was so overwhelming that others could see nothing but the work of the Holy Spirit. He did listen to others when they expressed a clear view of what the Bible taught or how social conditions would work with or against his insights. He might have lit the spark, but others made sure that the result was a safe flame and not a wildfire.[24]

It was extraordinarily important for Francis's earliest biographers to explain the growth of the movement in a comprehensive and ordered way. His earliest followers were listed name by name and where possible their characteristics described, though their names and the sequence of their joining may vary. We don't have any documentary evidence from the early phase of the movement, only the memories of that phase written down. Perhaps Celano had been well advised when in his *Second Life* he decided not to include an inventory of early members, but instead wrote: "In a short time many others were converted from the corroding cares of the world and returned into their country under the guidance of Francis, unto infinite good. It would be long to tell of each one how they all attained the prize of their heavenly call."[25]

We can therefore surmise that Celano had himself given up on the attempt to bring order to the jumble of followers. Indeed, in the following pages, while we try to track with the account provided by the Three Companions to provide some resemblance to the traditional narrative of the movement's growth, we recognize nonetheless that things may not have been as neat as suggested, and so from time to time we refer to alternatives too. What proves historically reliable is not the precise sequence but the general shape of the differing reports of the brothers, each of whom brought to their account their own background concerns. This is also true of Brother Giles as recounted by the Companions, for example, who joined the fellowship only after it had found a place to call home. This narrative suggests an intentionally arranged effort to show how orderly the foundation and expansion of the community was. After Giles joined, other followers from Assisi were named. The Companions list "Sabbatino, Morico, and John of Capella," and Celano includes Philip the Long. The difference between these two accounts is especially noteworthy because the Companions in the letter accompanying the *Legend* named Philip as their source. Would Philip have forgotten his own place in the story, or might he deliberately have underplayed his role? Or did Celano get the episode entirely wrong? After this point, the relationships presented by the Companions get murkier still. Being received into the community was not the responsibility of Francis alone but was decided by the fellowship, even if at least some of them were separated by travel from time to time. The Companions describe how four other brothers then joined the community too.[26]

Despite some confusion about details, it is safe to say that in the first two or three years after Francis rejected his father, a strong core of the fellowship took shape, and it continued to grow. The very first companions were united in their task only by their deep sense that Christ had sent them. In traditional language, these brothers were laymen, not clergy. And even though they enjoyed a community life at the Portiuncula, they were not monks who belonged to an order either, even if the consuls of the city had bestowed this legal honor on Francis himself. This was a committed lay fellowship whose authorization to preach came not from any ordination or any other order but from the commission of Jesus Christ himself. After the early accounts of Francis as a preacher in the writings of Celano, biographers tried to correct the story, as preaching by the laity was not permitted. For example, in the two years immediately after these events, the Companions noted that "Francis did not preach sermons to the people they met" and attributed his later permission to preach to Pope Innocent III. Of course, this may sound like canon law was trying to catch up with actual events, but we should not thereby assume that Francis was consciously rebelling against church authority. Perhaps he was merely trusting that Bishop Guido's protective hand covered him. The pope's eventual approval did indeed make a difference to the effectiveness of the brotherhood.[27]

It was perhaps just after the trip to Rome, which provided permission for the brothers to preach, that a priest joined their cohort: Silvester, who had previously sold rocks to Francis for his rebuilding effort. According to the Companions, he did not agree with the way that Bernard ultimately had chosen to spend the brotherhood's money. His opinion provides further indirect evidence that the fellowship was negotiating a new way of establishing its direction at this time. Silvester had willingly sold the stones cheaply to Francis for his renovation work, yet now he demanded that the money Francis saved should be given back to him to help the poor, though his motives may have been impure. And Francis generously—or perhaps contemptuously—returned some money to him. He reached for a handful of coins from Bernard's cloak pocket, gave it to the priest, and then contributed still more, without estimating or precisely counting the amount. He gave back so much that the priest left satisfied—surprisingly, given that the Companions suggested that Silvester was avaricious, one of the seven deadly sins. But his feelings of contentment didn't last, for these actions of Francis had a profoundly transformative impact on him. Confessing his own sinfulness and acknowledging the divine love that Francis reflected, he followed immediately in his steps. At this point, the Companions draw attention to the contrast between old age and youth. Despite Silvester's advanced age, he lacked wisdom and composure, both of which Francis demonstrated. We might see here too a contrast between the laity and the clergy, for it was not long since Francis had turned to a priest to explain the meaning of the commission to the disciples, but now it was a priest learning from him. In Silvester following Francis, the layman was now a leader for the cleric. Relationships had not just been turned on their head but were thoroughly confused, as Francis made abundantly clear in his aspiration for priestly office.[28]

In the *Legend of the Three Companions*, Silvester was possibly counted as the eleventh brother, for after the first six were named, there came four others, making twelve in all. This of course includes Francis but is still a fascinating way of counting. The accounts are historically reliable only in a very circumscribed way, showing some tension between their earliest iterations, especially the details concerning that unknown man in Celano's *First Life* and the uncertainty around Silvester's entry into the community. No explanation is required, however, for the number totaling twelve, which for a group of men who were pursuing an apostolic form of life was no coincidence. Symbolically, Jesus had gathered around himself twelve disciples to create the new people of God, according to the Gospel writers, based on the number of tribes of Israel. In light of this background, it is worth noting that the Three Companions (in agreement with Celano) did not place Francis outside the twelve but stressed that it was Francis who was the twelfth, and described him as their "dux et pater," their "leader and father." It doesn't mean that at this moment there were only twelve men and no others in the community; rather, the Companions note that there were twelve because Francis and his brothers had started out for Rome to demand recognition of their community from the pope. It was not necessary, and indeed would have been highly unlikely, that every last man of the community would have traveled to Rome. Even though Assisi was not too far away, there is good reason to assume that the group was now sufficiently large that only a selection of them would need to present their case. The Companions would nonetheless stick with the number twelve to give the impression that all the brothers and not just a delegation of them had had an audience with the pope.[29]

Whether we follow the precise details of the Companions or not, the number twelve was not the result of isolating a group for the journey to Rome but was a way of the brothers symbolically holding onto that moment when they as a group sought Rome's authorization. This then amplified the meaning of Francis belonging to the twelve, for he did not presume to position himself as a contemporary counterpart to Jesus among the twelve disciples, instead counting himself among, not apart from, his apostolic band. Even if he did at his life's end see in his story someone resembling Christ, this was not the case at the beginning. Instead, he counted himself among these apostles, raising the question of whether being named the leader and father of the group was the careful attempt of the Companions at just this juncture to show how later developments were outgrowths of early hierarchy, which might not have corresponded exactly with reality on the ground.

The Companions nonetheless reinforced the notion that the early brotherhood—they were already using the term *fraternitas* for themselves—had developed a thoroughly egalitarian structure. If anyone stood out, it was not because of his capacity to give commands to others but a function of his spiritual gifting, like Francis, or of a particular role, like Bernard, who had responsibility for the common purse, not an easy task given that he stood out from the others like Judas among Jesus's disciples (John 12:6).

More striking is the fact that, according to John of Perugia, it was Bernard who was elected leader of the brothers. This was likely to be only a temporary exchange of responsibilities, for shortly thereafter in Rome Francis took the lead in speaking. The election of Bernard nonetheless highlighted the nonhierarchical character of the brotherhood for two further reasons identified in the report of the Companions. The first was mentioned previously: entry to the brotherhood was not within the gift of Francis alone; any brother could welcome new members to the fellowship, for the Companions somewhat awkwardly explain that Francis gave them just this kind of "auctoritas" or "authority." We don't see any other particular processes for exercising authority, which might suggest that the relaxed nature of the organization enabled the culture to affirm equal rights between members as a matter of course, which expressed itself in the matter of the requirements of joining, without Francis necessarily approving the process, though the Companions do presumptuously designate the movement as an "ordo," an "order," even at this early stage.[30]

Second, we see how the community was characterized by an equality among members when it came to preaching, and this too emerged from the report of the Companions, perhaps despite their best intentions. According to the Companions, at a very early stage, when the fellowship still consisted of just four men (Francis, Bernard, Peter, and Giles), the brothers divided the group to go and preach repentance. As well as positive motivations for this dispersion, we might also include the unfortunate opposition that these sons of Assisi increasingly faced in their hometown. The Three Companions noted this for Sabatinus, Morico, and John of Capella at some later date with the interesting comment that the growing hostility in Assisi contributed to their lack of success in begging. Again assuming the later Franciscan ideal, this mention of begging suggested a broader horizon. The small but growing community of the brothers in Assisi was provocative enough. What exactly the denizens of the town held against these enthusiastic young men, even with a sympathetic reading, we just can't tell. If they hadn't given away their possessions, they wouldn't have been forced onto the margins of society to live a desperate life. The behavior of these formerly entitled brothers appeared simply absurd, one of the consequences of which could have been taking up new work, as they soon did. But on the other hand, it may have been a wiser possibility to spread out to preach with the hope that they might find greater acceptance elsewhere right from the beginning of the movement. And so according to the Companions, the path of the first four brothers led away from Assisi. Francis and Giles set out toward the northeast into the Marches of Ancona, and the other two went in a different direction. We might naturally sense some hierarchy here between Francis and Giles on account of their previous experiences, but it is not so easy to comprehend a hierarchical relationship between Francis on the one hand and Bernard and Peter on the other. The first mission trip can only really be understood as an expression of the equality of members of the brotherhood.[31]

This is true of Celano's description of the commission too, for he placed it later in the story and grouped the men together in a different way, with only eight companions in the cohort at this stage. According to his report, it was Bernard and Giles who set out together in the direction of Santiago de Compostela, the famous pilgrimage destination on the northwest coast of the Iberian Peninsula, while Francis set out with an unnamed brother in a different direction. In any case, Celano's narrative is notable for not naming two pairs of brothers, who simply went "two by two to other regions." Apparently he was concerned to present this early missionary activity as a mission to the four corners of the world, in which case the path to Santiago was not just a reminder of the importance of this pilgrim path to medieval believers but should be understood as well as a destination at the outermost corners of the known world. However, the fact that Celano mentioned the unnamed first brother points to the fact that his memory was not inferior to that of the Companions, and conversely that Celano's way of constructing events highlighted how the Companions were not always correct in their own telling. Both indeed support the claim that while many details in the origins of the brotherhood might have been unclear, their purpose in narrating Francis's life was not, taking up notions of completeness and numerology and not just historical memories. Possibly John of Perugia's account of their dispersal to the four corners of the earth got to the kernel of the matter when he reported that Francis and Giles left Bernard and Peter behind.[32]

All this meant that any conspicuous parallels in the symbolic attribution of numbers must be treated seriously, for example, the way Francis was numbered among the twelve, given his later veneration, is hard to fathom. Francis at the beginning of this account was just one among others, certainly the father in the sense that he stood at the beginning of the movement but recognized as its leader only with some hesitation. This kind of exceptional role was expressed ably by Julian of Speyer—again in hagiographic language—when he wrote: "Now the father rejoiced in the joyful company of six brothers, he being the seventh; and in all things he behaved not as someone greater, but as the least among the lesser." Reflections like these make very clear that the fellowship that set out in 1209 for Rome to seek recognition of its rule consisted of a group following the call of Jesus with great enthusiasm, recognizing him alone as Lord and listening to the pope as his representative, but with no requirement of a strict leadership cadre within its own organization.[33]

The biographies that told the story of the brothers as they headed out in all directions also narrate how they returned: at God's behest, as Celano relates, they came back and regrouped without human planning. This almost unbelievable construct is avoidable if we follow John of Perugia, who assumes that their travels were unplanned but on the whole were conducted within a short distance of Assisi, never reaching the Atlantic coast. This suggests a model of life that saw the early brothers traveling to preach but returning at regular intervals to the same predetermined meeting point.[34]

These first preaching circuits allowed for an easy parallel with the homelessness of the apostles: "Foxes have holes, and birds of the air have nests; but the Son of Man has nowhere to lay his head," as Matthew 8:20 describes the practice of following Jesus. This biblical background shone through when the biographies presented the followers of Francis having no place to call home, but the narratives are too dense and too concrete to explain exactly how their apostolicity of life might have been understood and exemplified in the light of biblical instruction. It was more that the brothers simply exerted themselves to live like the apostles as best they could, accepting all the consequences that might come their way. They simply found a place to lie down in the porticos of churches or houses, so that it appears believable that they were called "ribald," or vagabonds. Occasionally they were offered hospitality, but mainly they were denied a place to stay. John of Perugia once described how people related to them, a reflection not just on the fate of this movement devoted to poverty, but also an account of how in the thirteenth century those who lived on the margins of society (without bridges being built to offer inclusion) were further and further marginalized: "Although they were treated by this man with kindness, others considered them good-for-nothings, so much so that many, the small and the great, treated them and spoke to them 'as masters with their servants.' Although the brothers wore the poorest and cheapest clothes, for amusement many people still took these away from them. And so, even though they were left naked, for they had only one tunic, the brothers nevertheless always observed the form of the Gospel by not demanding back what was taken from them." John may well be prone to generalizations, but that the poor were treated contemptuously in medieval society and that the early Franciscans faced similar treatment was doubtless true.[35]

It is, however, quite easy to imagine that it wasn't the whole community that went on preaching tours, but rather small groups of brothers or, as the tales relate, pairs of brothers going out to the four corners of the world. But it remained true that the brothers believed themselves to be a unified community and reinforced this ritually. The Three Companions report that they tried to avoid any speech that would involuntarily injure others. But if one did speak hurtful words, he should throw himself on the ground, while the one who had been offended set his foot over the offender's mouth. In this way, internal punishment and humiliation were meted out in order to strengthen solidarity, which in turn would suggest common living quarters.[36]

But common quarters were not always easy to come by. As the brothers gathered together again after their preaching tour, the Companions reported that they erected a small house near the Portiuncula, which is not entirely implausible, for Francis himself had spent much time there—but it appears that Rivotorto emerged as their base after the trip to Rome. These options may not prove too hard to reconcile, for Rivotorto, named after a small stream, the Rivus Tortus, lies just below San Damiano and not very far from the Portiuncula. It only takes about an hour to walk from one to the other. So perhaps the brothers did seek out a location near the familiar Portiuncula but eventually decided on a location closer to the main trading street, which we learn about through a most memorable encounter. In 1209, when Otto IV (r. 1209–18) of the German Welf dynasty was passing through Assisi along the main road on the way to his imperial coronation in Rome, Francis and his community—according to Celano—refused to offer him any token of their allegiance. By any stretch of the imagination, Rivotorto could only have been a temporary solution, for the hut they occupied did no more than protect them from sun and rain. They denied themselves the construction of houses and instead took refuge in whatever kind of accommodation was available. The Companions mentioned how cramped their quarters were, for it was a great challenge simply to find enough room in which each of the brothers could lie down. The wretched condition of their quarters gives us insight into another one of their spiritual priorities in this period (after their preaching rounds): their asceticism. We can't even assume a more or less regular monastic religious life, especially when we read in Bonaventure's reliable account that they didn't even possess books of hours to shape their daily prayers but instead learned the liturgy by rote. They spent their day in ex tempore prayer, breaking frequently for silent meditation or to care for the lepers. Something of this lifestyle was echoed in the words Francis later wrote, assembled as the unauthorized *Rule of 1221* (the *Regula non bullata*): "They [the friars] should be glad to live among social outcasts, among the poor and the helpless, the sick and the lepers, and those who beg by the wayside."[37]

It is important to note how the last two categories hang together, for the brothers had apparently decided to imitate the behavior of the lepers in asking for alms, so their location near the main street through Assisi was an easy place to beg, though the disadvantage was that they were not close to a church. Even if Silvester, who later joined the brotherhood, had brought with him a portable fold-up altar to celebrate the Mass—something frequently used by traveling priests in the Middle Ages so entirely possible— they would still have been dependent on a local church closer to them in the valley (where the growing brotherhood eventually moved), for example, San Damiano or the Portiuncula, to receive other sacraments. The biographies drape the move in a legendary story: a farmer asked to stay in their hut with his donkey, ostensibly because he feared that the brothers were about to spread out and take land away from local farmers. This conflict made Francis realize that their ascetic ideal of withdrawal to a remote place did not necessarily support them in their spiritual task, which should be more focused on the church, so the community left for the Portiuncula. It wasn't merely that they needed a larger space; they had other logistical reasons too: they left the hut to the lepers of the town. They thus created a kind of hospital, even if it was only provisional. Francis's unplanned approach to the lepers at the beginning of his spiritual quest had become a more structured form of care. His alternative to the established world of Assisi was now becoming something permanent. This alternative reality formed around the life of the brotherhood, to which they gave an intentional shape.[38]

Even at the beginning of their life together, the brothers began to look for work so that they could better support the lepers. As strange as it may sound, this approach to daily labor represented a further radicalizing of the movement, a further step away from traditional piety in Assisi, even more radical than a life of begging, as they sought to create an alternative world. Whoever gave alms to the poor did a good deed, which could be reckoned to that person's spiritual account. In this way, through money or a gift in kind, a person could assuage his or her conscience before God. This was part of Francis's earliest understanding of the role of almsgiving. But now the brothers were doing work to support the lepers. Implicitly, they were calling an end to the strategy of religious and social solidarity built on almsgiving by making clear that the call to repentance was more radical than anything that European Christian society had known.[39]

But even this thought stands on shaky ground. Franciscan research over the last few decades has established that although begging was central to their lifestyle from the beginning, this was not in the sense of a self-conscious ideal but rather more like an unavoidable alternative. In Jesus's commission, he had provided this proverbial wisdom: "Laborers deserve their food" (Matthew 10:10). Reports emanating from the period of Clare's canonization also attest to the role of work for Francis and his brothers in the early stages of the movement. Only when work was lacking should the brothers turn to begging, according to later *Rules.* This loophole in the regulations of the early brothers led quite quickly to an increasingly important role for begging, a concession that in the so-called *Regula non bullata,* or unauthorized *Rule of 1221,* developed considerably to become a whole chapter explaining the conditions under which it was permitted. Among other things, it allowed the brothers to disregard prescriptions concerning fasting in a case of emergency. Slowly, begging became central to the Franciscan movement. In this way, the lifestyle and indeed the rule of Francis himself went beyond what was clearly demanded in the Scriptures. One can perhaps assume that here we see the first adaptations of the practices of the disciples of Christ to the particular situation of the brothers from Assisi.[40]

Through the vicissitudes of these developments, we sense Francis's emerging spiritual identity, which he articulated as he looked back on his life: "I worked with my own hands." It might be easier to imagine and more satisfying to conclude that all the reports of begging in the early years were the interpolation of a later period, but it is simply not the case. This quotation from the *Testament* of Francis is a barely modified sentence from Paul's farewell speech at Miletus to the Ephesian elders (Acts 20:34). The apostle of Assisi leaned on the words of the apostle of Tarsus in giving his own farewell address. Of course, this doesn't rule out the possibility that Francis had begged for his keep during his youth, but the way he stressed his preparedness to work might nonetheless speak to a situation where others in his order were increasingly refusing to work, with the hope that their desperate begging might lead them to some generous donor and the chance of a comfortable life. Francis's recollection is, however, likely to be slightly exaggerated, talking up the virtue of work, which may not have been precisely representative of original conditions.[41]

We see this dual intention as Francis further wrote: "And I am still determined to work." A couple of lines later, there is an interesting parallel: "When we receive no recompense for our work, we can turn to God's table and beg alms from door to door." Notice the explicit reference to his contemporary readers in using the word we. And even if the language of "turning" to God's table, recurrere, is not precisely biographical or literal, it is at least true that begging was not foreign to Francis's experience. It was one option alongside work, and—importantly—was valued next to work. An emergency solution, but a solution nonetheless. For both begging and work, the Portiuncula was the starting point. There the brothers built or requisitioned their small house, as one can still see today. Later they were given the church too, which meant all the buildings they needed were in proximity to each other, allowing for the formation of a type of monastic lifestyle, at least outwardly, though this differed markedly from the mighty monastic foundations of the Benedictines of the period. It appears that around 1210 this small group located in the valley beneath Assisi was the center of the community. The Franciscan scholar and friar Michael F. Cusato has emphasized how the brothers deliberately remained outside the city, although they had to walk into the city each day to beg. At least this was some kind of acknowledgment of an ascetic withdrawal from the wider society. Their biographers have trouble in describing the houses where they found residence: they were certainly impoverished but nonetheless solid and respectable. In his Second Life, Celano tells us that Francis tried to demolish the house near the Portiuncula all by himself, until he was advised that it didn't belong to the brothers at all but to the town council.[42]

The fellowship that was drawn to Francis was increasingly egalitarian, characterized by a religious vision to combine forms of ascetic living with a call of repentance to society at large. At the beginning of this process, Francis had recognized that his ideals stood in marked contrast to the realities of bourgeois society, but significantly not in contrast with the values of the church. Not surprisingly, then, he sought out papal recognition of his movement. In this cause, he set out for Rome in 1209 with eleven companions. This was clearly a signal that he believed any authorization for his fellowship needed to come from the pope and not the bishop of his own diocese. Here Francis showed that he was committed not just to the local but to the universal church.

The Search for Recognition

Francis had just returned from his preaching tour when the brothers undertook their journey to Rome in 1209, probably between Easter and Pentecost. We can date this event quite accurately because we have already learned that Francis encountered Otto IV as he passed through Rivotorto around that time on his way to his coronation. This small band of twelve poor brothers left shortly afterward for their own meeting with the pope in the richly appointed Lateran Palace in Rome, which was at this time the headquarters of the papacy before it moved to the Vatican. There will be more to say later about the misunderstanding between the then reigning Pope Innocent III and the *poverello,* but suffice to say here that Innocent is rightly depicted as one of the most grandiose and powerful popes of the Middle Ages. His lifestyle was far from the ideals of Francis, who did not, however, pay much attention to the contrast. Since Bishop Guido's offer of protection to Francis, he was persuaded that he could trust the church and its highest representatives. And happily for Francis, when he got to Rome, Guido was also there. Francis was counting on Guido's support as he presented his petition, demanding recognition of his community as an order of the church.[43]

There is no way of understanding Francis's presentation other than as a claim for recognition of his "regula," his rule for the order. This original rule appears no longer to exist, and it would be in vain to try to reconstruct it from the later *Rule of 1221 (Regula non bullata)*, which was never authorized by a papal bull anyway. There is just no way of knowing what might have been taken over from the document of 1209, assuming various versions of it in between those years, and it appears that the original version had next to nothing in common with the later rule anyway. The purpose of a rule, as we will see later, was to determine exactly what philosophy will guide a community, its lifestyle, and its leadership structure. Even the development of the unauthorized *Rule of 1221* underwent significant changes before its authorized edition in 1223, especially concerning questions of leadership. The rule for an order naturally contained some theological basis, but its function was more as a legal text that normalized the shape of the order.[44]

For all intents and purposes, Francis's original rule contained no provisions for the order's leadership. Francis recollected in his *Testament* that he had drafted this rule "briefly and simply." In fact, he never even referred to it as a rule at all, but he did speak of a "forma sancti Evangelii," a lifestyle according to the holy Gospel that the Lord had revealed to him. Even though Celano used the words "forma et regula," giving the impression that something more substantial was being presented to the pope, it was actually something less like a rule than we might imagine, for Celano went on to say that Francis used "for the most part the words of the holy Gospel" along with "a few other things that were necessary." The later rules also contained frequent quotations from the Scriptures, but Celano's comments suggest that the original draft of the rule consisted of not much more than a collage of sentences from the Gospels, which had become especially important to Francis and his colleagues, perhaps just what the Lord had revealed to him, as he remarked.[45]

In this early version, we can assume that the genre of a rule was almost completely absent, and perhaps it was never Francis's intention to write one anyway. It is likely to be a wrong assumption that Francis intended to found an order. He just didn't think in categories like this. It can be no coincidence that the Three Companions in their account never mentioned a rule, and it is also not surprising: Francis was the son of a merchant with enough education to exercise his trade but not much more. Whether he knew other literary models, like the famed *Rule of St. Benedict,* is of course open to debate, but his later rules by no means required this assumption. He had written his rule just as it seemed plausible to him. And what seemed plausible to him at this juncture probably emerged from Jesus's commission in Matthew 10, in which his conversion to a new way of living was grounded and that for him had great resonance. It forbade bags and shoes, a second shirt, and a walking staff, conditions that he had from the beginning applied to his life, though his handling of money was not aligned completely with the words of commission. Jesus had said to his disciples that they should "take no gold, or silver, or copper in your belts" (Matthew 10:9). These words stood in tension with other Scriptural passages, according to which all goods were to be sold and the proceeds given to the poor, which of course meant that in the meantime gold could be possessed. And it was Bernard who in the early movement took up responsibility for handling what money the fellowship did have. We just don't know if in that first draft all money was to be renounced, but any hesitation concerning wealth would likely have influenced developments anyway. Rejection of his earlier life in the home of a wealthy merchant no doubt still played its part, as might Jesus's instructions in Matthew 10. Just as regulations against owning property shaped their lifestyle, so too the admonition from Mark 6:12 concerning repentance and the importance of preaching conversion might have been included in the *forma* of their first rule, which Francis wanted to have sanctioned. What Francis brought to Rome was unlikely to have been a polished legal document, and the reaction he got was fittingly restrained. When Francis later claimed that the pope had confirmed his way of life, he didn't mean that the pope had provided a formal recognition of the rule, but merely an acceptance of his community's life.[46]

More indelible than the first form of the rule was the meeting between Innocent and Francis. In this narrative, which has seared itself into the annals of the movement, we learn of Francis's dream about the pope, which was actually more like a combination of parable and dream. Bonaventure made much of it in his *Major Life*, and along with Giotto's frescoes, the dream has established itself as a powerful element in the biography of Francis. The scenario of the dream reminds us of the audience of Old Testament prophets before powerful rulers. Just as Daniel interpreted a dream for Nebuchadnezzar in Daniel 2, or the prophet Nathan made an accusation in parabolic form against King David in 2 Samuel 12, so Francis recounted before the pope a story, which according to Celano's *Second Life* had been revealed directly from Christ himself. In this tale he described a rich king whose beautiful but poor wife had given birth to children who were just like their father and had raised them at his own table. We might assume that any father would do this, but we learn more about the background to this particular situation when we read on. His wife had never been invited to live in the palace but remained with her other children, born out of wedlock, in the desert. It was only when the children had grown up that she sent them to the court of their father, where they were welcomed in without her.

This kind of parabolic structure has New Testament parallels, where something good might be represented in a problematic person or series of difficult events. Here we discover that the relationship between the king and his wife was not all that it appeared to be, for in fact it was illegitimate. In Celano's account, the king first had to do some research to provoke his memory of their amorous encounter. Bonaventure, in abbreviating the whole narrative, veils and confuses some of its details. Biblical allusions play a role here, reminding us of the proclamation of the prophet Hosea, who argued that Israel's relationship with God was like his own relationship with his wife, a prostitute (Hosea 1:3). What Francis said is by comparison not so offensive, but the great distance between the eternal God and the woman is recognizable yet becomes more striking still when we learn, counterintuitively, that in early accounts this woman was identified with Francis himself. The good king was of course Christ. It is worth noting that in the accounts by both Celano and Bonaventure, Francis presented his request to the very pope who now had begun to see his office no longer as a follower of Peter but instead as the representative of Christ on earth, drawing him into the dynamics of the story. In their world of visual representation, the pope's wealth was legitimized as a reflection of Christ's own glory. The tale has the further meaning that poverty is not viewed in contrast with the riches of the church but is seen as complementary to its wealth.[47]

In Bonaventure's account, the parable needed further explanation, which became one of the most famous and loaded episodes in the life of Francis, where the chief protagonist is not so much Francis as the pope himself, and perhaps therefore God, who could use others to guide and direct the life of the *poverello* from Assisi. The pope interpreted this encounter with Francis by means of a vision that he had himself received, in which the mighty Lateran Basilica, first built in late antiquity, was shaking but didn't finally collapse. Should this church, connected to the papal palace in which they now met, shake, so would the power of the papacy shake, as they both understood clearly. But there was also someone in the vision who could save the building from collapse, a "homo pauperculus," a "poor beggarman," who put his back to the wall of the enormous building to stop it from falling, whom the pope immediately recognized in Francis: "This is certainly the man. By his work and teaching, he will uphold Christ's Church." All at once, Innocent solved the not too complicated vision according to Bonaventure's report and identified the man from Assisi with the man in his dream.[48]

Even if a reader was generally skeptical concerning visions like this, it is not too hard to see how literary models could be at play here. First of all, the work's late composition lends this impression. Celano knew as little about the parable or the vision when he wrote his *First Life* as did Julian of Speyer, and in Celano's abbreviated *Life*, the *Vita brevior*, both are entirely lacking. John of Perugia is aware of the dream but not of the collapse of the Lateran church. It was only in Celano's *Second Life* and in the narrative of the Three Companions that all these components appeared together, and then Bonaventure passed them down in a more complete way. We may not see this development as particularly important, given that there are several other stories from Francis's life that appear only in later versions. But can we really believe that such an extraordinary account of the pope's vision, unknown in the 1230s, reemerged only when Crescentius appealed for stories about Francis for a new collection, only then being rescued from oblivion? Barely any other story could validate and strengthen Francis's movement better than this one, which was ignored by Celano in his earliest account. Rather, a theological conviction seems to have generated the story that was present in other parts of Francis's biographies: the call of the speaking crucifix in San Damiano for Francis to rebuild the house of Christ. This command and its reception by Francis thrived because of its splendid ambiguity, which colored Innocent's dream too. Just as Christ's instruction through the crucifix was of course meant to be understood figuratively as referring to the institution of the church, though Francis heard the command to refer to its very literal buildings near Assisi, so also the pope's dream describing a real building might best have been interpreted symbolically, representing the church universal on earth. Both tales have a similar idea at their core and both shaped the Franciscan tradition in the few short years after Francis's death. Their value lies not in literal historical sources but elsewhere: in these stories, we see how his contemporaries viewed Francis as someone who could save the church of their day. In this spiritual sense, he did indeed build up Christ's church again. His earlier renovations of physical buildings gave credence to the dream, in which, with all its ambiguity about what the church is, God's role in leading was nonetheless discernible.[49]

At one level, this whole encounter comes across as so impressive and therefore true, even if events from a more mundane perspective played out more laboriously and diplomatically. At first, Francis was not allowed to appear before Innocent at all—and in one sense this shouldn't surprise us. The first conversations involved Bishop Guido of Assisi, who no doubt feared that the "Francis matter" would get in the way of his own negotiations with the pope, which is why he was in Rome in the first place. Along with the bishops of Perugia and Foligno, Guido had been instructed by the pope a year earlier to dissolve a monastery within his diocese and place it under the authority of another. These diplomatic tensions provided the least propitious context in which to advocate for Francis and his friends. This is probably also the background for Guido's annoyance when Francis arrived, despite earlier being such a champion of Francis's cause. Celano's comment that Guido just didn't want such good men to end up leaving his diocese may obscure his more pertinent disappointment that they were getting in the way of his diplomatic hopes. He didn't appear to want to lobby for their papal recognition, especially in the confused form in which the claim was presented. What Francis was asking for was so different from established forms of monasticism, yet his appeal was never more likely to succeed than then. Traditionally, monasticism was defined around the evangelical counsels of poverty, chastity, and obedience. They were called evangelical counsels because their origins lay in the Gospel that Christ preached, but unlike other commandments, they were not applicable to all Christians. They had a different status from commandments like "You shall not kill" or "You shall not commit adultery." But such values were nevertheless grounded in Christ's message. It appears that consideration of these evangelical counsels reinforced the commitment to a life of poverty and especially to chastity or sexual abstinence that belonged to the Franciscan form of life. It was the question of obedience, which was less well thought through within this egalitarian community and yet found particular expression in their submission to the pope, whom according to John of Perugia Francis and his brothers praised.[50]

If Francis and his brothers had adopted and adapted one of the many rules that monastic movements had previously written, it would have been quite straightforward for them to have found their place in the church and not to have needed any particular papal permission or recognition of their community life. Perhaps it is for this reason that Guido referred the group to someone else who might be ideal to act in their interest, John of St. Paul, the cardinal bishop of Sabina, whose name alerts us to his role as a member of the Benedictine order in the monastery of St. Paul outside the Walls. As cardinal and scion of the great Roman Colonna family, he no doubt had more influence with the pope than the Umbrian bishop Guido, and as a Benedictine he knew well the ascetic tradition that Francis had come to commend. It is for this reason that he attempted to guide Francis into a traditional form of the ascetic life, engaging him in conversation about the *vita monastica* and the *vita eremitica*, according to Celano. However, these older models of piety didn't prove to be to Francis's satisfaction: he could see how they supported some of his concerns, but they gave no obvious place to Jesus's commissioning sermon. Besides, if we take it that the biographies are not at this point stylized, Francis had already in vain sought out help from the Benedictines and had worn the garments of a hermit, though he had now given up on this practice.[51]

In any case, Francis found support from Cardinal John, who offered to function as "procurator," a kind of spokesman, for the young fellowship within the curia and to bring their request to the pope. It is likely that he was the one who secured for Francis an audience with the pope. Acting in this regard for Francis would not have proved easy for John, for their conversations were about more than how challenging the church would find the demands of the Franciscan movement, whose ideals were fed by their apostolic roots. Bonaventure too sharpened the question of novelty when he described their encounter with the pope. As Innocent paused, John of St. Paul spoke up: "Anyone who says that a vow to live according to the perfection of the Gospel contains something new or unreasonable or too difficult to be observed, is guilty of blasphemy against Christ, the author of the Gospel." This report gave focus both to the problem and the solution. Anything new was unwanted, for the church yearned for stability at this moment, given the threats it felt by the heretical movements of the Waldensians and the Cathars. But everything turned on the way newness was defined, whether measured against contemporary conditions or, alternatively, against the venerable origins of Christianity. John's speech in Bonaventure's account pled for the Franciscan movement to be weighed against apostolic ideals, thereby recognizing that its life was animated by the inheritance of earliest Christianity.[52]

Nonetheless, one could not close one's eyes to the very real concerns that arose in canon law. The reports were clear that alongside the question of novelty there was still a concern about the legality of the kind of preaching to which Francis and his band felt called. And it was exactly this concern that was front and center in conversation with Pope Innocent, who began "exhorting them concerning many things and admonishing them," as Celano reports, and concluded their audience with a blessing that gave them permission to preach: "Go with the Lord, brothers, and as the Lord will deign to inspire you, preach penance to all." What Francis recalled in his *Testament* as the pope's confirmation found its earliest shape here, for the pope wasn't rubber-stamping a final legal text but affirming the spirit of the Franciscan movement and excising it from the episcopal hierarchy. The brothers were not dependent on the bishop to exercise their preaching ministry but drew their inspiration only from God. When other church leaders came to terms with their preaching—as Jacques de Vitry recalls—it was because of the "great esteem" in which they were held. If this was true, it was a weak foundation that nonetheless fitted well with the vague narrative of Celano. The word *inspirare*, which Celano used in his Latin text, was not unintentionally connected to the "Spiritus sanctus," the Holy Spirit, whom the pope assumed to be leading their fellowship without them being formally incorporated into the church hierarchy, apart from its highest authority. Their connection to the pope was now of course official and remained so, for the pope not only authorized the brothers to preach but placed them under his own watch. His blessing assumed the announcement that he would grant further concessions if the number of the brothers increased accordingly. This meant, in short, that he wanted to keep his eye on them. He was providing them with a test to see if the Franciscan movement could prove itself, with the nod that any further commission could come only from him.[53]

It was in 1209, just a few years after Francis had either left bourgeois society behind or had been pushed out, that he received the highest acknowledgment that the church could bestow. As Michael F. Cusato avers, here we witness a "watershed in the history of the Franciscan movement." Though the life of Francis's soul is more closed to us than many other historical figures whom we learn about through textual and visual testimonies, and the stories about him have only the most marginal interest in psychological processes, we can nevertheless try to imagine the magnitude of the transformation that must have taken place. Within just a few years, his friends and family had begun to feel a deep contempt toward him, or in the best case perhaps just ambivalence. Now he had stood before the most powerful man in the world and had received his recognition, which was not just legal in its outworking but had stabilized his conflicted identity. The man who had once been unrooted had now found his place in the world.[54]

Here began a new quest for Francis, one that was to prove so challenging for him in the remainder of his life. He was on a quest to find structure and order. Most fellowships can't really function without some rules, and the larger they are, the more important the rules become. It appears that it didn't take long before that original rule for the community's life, which Francis had presented to the pope, no longer proved adequate. Celano makes clear that very soon after his audience, the first drafts of a new rule were being prepared, a rule that would much later be presented to the pope and has come to be known as the *Regula non bullata*, the *Rule of 1221*, which was not formally authorized. As confirmation, we learn here too that Francis also gave the brothers a name, the *ordo fratrum minorum*, or the Order of the Friars Minor. This description was not only drawn from the label of *minores*, a social grouping in Assisi that represented the lower middle class and that had steered the fortunes of the city since the peace treaty or "freedom charter" was signed. No doubt the Franciscans had to wrestle this epithet away from the town to fill it with new theological content. For them one was a *minor* not because one was socially inferior but as a result of one's humility and penitent heart. And just as important was the description of the movement as an order, for under this label, even without official papal recognition, we sense the beginnings of structure and the formalizing of its shape. It was of course still a long way off, another decade, before the order in 1223 was officially sanctioned.[55]

Beloved in the Spirit: Clare

When the first followers of Francis formed a community and sought the sanction of the pope for legitimation, men were at the center of the action. And it is easy to imagine why (even if a rash interpretation proves inadequate): Francis wanted to follow the call of the apostles, and the earliest apostles were all men. However, Paul was aware of female apostles in the church when he sent his greeting to Junia, who according to Romans 16:7 was "prominent among the apostles," though this had long since been forgotten in the thirteenth century. The apostolic office of the bishops had become, like the office of the priest, a purely male affair, though women had responsibilities in the congregation as widows, or later as nuns in monasteries.

With this background in mind, we note nonetheless that Francis's rule of life would not necessarily be one for men only. The thought that life as a believer might be expressed as someone naked following someone naked would of course be even more problematic in the Middle Ages for women, who thus had more chance of offending against social propriety, yet leaving behind traditional social norms was part of the movement's identity from the outset. Feelings of dislocation could be shared by women in Assisi too. We know this through the story of Clare, born in 1193, who soon became acquainted with Francis and was a scion of the noble Offreduccio family. It appears that Celano had drafted a *Vita* for Clare too, where we learn that her mother, Ortulana, had often undertaken pilgrimages herself. We sense something important in the comment that she did so "even though she was bound by the bond of marriage," suggesting that her husband was not especially supportive of her pilgrimages, or that this was one of the few opportunities she had to get some distance from her husband's sexual demands, although she did not want to escape her responsibilities but instead appears to have devoted herself to care for her family.[56]

The evident tension between her parents led Clare to a kind of behavior not unlike what we have seen in Francis's life. At least formally, she tried to uphold her family's expectations of her while coming to terms with the possibilities of a more radical path. In the context of the investigation around her canonization, her friend Bona de Guelfuccio reported that even as a young girl, Clare had given food to the poor, which sounds like an exaggerated description of common assumptions of religious responsibility (similar to the origin stories of Francis or Bernard) that her parents would also have undertaken. To give alms to the poor was central to the external forms of piety that Clare shared with her world, even if we learn in Celano that—quite proper for Clare's class—she didn't hand over the alms herself but sent servants to provide for the poor. Such aspects of diaconal service were greatly stressed in accounts of her life, perhaps to shore up parallels with Francis. From the very beginning, the ascetic way had a large place in her life, as Celano reports, "Under her costly and soft clothes, she wore a hairshirt." Francis was also depicted from time to time in such a way. But more pronounced than in the story of Francis, the theme of sexuality—or rather its denunciation—can be seen in the narratives about Clare, picking up features of her mother's marriage and reframing them as elements in a new story. Several witnesses in her canonization process point out that

Clare, like many female religious contemporaries, resisted her parents' plans for an arranged marriage, the strongest kind of protest against the expectations of their class. And it apparently happened even before her parents had given their approval for the normal life of singleness in becoming a nun. The remarkably similar irritations that both Clare and Francis experienced in their youth—along with others like Bernard and Peter—point us to the fact that this was a generational conflict that was in part determined by the many social changes experienced in Assisi itself. Clare experienced this even as a child when her family had to leave Assisi due to the conflict between the middle class and the nobility. She saw from the perspective of a noble family how the rise of mercantile wealth bought the decline of her own class, and she felt the hollowing out of forms of piety in her own circles too. These kinds of experience of difference and tension she shared with Francis, but she didn't know it yet.[57]

She first heard about Francis when she was sixteen years old. After the brothers had returned to Assisi from their trip to Rome and had taken up residence around the Portiuncula, Clare sent some money to them. In the fellowship of the brothers, she noticed a potential model to escape the feelings of dislocation that she had experienced too. This was exactly the time (Francis's biographers tell us) when his message began to reach women and not just men. Because she was a noblewoman, she couldn't run to Francis and the brothers as other women did, so it was cousin Rufino, who got to know the group after their return from Rome, who was able to introduce her. It was thus that Clare and Francis's friendship was kindled, which in Celano's account resembled a love story. When Francis first appeared, he was like a *paranymphus,* a ceremonial assistant helping to prepare Clare for the heavenly marriage with her bridegroom Christ, which may have obviated the implication that he was himself her lover. More suggestive is the way their meetings were described almost as rendezvous, as they sought each other out secretively. Of course, such clandestine meetings were designed to avoid the rumor mill, the "rumor publicus," as Celano phrases it, but this in itself shows that Celano was aware that this kind of tryst between a young man and a young woman was normally attached to scandal. Such secretiveness is attested to in other stories of those who were close to them. Whenever Clare left the house to visit Francis, she was accompanied by a friend, which as we have seen was confirmed in the canonization process by Bona de Guelfuccio, though Francis visited her without any chaperone, or at least that is the impression we have from Celano's account. Whether Philip the Long, whom Bona names in this context, accompanied Francis, or whether he was just another companion who visited her, we simply cannot tell. Regardless, these secret meetings were likely to be understood as literary devices suggesting a love story. Just a hint of eroticism wafts in the air of the meetings between this almost thirty-year-old man with this sixteen-year-old girl.[58]

However, drawing a hasty conclusion about their relationship should be ruled out for twenty-first-century commentators as well as for their thirteenth-century neighbors—and not because the power of sexuality was unknown in the Middle Ages. We note, for example, the story of the almost forty-year-old Parisian master Peter Abelard (d. 1142) who gave private instruction in the liberal arts to the sixteen-year-old girl Heloise (d. c. 1164), from which a tale of love—one of the most dramatic and touching in the whole medieval period—developed, consisting of intellectual fascination, spiritual companionship, and physical attraction. But this story does not necessarily have to repeat itself in the lives of Francis and Clare. To suppose this, we would have to overlook the deliberate ambiguity in Celano's telling of the tale. Even the fact that he is telling this story, with such evocative language, thirty years after Francis's death speaks against the idea that he harbored a suspicion that their meetings were anything but spiritual encounters. It is highly unlikely that he would have provided an unprovoked suggestion about their relationship, only then to have to make a big effort to avoid the consequences that the suggestion created. His attempts to deny the possibility of an ordinary affair show clearly that such an illicit relationship lay far from his mind.

This does not mean, however, that there was no erotic dimension to their relationship. On the contrary, the clarity with which Francis later forbade any interaction with women lies in stark contrast with the potentially suspicious nocturnal meetings with Clare, from which Francis had apparently learned an important lesson: from his own experience he had come to understand that spiritual fellowship and physical attraction are closer to each other than his previous spiritual self-understanding had allowed. But feelings must not necessarily be expressed. Whatever had or had not determined their emotional chemistry on their first meetings, the enthusiasm of the young girl for a much older man resulted in a spiritual relationship that was to last a lifetime. Whatever we know about their social milieu, Celano emphasized that secrecy can be the result of both an erotic love story and a religious decision: Francis was a commoner from the middle class, while Clare was of noble extraction. Francis was effectively an outcast, whereas her parents cared for her deeply. Both these scenarios explained why their relationship had to remain secret. However we choose to approach their relationship, there will always be something that remains opaque to us, and so it must be.[59]

There is, however, much that we can learn about their conversations if we are prepared to concede their religious character. Clare's friend Bona declared that Francis always "preached to her about converting to Jesus Christ." He tried to warn her clearly that simply belonging to Christendom, participating in common liturgical practices, and doing good deeds were not enough to show that one was converted to Christ. And crisply the "Forma vivendi," or the "Form of Life," a text that Francis penned in 1211, the same year Clare and her sisters moved to San Damiano, made this clear too: "Because it was God who inspired you to become daughters and handmaids of the most high supreme King and Father of heaven and to espouse yourselves to the Holy Spirit by choosing to live according to the perfection of the holy Gospel, I desire and promise you personally and in the name of my friars that I will always have the same loving care and special solicitude for you as for them."[60]

Conversion to Christ, perfections of the Gospel: there is no way to understand this other than to assume that Francis imagined for Clare a lifestyle like the one he had approved for himself and the other brothers. Clare declared in her own *Testament* that she had wanted to follow the example, or "exemplum," of Francis. And if the above reflections prove true, at this stage there wasn't even for Francis a smoothed-out and well-conceived rule, just the words of Jesus, whose way of discipleship he wanted to follow and which he expected of Clare as well. Unfortunately, we don't know much more, but it is nonetheless likely that Francis was not as concerned as others to establish differing expectations for men and women, and indeed provided a form of life for Clare that resembled closely his and that of his companions. The noble daughter, like Bernard the noble son, became a beggar, with ensuing responsibilities for preaching as well. Men along with women would experience in this new kind of fellowship the apostolic way—and in 1216 Jacques de Vitry saw how men and women formed a united group. Astonished and admiring, he described this new community in a letter he wrote from Genoa naming the "Fratres Minores et Sorores Minores"—the Brothers Minor and the Sisters Minor—as belonging together.[61]

However, the path that Clare and her sisters took was distinct—and even Francis eventually came to realize that his *fraternitas* should not be open to women. In the unofficial *Rule of 1221*, he strongly maintained that no woman should enter the order or "profess obedience" to them, but instead they should "let her go and lead a life of penance wherever she likes," which is exactly what Clare and her sisters did. The *Rule* that Pope Innocent IV approved on August 9, 1253, two days before Clare's death, established their community much more clearly in the classical form of asceticism and the cloistered life. They maintained a close connection with the spirit of poverty, but this commitment was not expressed by begging on the streets, as it was for the brotherhood. They were permitted, however, to "confidently send for alms." The gap between them and the world grew larger, but this provision did minimize to some degree the distinction between them and the lifestyle of the brotherhood, ameliorating the potential degradation of these women. There was less confidence in their capacity than perhaps Francis had wished. Celano knew this when he described the meetings between Francis and Clare in 1209, even before she decided on a life in the sisterhood. Celano represented Francis's warnings differently from Bona's. The goals for her community were contempt for the world and virginity, befitting and expected of brides for Christ.[62]

In Celano's report, Christ's lifestyle was not the model for the community to imitate, as Francis had demanded in Bona's report and had required in the first *Forma vivendi*. It was Francis who was now the heavenly bridegroom with whom the sisters should be united in contemplation. If at the beginning, Clare's youthful experience was shaped by the powerful dynamism of tearing up social and sexual boundaries, at the end of her life more traditional roles had been reasserted. Women were largely constrained by their seclusion and passivity, so Clare's path toward the religious life had to be expedited. Clare had already turned down some marriage prospects, as she was at just the right age to be engaged and married, but still had to receive her parents' permission to enter a monastery. So there came to pass a proper abduction of the (heavenly) bride from her family home, though the course of events was less like an adventure novel and more like a set liturgical piece. The transition from the mundane to the spiritual world was planned for the night of March 27/28, 1211. March 27 was Palm Sunday, commemorating the entry of Jesus into Jerusalem riding humbly on the back of a donkey while the crowds strewed palm branches before both him and his disciples (John 12:12–19 and parallel passages). Every year this event was replayed liturgically and was thereby made present spiritually, with the citizenry of Assisi acting as the Jerusalem crowds who greeted the Lord. The blessed branches used in the procession were available from the Cathedral of San Rufino, right next door to the palace of the Offreduccio family. Clare was to have held back from the crowds pushing forward to get a branch until the bishop had climbed the stairs toward her to give her a frond. Even this account tallies well with what we know about the different groups in Assisi society, for members of the nobility were not expected to mingle with the crowds but instead to receive special attention from the bishop himself. In later veneration of Clare, this moment was a sign of things to come. Clare, like Francis, now could claim to have received a particular honor from the hands of Bishop Guido, or at least in later retellings the incident functioned as a premonition. Both Clare and Francis experienced rupture from their families through the intervention of an episcopal blessing.[63]

During the night, Clare slipped quietly out of her parents' palace. According to the report Christiana di Bernardo gave in the canonization trial, Clare's parents had apparently already done much to prevent her from absconding. Perhaps they had heard about Clare's frequent excursions, whether or not they really believed she was seeking out spiritual conversations or, more likely, thought she had a secret lover with whom she arranged nocturnal dalliances. In either case, they were bound to disapprove of this kind of behavior. They set a guard over the main door of the house, which of course made Clare fearful that she would be found out and stopped in her tracks. There was, however, another exit, which according to Christiana's report was barricaded with wooden beams and a stone pillar. Amazingly, Clare was able to push past these obstacles "with the help of Jesus Christ." Presumably another young woman helped her, as Celano notes the presence of a companion, but either way this must have been a feat of strength, for whoever barricades a door does so with the express intention that no one should be able to get past it.[64]

So Clare escaped, not only from her home but also from Assisi, despite its gates being closed at night. Perhaps her escape route passed through the bishop's palace itself. She rushed to reach the Portiuncula by the most direct route, where she was taken in by the brothers and brought to the altar.

Again we note how a change of status was flagged by a change of clothes, as we saw in the case of Francis. First, Celano notes how Clare took off her jewelry, a comment that deserves further reflection, for apparently her flight in the night hadn't stopped her from putting it on in the first place. But taking it off certainly paralleled Francis's own denial of his rich merchant's garb. Clare was letting go of these last visible yet symbolic remains of her wealth and beauty. Her entire inheritance she had already sold to give money to the poor. She had pursued a life of poverty even before her flight, but now she stepped away from the last tokens of material prosperity. But the change of status went yet further as she received "the sacred tonsure from blessed Francis himself," as we read in the bull by which Pope Alexander IV (r. 1254–61) canonized her. Such a haircut removed all the hair from the head, except perhaps a small fringe. It wasn't so much a symbol of rejection of physical attractiveness as an indication of transition into the spiritual state, the most external sign of a now legally and personally complete identity transformation. What this meant we discover in the reaction of the city consuls when Francis had received the tonsure: whoever belonged to the spiritual estate was no longer subject to the laws governing civil society, which included not just the legal rights of the city but also the family's rights over an individual. When Clare received her tonsure, she was making clear to all the world that she no longer belonged to the civil sphere and thereby declared her independence from her family as well.[65]

Not just anyone could pronounce this kind of legal act, let alone a fellowship that had only just been acknowledged by the pope and was still not furnished with a constitutionally recognized rule. Something new had been established with this performative act, and if Celano is accurate, this tonsure wasn't just Francis's action alone, for we learn that she was "shorn by the hands of the brothers." A corporate act of the young brotherhood transferred Clare, at least notionally and visibly, if not yet legally, into the spiritual estate. Insofar as Alexander IV regarded this tonsure as validated by Francis, who had by this time been venerated as a saint for some thirty years, he covered up the awkward legal context by which the papacy had to all intents and purposes been ecclesiastically mugged. And why should the tonsure as applied by the brotherhood have any real relevance to legal questions anyway, given that Francis was only canonized much later and no one knew in 1211 that things would necessarily turn out this way? The context of Bishop Guido providing protection for the brotherhood, even if the story of him giving the palm branch to Clare as a sign of his protection was not deliberately planned or approved, is of only limited merit. In the eyes of her family, legally speaking, the whole drama could be described as an abduction.[66]

Of course, we should also assume that Francis knew just how precarious their legal standing was. Clare had promised him her obedience, as she recalled in her *Testament,* which effectively served as her entry into the community. But she did not remain with the brothers in the Portiuncula, as we might have imagined, given Jesus's original commission to his disciples that they sought to emulate. Exercising great caution, Francis escorted her to the Benedictine monastery of San Paolo delle Abbadesse. Any naive thought that a woman could be sent out as a beggar and preacher quickly evaporated, so her future in a traditional contemplative order was accepted instead. Even though this step wasn't to be her last—Clare soon departed from San Paolo—we see here some early signs of the path she would later tread, which resulted eventually in the creation of her own order with a rule that took years of hard work to draft. But at least Francis had now achieved something he had long yearned for: administering the tonsure, even if a largely symbolic act, validated to some degree Clare's reception in the monastery, which in turn gave her protection from attacks by her family, who menaced her to return home. Her tonsure was sufficient proof that she was no longer subject to her family's will. In fact, her family achieved the opposite of what they wanted. Instead of Clare's return, her younger sister joined Clare just sixteen days later. All this goes to show the meaning of the tonsure. Before Agnes had received it, other family members tried valiantly to remove her from the cloister, though the sisters resisted more valiantly still.[67]

These later events took place in another Benedictine abbey, Sant'Angelo di Panzo, where Clare had taken up residence not long after her admission to the order. But even here she didn't stay long, taking Francis's advice and moving to San Damiano. This carried further legal significance as now she had moved back into the jurisdiction of Guido, bishop of Assisi. The monastery of the Benedictines apparently wasn't secure enough, as later attempts to forcibly bring Agnes home attested. In this way, we see clearly how Bishop Guido extended the protection he had afforded Francis to these his female companions too. San Damiano became the permanent home of the order, partly due to the excellent renovations that Francis had carried out in this complex of buildings, and partly given its location halfway down the hill between Assisi and the Portiuncula. Clare's affairs were so clearly connected to that location that in the Papal Decree of Canonization, her community was named the Sacred Order of San Damiano, today known as the Second Order of Franciscans or the Order of Saint Clare. But the path from these early years until her order was officially established was a long one. First of all, the move to San Damiano in 1211 meant that the church had once again, through its bishop, become a protector of the poor. And now this protection would enable an ideal of the common life to become possible for women, which despite many close connections with the community at the Portiuncula set out on its own path in several distinct ways.[68]

CHAPTER 4

Mission

Peace and Judgment: The Double-Edged Message

 O DO PENANCE AND TO CALL OTHERS TO DO PENANCE were the identity markers of the early Franciscan movement. John of Perugia tells us that the brothers, when asked where they came from or to which order they belonged, would answer that their background was Assisi, but more important they were to be known as the "penitents." They were committed to repentance, and they preached repentance. The later Dominicans were designated a "preaching order," but this was no less true of that first community of brothers who gathered around Francis: they were a community of preachers, for they followed the commission that Francis had himself once heard, which highlighted their responsibility to proclaim the Word of God. Of course, the appeal to repent, now an integral part of the message preached by that young man from Assisi, had been part of the message of Jesus from the beginning. When not yet thirty years of age, standing before Pope Innocent and driven by those negative impulses of defense against and renunciation of the world, Francis chimed a melody that would continue to resound within his soul for the remainder of his days. Penance, when it referred to more than participation in the sacrament of penance, meant a radical rejection of a sinful way of life. And Francis saw just such a sinful way of life as normal among the population of Assisi, and more pointedly among the extended families of those budding preachers who were his cohort.[1]

They believed that dependence on money and conspicuous displays of wealth (visible in the apparel of the nobility) were an expression of a wrongheaded spiritual posture. If the reports are true that Francis called on Clare to convert, it was because he couldn't see Christ at work in her life, despite her baptism. The life of the whole town of Assisi, which understood itself as Christian, would be damned by Francis as failing the test. The pursuit of profit, the pathway to success espoused, for instance, by the Bernardone family and other local clans, was in the end a commitment to false values. Mundane economic criteria had pushed aside what they should really have been seeking, something that the apostles had prized and preached: the Kingdom of God. It appears that Francis and his followers understood themselves to be part of this Kingdom now breaking into the lives of individuals in central Italy in the thirteenth century. Not surprisingly, then, his companions noted at one stage that Francis's preaching was a reminder to them that he was a "homo alterius saeculi," a man from a different age. Francis's ministry secured the hope that the expected future Kingdom of God had now arrived, extracted from his own age both to point back to Jesus Christ and to point forward to Christ's second coming. For those who received his teaching, this could mean two things. More radical Franciscans saw in Francis the end of the age, or perhaps the beginning of the thousand-year reign of Christ on earth. For others, less radical, he represented Christ's timeless rule on earth and kept alive Christ's memory in a world that still hadn't reached its consummation even centuries after Christ had been raised from the dead. That Francis can be viewed as a man from a different world has enabled something of his veneration through the ages.[2]

Of course, the comments of Francis's companions concerning his ongoing contested importance need to be further analyzed. Did they really represent the reactions of Francis's first hearers, or do they reflect the attitude of followers who came later? At least we can say with some certainty that Francis preached the Kingdom of God. The preaching of the Kingdom coming near was not merely a novel *threat,* for the call to repent is at the heart of Matthew 4:14. Preaching the Kingdom of God was also a *promise,* for the presence of the Kingdom was closely connected to the arrival of a universal reign of peace, as medieval believers well knew and as the prophet Isaiah proclaimed: "The wolf shall live with the lamb, the leopard shall lie down with the kid, the calf and the lion and the fatling together, and a little child shall lead them" (Isaiah 11:6). Repentance and the offer of peace belong tightly together. As Celano reported, Francis came to understand how confession and repentance would lead to a liberating experience of the nearness of God:

One day . . . he sought out a place of prayer, as he had done so often, and he persevered there for a long time . . . frequently repeating this word: "O God, be merciful to me, the sinner." Little by little a certain unspeakable joy and very great sweetness began to flood his innermost heart. He began also to stand aloof from himself, and, as his feelings were checked and the darkness that had gathered in his heart because of his fear of sin dispelled, there was poured into him a certainty that all his sins had been forgiven and a confidence of his restoration to grace was given him.[3]

Francis and his circle demanded penitence from themselves as well as from others. In all attempts to pursue Jesus in perfecting the path to life, they never assumed to be equal to him but always saw themselves as sinners who before the face of God needed to confront their own limitations. Though the discovery of personal piety was expressed clearly in this story, it isn't so easy to locate in the historical narrative, for it obviously concerned something that Francis had experienced alone, so was without witnesses. The best clue we have goes back to Francis's own explanation of this event, but this nowhere appeared in Celano's account. As is often the case with Francis, a certain skepticism is therefore appropriate regarding the exact details provided for us by his earliest biographers.

However, it is of no great advantage to assume that Celano invented the story or to deny its factual basis. In many micronarratives we should not be surprised by an intensification of dramatic prose to represent themes in the larger narrative. In one account, we might find elements that appear to bring into doubt the historicity of an event yet maintain that the power of the narrative has been amplified insofar as it conveys not a particular event but repeated events that the broader circle around Francis had summarized and passed on. The connection with Francis is reliable in that he might have shaped the piety at the heart of the story. We also should not place too much weight on the precise location of Celano's story at the beginning of the Franciscan movement, where it might constitute the point of departure for the description of Francis's visionary experiences and give courage to his followers. The idea of repentance must not be limited only to the opening phase of his community's life. Francis himself in his *Testament* summarized his whole life as an expression of the act of penitence. When, for example, he wrote to the brothers of the order, probably around 1224, to impress upon them expectations of behavior, he included in his instructions a formalized confession of sin. The profound experience of his own sin did not dissipate but shaped the life and piety of the community and its founder again and again. It is important to make clear from Celano's account that continual appeals to penance were not seen as something negative but rather as contributing to an experience of forgiveness. Just as the sacrament of penance in church found its climax in an experience of absolution, or the declaration of sins forgiven, so the pursuit of repentance as a lifestyle also climaxed in the same experience of God accepting and welcoming the penitent. This experience of God was tied up with the message of peace as well as the call to repent.[4]

The greeting of peace was a striking feature of the Franciscan movement. In his *Testament,* Francis declared: "God revealed a form of greeting to me, telling me that we should say, 'God give you peace.'" This revelation may have been mediated, as in other instances in his life, through the Bible itself, for these words can be found in Jesus's instructions to the disciples: "Whatever house you enter, first say, 'Peace to this house!'" (Luke 10:5), which was then cited in later monastic rules. But it has to be acknowledged that even if the revelation that Francis received was through the biblical text, it should not be seen as divorced from his life context, for we note the way his formulation deviated from the original. The greeting that defined the Franciscans was directed to individuals, whereas the greeting in Luke 10 that Francis cited in his *Regula non bullata* was directed to households, though of course secondarily it was then directed to individuals as well, but the change in address is clear. We must, then, seek for other background reasons to explain what meaning this form of address had for Francis and his movement. Indeed the formulation that Francis used in his memoir stands closest to the liturgical greeting, which only bishops or priests were permitted to use: "Pax vobiscum," "Peace be with you." It gave identity to the spiritual community that had assembled for the church service and demonstrated that the service was to be distinguished from the trials and challenges of normal daily life, lifting the congregation into a sacred world of communion with God and with one another. Francis's use of this formula of greeting certainly had liturgical overtones, which Celano drew attention to when he explained that, in the earliest phase of the community's life, the greeting and the sermon were connected: "In all his preaching, before he proposed the word of God to those gathered about, he first prayed for peace for them, saying 'The Lord give you peace.'"[5]

Francis made use of this liturgical greeting, and despite the fact that it properly belonged to the bishop, so did the ministry of preaching, which he nonetheless pursued. Most important, using the greeting of peace in his distinct way placed the task of preaching—wherever it was practiced—in the elevated context of an authorized, perhaps consecrated, liturgical form. Just as the greeting of peace in the liturgy divides the sacred from the profane, so also Francis was separating out the sacred from the profane when any sermons preached by his band of poor brothers from Assisi were heard. Celano also makes mention of other, nonliturgical uses of the greeting, for he relates that Francis greeted everyone on the road, whether men or women, with the words of peace. Unlike in the commission of Jesus, this greeting was not limited to entry into houses, and was not limited to liturgical settings either, but resembled both. The declaration of peace was appropriated as a universal activity. And as is often the case with Francis, he was not concerned whether others saw it as reasonable; indeed, sharing a greeting of peace with anyone whom he met on the road was an unusual practice from the beginning.[6]

Yet there are still more layers to be uncovered concerning the greeting of peace in Francis's life. Such a greeting pointed to deep connections between the beginning and the progress of Francis's journey. Celano, for example, in his *Second Life,* takes us right back to Francis's behavior in prison when an encounter with an ostracized fellow inmate was explained by his longing for peace. But this does remain speculation, for the language of peace belongs to Celano's interpretation rather than Francis's words. Francis's experience of war and later emphasis on the pursuit of peace are further considerations suggesting the value he attached to passing the greeting of peace, but we can't place the language of peace early in the life of Francis, despite the birth of the Franciscan movement under the conditions of readiness for, and execution of, war. Francis had not only experienced war with Perugia but also had felt the ramifications of war in his hometown. Peace was not a settled part of his daily routine. One could only encounter peace as a promise and then pass it along.[7]

However, we can see how this greeting of peace was later applied more explicitly. It has already been noted how Francis chose to exchange a kiss of peace, the "osculum pacis," with people on society's margins long before he had worked out what his calling was to be. The original context for understanding such a kiss was the liturgical setting of the Eucharist. His commitment to the ostracized of society was not to be understood as somehow a loving act distinct from other religious obligations; rather, it was in the end something like a sacramental event too. Even among the marginalized of society, Francis encountered the presence of Christ as he might have done in the Eucharist. This reminds us again of that passage in Matthew 25, in which we learn that whatever has been done to the least of the brothers has been done to Christ as well. But spiritually there is yet further depth, for when another human being dwells in such a sacramentally loaded world, we become increasingly aware of how close the sacred is to our mundane reality. This dimension is central to understanding why Francis's activities, both his miracles and his affirmation of the creation, matter so much.[8]

But these don't exhaust the various meanings that lie behind the greeting of peace either. Surprisingly, we learn the following in the account of the Three Companions: "It was certainly remarkable, if not miraculous, that, before Francis' conversion these same words had been proclaimed in Assisi by a forerunner, who often greeted the folk he met in the streets with 'Pax et Bonum'—Peace and All Good!" The Companions of Francis of course couldn't help but see the parallel with the role of John the Baptist as going ahead of Jesus, for John didn't just *announce* Christ, his call to repentance *anticipated* Christ (Mark 1:4). When the Companions suggested that Francis might have a forerunner too, they raised his calling into something like a divine revelation, which he then claimed for the greeting of peace as well. His impact, as much as it appears a spontaneous development, was not without precedent, meaning not only that there were similar movements that shared concerns with the Franciscans, but more concretely that there was a man in Assisi whom this young merchant's son must have encountered and probably had looked down upon, just as others in the town would in time look down upon him. Assisi and its denizens, like Francis before his conversion, had had experience with such dropouts before Francis dropped out too. He was special but he wasn't unique.[9]

This reinforces the insight that the movement around Francis of Assisi reflected a generational shift. The rejection of wealth and the suspicion of both middle-class and noble habits were already in the air, with Francis's example a concrete expression of that mood. For apparently that man on the street, if he had not been summarily mentioned in the account of the Companions, would have been forgotten. He neither sponsored a movement nor rallied supporters around himself. He remained, so it appears, a strange and solitary figure, but at least in his unusual greeting of peace he found some longevity in the community of the Franciscans. So it can be seen that in the gesture of a greeting of peace many different levels of meaning can be captured, as much in the life of Francis as in his immediate environment. It points back to his youth, apparently a time before his calling was clarified. Or, expressed the other way around: his task in life contained within it a proclamation of peace built around his call to challenge others to repent, spiritual postures that he had long since cultivated himself. This personal development in the life of Francis was shaped by a multitude of ruptures, which he pursued and cultivated to renew his creaturely experience.

It therefore remains noteworthy that the greeting of peace belonged to the center of his activity, his preaching. Of course we must consider that his preaching might not have been as central as we imagine. As Jan Hoeberichts has quite rightly emphasized, when Francis wrote about the early brotherhood in his memoir, he never mentioned his preaching. But this silence alone is not enough for us to conclude that preaching played no meaningful role in his early ministry. Such homiletical assumptions are deeply anchored in the hagiographical accounts, as well as in other sources by Francis, not least his own writings like the *Rules*. As considered earlier in this book, memories in others' sources can still constitute autobiographical fragments. These may be selective, but Francis's *Testament* was not intended as a comprehensive review but as an exhortation to his brothers before his death. Despite some lacunae, yet with some modesty regarding the exact genesis of his ministry of proclamation, this activity can still be affirmed from a range of other sources, even if in this particular account we do not see its inclusion as a central element of this new and young movement, although we might have expected it.[10]

Francis's appearances can be described as charismatic. Celano tells us that he "so very often preached the word of God to thousands of people." Of course this might be an exaggeration, but even exercising some caution, this amounted to a very large number and proved how inspiring his preaching was. This enormous reach was due more to his personal presence than to the content of his sermons. The accounts of his preaching in the biographies are thin. It is only really through indirect means, especially other statements of Francis, that we can piece together what occupied him in his preaching, though we recognize that other texts had different audiences. His sermons nonetheless had a distinctly missiological character. The other extant writings chiefly addressed members of the brotherhood, or at least those who sympathized with its agenda, such that there was no pressing need to persuade the audience of the merits of his better Christian way. And in all this, there is the proviso that he may have engaged with many other topics although these are not mentioned in the few original texts that remain to us. Much has been lost, and potentially many of his thoughts have been lost as well.[11]

Despite these methodological reservations, we do have a most interesting collection of random statements from Francis, known as *The Admonitions*, containing both doctrinal and ethical reflections. It is not easy to order them chronologically, but they do provide easy access—perhaps in a limited fashion—to the way Francis likely spoke to others, either in one-on-one conversation or in addressing a crowd. Alongside the debates around the date of their composition, we must also be wary of the sources used to compile them. Quotations from Francis were not dictated and were perhaps even written down long after they were spoken to summarize what the author wanted others to hear. This is probably true of the compilation itself: others had to decide what was worth preserving, with some statements being forgotten entirely. Also, how exactly they were transcribed might say something about the process of transmission: we might hear Francis, but perhaps also other voices that sharpened some feature of the quotation or decided to present only one side of Francis to posterity as they saw fit. These concerns of course pertain to his biographies as well.

All this aside, we can still uncover something of Francis's central message in *The Admonitions*. Here, the call to repentance echoed around his reflection on human sinfulness, which begins, as all Christian theology does, by recounting the story of the fall of Adam and Eve into sin, a story now proverbially famous as they ate the forbidden fruit plucked from the tree of knowledge of good and evil. Francis shared the opinion of his day that his very own sin was punished as a natural consequence of the penalty due to all humankind, but the story wasn't merely about a discrete historical event. Indeed, everyone eats from the tree of knowledge when they follow their own will or desire. A strange way of understanding sin is further elucidated by Francis when he wrote that a sinner is a person who "claims that his good will comes from himself alone and prides himself on the good that God says and does in him." These few words represent a profoundly theological approach to radical humility. Good cannot come from a human being but only from God, which means in a roundabout way that human beings must always keep their sin or their incapacity at the forefront of their imagination in order to achieve anything that is good. Every person is a new Adam or Eve, as Francis saw in his own battle with the devil and his lies. It might be difficult, however, to work out from this admonition without any context how much this applied to those not living in his order. In the context of other admonitions, the instruction to give up one's own will has an easy application in the instruction to submit oneself to superiors in the order, with the interesting exemption that commands must not be followed if they are against one's conscience, *contra animam*. The role of one's conscience in ethical deliberation is not something that was invented in the modern period but arises from monastic culture in the medieval world.[12]

Even if this instruction concerning submission to those over us in the Lord was intended to address members of an order, Francis applied this admonition to surrender one's will in his sermons to broad sweeps of the population as well. How this might be seen concretely was explained in the so-called *Letter to All the Faithful,* which captured the content of Francis's preaching of repentance: "All those who refuse to do penance . . . indulge their vices and sins and follow their evil longings and desires, without a thought for the promises they made. In body they are slaves of the world and of the desires of their lower nature, with all the cares and anxieties of this life; in spirit they are slaves of the devil. They have been led astray by him and have made themselves his children, dedicated to doing his work." Though one and the same man, this Francis is different from portraits of the loving and tender *poverello* who preached repentance so passionately. His condemnation was not just directed to the rich, but, dividing the world into two—on one side the Lord Jesus Christ and on the other side the devil—he preached just as pointedly to anyone who was caught up in the ways of the world. And this rhetorical contrast fitted well into what we know about his preaching in his early days. Decisions were demanded, and clear alternatives offered, and these not through friendly invitations but by threatening sinners. Francis warned that whoever should die without true repentance— and presumably he meant here having been absolved through sacramental penance—had dire prospects: "The devil tears his soul from his body with such anguish and distress that only a person who has experienced it can appreciate it." We can barely imagine in our day a sermon so full of terror and anxiety, in which Francis would warn about leaving our mortal possessions to ungrateful relatives, about our body being eaten by worms, about our soul ending up in hell to be tortured for all eternity. And this kind of preaching could easily be connected to the concerns of the brotherhood. If in death one loses all one's earthly possessions, as Francis was to have written in a more literary and minatory version of this letter, then there should be nothing stopping his listeners from following Franciscan ideals and giving alms. This was the first step toward freeing oneself from the prospect of future terror, and the second consisted of joining the fellowship, and thereby escaping the devil's tentacles.[13]

We can assume that this style of terrifying and alarming preaching was normal for Francis, as we note in a kind of sample sermon in the unauthorized *Rule of 1221* sent to all the brothers, not just to those who otherwise were described by means of their preaching ministry. This proclamation was recommended to be preached by all:

> Whenever they see fit my friars may exhort the people to praise God with words like these: Fear him and honour him, praise him and bless him, thank and adore him, the Lord almighty, in Trinity and Unity, Father, Son, and Holy Spirit, Creator of all. Repent, for the kingdom of heaven is at hand (Mt 3:2); remember we must die soon. Forgive, and you shall be forgiven; give, and it shall be given to you (Lk 6:38); if you do not forgive, neither will your Father in heaven forgive you your offences (Mk 11:26). Confess all your sins. It is well for those who die repentant; they shall have a place in the kingdom of heaven. Woe to those who die unrepentant; they shall be children of the devil whose work they do, and they shall go into everlasting fire. Be on your guard and keep clear of all evil, standing firm to the last.[14]

In this sermon, repentance did not mean simply compliance with a rule of life, but, entirely consistent with the teaching and practices of the church, it meant at least confessing one's sins as one might before the priest in the sacrament of penance. We sense here some loss of the wild and unrestrained energy that characterized the beginning of the movement, which Francis recollected in his *Testament,* but there was still a (different) kind of wildness that he expressed in the threats of Judgment Day. The fear of death provoked repentance first of all, and was surely the point at which the brothers would most scare their listeners. What is enjoined upon the brothers in this unauthorized rule did little to achieve edification. It was a mixture of threat and admonition, a message of judgment in which the devil had a clear role.

In dualistic fashion, Francis starkly contrasted penitents with children of the devil, who cannot reach the Kingdom of Heaven but will instead wind up in hell, as this quotation suggests.[15]

Francis's proclamation was not as tender, not as optimistic, not so compatible with today's sensibilities, as we might have imagined if we had only read the famous *The Canticle of Brother Sun*. This Francis is prepared to speak of "everlasting fire," and in the unauthorized rule its context expressed some measure of cynicism, formulated as thanks for the destruction of God's enemies: "We give you thanks because your Son is to come a second time in the glory of his majesty and cast the damned, who refused to do penance and acknowledge you, into everlasting fire." It takes a lot for us to get used to this kind of Francis—but get used to him we must. To this worldview belonged belief in a devil whose threats aroused fears and whose presence required exorcisms. Celano recounts a story in a multi-layered narrative that Francis saw devils dancing in the sky over Arezzo, devils who were stirring up the citizens of the area such that the town was "shaken by civil war." So he sent to that place—again according to Celano—a brother who would "at the command of our father Francis" drive the devils out of the town and so restore order. One does not have to read this account as historically accurate to come to the conclusion that it contains elements common to Francis's view of the world—a world not just full of the glory of God but full of demons as well.[16]

How this background played out in the real political world Francis inhabited can be seen in another incident that was like the episode in Arezzo but was perhaps more important because it was more believable in that it didn't depend chiefly on hagiographical accounts. Thomas, bishop of Split, wrote between the 1240s and 1260s an account of popes from his hometown and from nearby Saloniki, into which he wove memories of his student days in Bologna, where Francis came to preach in the marketplace on August 15, 1222 (supported by the archbishop of Pisa, Federico Visconti). His theme that day was angels, humans, and demons; content with the stir that alone would have caused, Francis added a direct admonition to the townsfolk to end their long-standing conflicts and make peace. According to Thomas, Francis proved successful in his goal and helped reconcile the estranged noble parties. Dramatically, this story illustrates how Francis held together themes that our contemporary ears have trouble combining: preaching the difficult topic of the supernatural world with a welcome message of peace, even though instructions concerning the greeting of peace were not included in Francis's letter—though this should not be read to mean it was of no significant value. It was quite clearly an organic part of the message of repentance. Peace was an act of repentance as well as the consequence of repentance, as summarized in the *Admonitions* with reference to the Sermon on the Mount: "'Blessed are the peacemakers, for they shall be called the children of God' (Mt 5:9). They are truly peacemakers who are able to preserve their peace of mind and heart for love of our Lord Jesus Christ, despite all that they suffer in this world."[17]

Of course, painting a supernatural world in which the devil was at war with human beings for their souls while at the same time exhorting his listeners to work for repentance and peace was a difficult task that required Francis to give clear pastoral and theological advice regarding everyday discipleship. When Francis warned his listeners against attending church services or persisting in their prayers while yet caught up in their own desires, he was surely not just addressing brothers in the fellowship, whom he addressed in the very next breath, exhorting them to avoid the danger of forgetting love of neighbor because of their own outsized devotion to ascetic living. Surely he had in his sights any Christians in towns and villages who were obsessed by their middle-class or noble existence and were unrestrained in their envy. No matter what one's social station, this kind of admonition would serve to encourage an ethic freed from self-interest. Resulting in self-critique or self-contempt, in repentance and humility, or in release from self-will to contentment, Francis's message could make a difference inside the brotherhood or outside among the population of the city. It was indeed a simple message deeply rooted in the ethics of Jesus.[18]

The impact of Francis's sermons was not due merely to their content but was also a function of how they were preached and the form that they took. Even in his earliest preaching, Francis expressed himself through visual actions, making his clothes or his body expressions of his message. For example, Celano relates the story of Francis bringing a lamb before the bishop of Osimo as a sermon illustration. He had found it among a flock of goats and compared it to Jesus Christ himself, who biblically and liturgically was called the Lamb of God. Just as Jesus lived humbly among the Pharisees and the High Priests, so too this sheep had lived peaceably among a hostile herd. Nature became a parable for Francis, and he didn't hold back from using it powerfully and concretely. However, such object lessons were not strictly necessary to explain the impact of his message, as Celano made clear when describing Francis's conversion, from which he achieved such renewed assurance: "From then on he began to preach penance to all with great fervor of spirit and joy of mind, edifying his hearers with his simple words and his greatness of heart. His words was [sic] like a burning fire, penetrating the inmost reaches of the heart, and it filled the minds of all the hearers with admiration."[19]

Of course, this description of his preaching is generalized, but something of what made his preaching so electric does break through here. He may not have been very learned, nor did this style of preaching necessarily relate to his gifts in rhetoric; rather, it was his personal manner that reached his hearers, not just cognitively but more importantly affectively. Contrasting Francis's sermons with those preached decades later by Bonaventure about Francis, we can see just how medieval sermons could differ. In Bonaventure we see a Scholastic intellect, whose content was well proportioned and who divided his sermons into sections to treat individual points distinctly. But all this was, according to Celano, so different from the approach Francis took, whose impact was like a "burning fire" that left his hearers amazed. The Three Companions give us a taste of this: "From this time onward Saint Francis wandered through cities, villages, and hamlets, and began to preach with increasing perfection, not using learned words of human wisdom, but through the doctrine and virtue of the Holy Spirit most confidently proclaiming the kingdom of God. He was a genuine preacher confirmed by apostolic authority; therefore he spoke no honeyed words of flattery or blandishment; what he preached to others he had already put into practice himself and his teaching of the truth was full of assurance."[20]

Yet even the Three Companions didn't merely describe his preaching, but instead presented Francis through the lens of theological interpretation: his rejection of the arts of rhetoric and human wisdom came from 1 Corinthians 2:4, aligning his preaching with the assumptions of the apostle Paul. In the reports of both the Companions and the early biography of Celano, Francis had expressed some skepticism concerning human wisdom. We read this warning from the unauthorized *Rule of 1221*: "We must all be on our guard against pride and empty boasting and beware of worldly or natural wisdom. A worldly spirit loves to talk a lot but do nothing, striving for the exterior signs of holiness that people can see, with no desire for true piety and interior holiness of spirit."[21]

With this background in mind, we might be surprised to read the summary of the office or duty of the preacher, which Celano recounted later in the *Second Life*, where Francis made a distinction between the task of the minister of the Word of God ("ministri verbi Dei") and those who appeared to belong to a cohort distinct from the brothers, for ministers of the Word were to be free from other tasks ("officia"). They should also aim not to get caught up in cold and heartless preaching, though Celano's Francis also gave good instructions on how they might do this, by praying intensively before preaching. And this may well have arisen out of Francis's own experience that the preacher's relationship with his audience would assume the preacher's devout and prayerful relationship with God, which as a rule of thumb characterized Francis throughout his ministry and produced a degree of spontaneity and thereby spiritual authorization. Such spontaneity in preaching was in evidence elsewhere in Celano's *First Life*, where we learn that Francis only rarely prepared his sermons. His message did not require what was not already accessible to him in head and heart, though the downside of this kind of spontaneity was witnessed on one occasion when nothing came to him to say in a sermon despite the fact that it had actually and unusually been prepared. He simply dismissed his listeners with a blessing, leaving them "feeling that from this alone they had received a great sermon."[22]

However, in Francis's later instructions concerning preaching, we don't actually see much that reflects this commitment to directness or to such a carefree attitude. Later statements about the task of preaching are rather more connected to Francis's esteem for learned interpreters, those "sacrae ... theologiae doctores," or "doctors of sacred theology." For someone who had described himself as an "idiota," this was perhaps surprising. In his *Testament* he wrote, "We should honour and venerate theologians, too, and the ministers of God's word, because it is they who give us spirit and life." Celano quoted this at the parallel moment in his own *Life* and described how Francis taught this in general terms. He remained true to the teachings of Francis, though the traditions that swirled around him were more notably in tension with each other. In the *Legend of the Three Companions* or in early Celano, we see the simple Francis who didn't lay much worth on big words, but in Celano's *Second Life*, we see a Francis who admired learning, both of which aspects, of course, can find some points of reference in his life. Chiefly, the differences can be explained in terms of the gradual development of his teaching. As mentioned previously, Francis was not nearly as untrained as the self-description "idiota" might leave us thinking. It is true that he didn't have any formal higher learning, nor had he sought it out. As a budding merchant, he didn't need more than basic skills in writing and mathematics. But it wouldn't be long before well-trained scholars joined the order, for example, the lawyer Peter of Catania, or later in 1220 the priest from Lisbon Don Fernando—known to us as Anthony of Padua, the city where he died and is buried—who was well versed in theology and quickly made himself known through his preaching. Francis followed this new brother's sermons, for example, his sermon to the Cathars, with interest and admiration, shown by his addressing Anthony as "my bishop." Of course, a title like this could be used to express friendship along with irony, demonstrating that Francis saw in his learned colleague someone who could and should set him right in questions of correct doctrine. We immediately see here with great clarity how Francis was more and more prepared to accept academic training as a help for a ministry of preaching. He appeared troubled in 1223/24, just a couple of years before composing his *Testament,* when he wrote to Anthony: "To Brother Anthony, my bishop, Brother Francis sends greetings. It is agreeable to me that you should teach the friars sacred theology, so long as they do not extinguish the spirit of prayer and devotedness over this study, as is contained in the Rule."[23]

This letter was to become very important for the Franciscan movement when the brothers opened themselves up to participate in academic learning. Indeed, the universities were founded in parallel to the Franciscan movement in the early thirteenth century. It was in 1215, more than ten years before Francis died, that the chancellor of Paris enacted statutes to establish a university, and at almost the same time a university began teaching (chiefly law) in Bologna, while in Oxford a more encompassing university system was organized. Originally, Franciscans had kept their distance from these kinds of institutions, but when the Paris master Alexander of Hales entered the order, Franciscans now had representation in the most important university of Europe, followed by several other outstanding Franciscan academics like Bonaventure, Duns Scotus (d. 1308), and William of Ockham (d. 1347). They recalled with pride that Francis had once promoted and praised the theological learning of Anthony, and it is in this context that we should understand the comment by Celano in his *Second Life* concerning the gradual opening of the order to academic activity.

On the other hand, the letter to Anthony was not a simple advertisement for the study of academic theology. If there is such a thing as faint praise, then it comes packaged in these words, "it is agreeable to me," which are not an expression of joy but more like a concession and permission, by which someone might approve another's request. He did support academic inquiry, but not wholeheartedly. His warning not to let academic study get in the way of godliness and prayerfulness and thereby fall foul of the authorized *Rule of 1223* was not just a platitude. It was here that Francis showed beyond doubt what he held to be the great danger of the rise of Scholastic theology, with its delight in definitions and distinctions. With this letter in mind, it proves difficult to work out exactly how Francis's differing views on education should be reconciled as they moved from skepticism to goodwill, though that is just one part of the story. Truth be told, there remained a good deal of skepticism lurking within his goodwill. Even his acceptance of the theological project in his *Testament* may have been grounded in his worry that knowledge could distract believers from the pursuit of their own simple piety, which the early Francis had lived and represented. No doubt Francis could see, as his community grew and diversified, that theological education had a place, but it was never for him a matter of the heart. This accounts for the difference in the way preaching is presented in Celano's *Second Life* on the one hand, and how it is described by the Three Companions as well as Celano in his *First Life* on the other, and how tensions were resolved, given that they went back to Francis himself. His legatees sought to discover in the variety of experiences in Francis's life what might count as the most general of his views, or what might fit best into their own, thereby attempting to unify or perhaps homogenize such a range of opinions.[24]

Of particular importance in the report of the Three Companions is that we learn more about Francis than his simplistic use of language. They say something much more authentic about him, for they summarize the validation of his preaching by means of his own actions: in the course of his ministry Francis had become and remained the master of performative acts. His life was a kind of message in itself, one that did not displace the value of words but gave them form. His whole life path was grounded in clear biblical instruction, though it was not of course the case that such instruction had never been known before. What had been held at arm's length and resisted was now a critical element in the path of discipleship: Jesus's massively irritating words about giving up one's possessions were bound to have implications in a society that was rapidly being transformed economically. The poor son of a rich man embodied this challenge, bringing lifestyle and proclamation tightly together. The way he presented himself publicly to the world was part and parcel of his message about simplicity and humility.

Like other accounts, Thomas of Split's gives us a sense of the importance of this in his eyewitness report of Francis's preaching in Bologna in 1222: "He was held to be vile, with a contemptible face and unseemly figure." Since the time Francis hid from his father in a cave, it is not surprising that we think of him in this way: messy, with dishevelled beard and shabby clothes. Here Thomas gives us further insight that stands at odds with later representations of Francis's preaching and its conformity to canon law. Bonaventure later recounts how Francis preached most every Sunday in the cathedral in Assisi and would arrive back in town on the preceding Saturday to prepare himself. This would hardly have been possible without the permission of the bishop, so it must have accorded with canonical regulations, but in all likelihood it wasn't understood to be the regular preaching ministry of a layman, nor conforming to the status of a cleric either. Perhaps Bonaventure meant to show how the same opportunity given to later Franciscans to preach in city parishes had applied to Francis too. It is of course true that the *poverello* did have permission occasionally to preach in churches, but it was more normal for him to preach in the open air, which Thomas of Split affirms. Given this distinction, he was more likely to use different words to describe preachers ("praedicatores") in liturgical settings and speakers like the Franciscans ("concionantes") who were not. Francis acted as he exhorted other brothers to do in the unauthorized *Rule of 1221*. After giving exacting details in chapter 17 concerning preachers, he granted permission to the brothers in chapter 21—not just to the preachers but to all the brothers—to proclaim a sermon "whenever they see fit" to "exhort the people." This distinctly does not sound like a limitation to preach only in church buildings on authorized liturgical occasions, but rather opens up the possibility, given the technical distinction in canon law between the two categories of speaker, of promoting the Gospel on the streets and (like in Bologna) in the public squares of the cities.[25]

Francis's shabby appearance was only one element of a whole range of attitudes or activities that the Franciscans felt themselves obliged to uphold given the commands of Christ. As Francis himself was reported to have said to his brothers, "We have been called to heal wounds, to unite what has fallen apart, and to bring home those who have lost their way." And in the unauthorized *Rule of 1221,* he wrote, "All the friars . . . should preach by their example." He is giving instruction in this phase of his ministry, probably around 1221, regarding how the brothers should understand their ministry responsibilities, which Celano refers to as well. In the same context, Francis made clear that no one can take up of their own volition a preaching ministry, or "officium praedicationis," for this can only be exercised by special commission, even when it was understood by him that preaching by word and preaching by deed were complementary activities. He had to live out what he proclaimed with his words, and his words functioned as a plumb line for his life. In a sense, this made verbal proclamation all the more simple and strengthened the implicit challenge when he set his verbal proclamation within the quasi-liturgical context of his greeting of peace.[26]

We have noted the importance of Jesus's commission to the apostles to go out to preach, which for Francis proved a powerful model for his movement. The brothers traveled far and wide to preach the apostolic message of repentance and the Kingdom of God. But there were other scenarios in which it was less the Lord Jesus and more John the Baptist who functioned as a model to imitate. Just as in the Gospels people came from Jerusalem and many other towns to hear John at the Jordan preach repentance, the Three Companions tell us that many people "hastened" to hear Francis as well. It wasn't so much that they wanted to see him as to hear him. Both Jesus and John were models. And Francis imitated John the Baptist in another way, too, for his clothes, like John's garment of camel hair, were designed to picture the nature of repentance that he preached. According to the Companions, this rush to hear him must have begun early, when Francis was in Rivotorto, probably late in the year of 1209 just after he had returned from Rome. People from all different levels of society ventured up the hill to him: "many learned and cultured men . . . nobles and commoners alike." Though he wasn't used to thinking in these terms, this experience reflected a kind of victory, for it hadn't been long since those same rich and fashionable inhabitants of Assisi had mocked Francis and the brothers. Now they were hurrying (at least some of them) to listen to him, or to God speaking through him. Just as the first brothers had rushed to hear Francis, so others were now rushing to him too, though it must be said that unlike Bernard, Peter, and the others, these new crowds didn't always stay. They returned to their families and homes, such that a new circle formed, those who sympathized with Francis in distinction from those who became close followers, but these sympathizers proved a boon to the movement anyway, for the brothers out on their preaching tours now had friends they could turn to with their needs. Celano reports that at the high point of the early movement, entire cities had become congregations of sympathizers: "When he entered any city, the clergy rejoiced, the bells were rung, the men were filled with happiness, the women rejoiced together, the children . . . taking branches from the trees . . . went to meet him singing." It is easy to imagine that all this is exaggeration, but we can safely say nonetheless that these highly condensed accounts represent a genuine enthusiasm among the people as the brothers entered a town and encountered the people at close quarters.[27]

There had always been sympathizers. Even in the earliest phase of the brothers' itinerancy, the Three Companions reported an incident that would also fit well into the later period, given that the episode might be modeled generically on the commission that Jesus gave the apostles. Two of the disciples had traveled to Florence and had stayed overnight in the portico of a house, where they found an oven. The ensuing story is typically symbolic. While the lady of the house had wanted to offer them floor space near the warm oven, her husband wanted to get rid of them and refused them even a blanket. Whatever may be historically accurate, the whole account shows just how much the brothers were like the early followers of Jesus. They too were dependent on the goodwill of those they met along the way, though those others who had not decided to renounce their worldly possessions with the same radical intentionality were now able to accommodate their guests and could do so more generously and with a different motivation than those who merely gave the mendicants alms along the way. Indeed, it was a social norm and an expectation of the Christian's obedience to give beggars a small gift, whoever they were, as Francis had done while still living as the son of a merchant. To give alms was the duty of a Christian, which would be calculated to a Christian's advantage when the divine Judge after death inquired about a person's good works. In a dialectical kind of way, the Franciscans were forcing the hand of others to give, even though they themselves had become beggars only by renouncing daily labor in order to receive alms. Those who sympathized with the Franciscans stood apart from the normal round of dutiful Christian giving, and therefore rushed to hear Francis preach or to offer the brothers lodging. They did both because they keenly supported the insights of Francis and his brothers, though they couldn't live in the same way themselves.

In the case of Bernard, who himself had originally been such a sympa-thizer when he invited Francis in, we learn that sympathizers sometimes became active followers too—and were at the same time a source of food, enabling the brothers to eat. The transition from the status of sympathizer to that of member of the community could happen quickly and with mas-sive consequences. Celano tells us that Francis, after preaching in Ascoli, vested thirty men, including some clerics, with the habit of the Friars Minor. Though the actual number might be slightly exaggerated, the fact that some-thing very much like this happened cannot be doubted. It is, however, more difficult to answer the question of whether this significant entry into the fellowship took place merely as a spontaneous response to Francis's preach-ing, which is the impression Celano's account leaves, or whether there had been some other kind of preparatory softening. Ascoli is the very town from which reports are given of the children who came to meet Francis. He was expected here, in short, so the episode of vesting the men might well have been a planned event, including an evangelistic message that with Francis and through Francis miracles were possible.[28]

We discover, then, that the sympathizers of the Franciscans stayed living in their own homes and didn't join the crowd in its enthusiasm, but also that they offered their homes as hospitality and thereby sought for their households Francis's protection. People let Francis bless their bread, as Celano says, in order that they might store it to eat later as a kind of medicine to cure sickness. A notable change had taken place: where once Francis had called people away from their middle-class values, he now confirmed their status through his blessing. We get a glimpse here of how the tertiary order of the Franciscans later emerged: as an association of the bourgeoisie oriented toward Francis without having to surrender all links to heritage or family. And indeed Celano might have had this kind of trajectory in mind in his narrative. He didn't have to invent the story in order to legitimize this kind of sociological development, for here we witness a phenomenon that has often occurred in the formation of social groups. A radical message becomes so successful that its own power is blunted when the number of those who can actually live out its necessary radicalism is limited. And it appears that Francis, too, had to some degree learned to live with the softening of the movement's claims. Even if Fran-cis later in his *Testament* appears to have regarded the laxness that had gripped the brotherhood with grief and worry, earlier he seems to have actually promoted, at least for a short time, a weakened and less robust group of followers among his sympathizing circle. Just as in the previous discussion of Francis's view of education, some measure of compromise with the world was in part understandable. Only in this way could his movement unfurl its potential and make his small community increasingly effective in the world and provoke new approaches to reform in the church more broadly.[29]

This compromise was at the same time a kind of success that was to determine and sustain Francis's legacy. The blessing of one's bread that so many sought from him was part of the move toward him being venerated as a saint. People sensed in Francis a holiness that irradiated everything it touched: "So also they very often cut off parts of his tunic in their very great faith, so much so that he sometimes was left almost naked." Again his clothes took center stage, and his nakedness too, which had once already been exposed before the bishop. These remain of significance in the story of Francis, and not just incidentally. Significant background to this story in Celano is the tale of the woman who was healed by Jesus of her hemorrhaging menstrual flow in Mark 5:25–34 when she touched his cloak. Reliquaries known to heal by touch were common in medieval piety, for they represented the longing for increasing holiness enabled through material means. Objects like this reflected the divine presence and were like precipitation from a higher sphere. In philosophical discourse, these commitments had been expressed since antiquity in Neoplatonic philosophy, which had in part impacted the Scholastic thinking of the Middle Ages. Accordingly, the pure and spiritual divine essence had been poured into the material world though a sequence of downward and overflowing cascades, with the divine both preserving some of its integrity and losing some of its efficacy in the process. And this was exactly how the holiness of Christ had been taught—it found some of its power expressed in the saints of this world, which accounted for the view in the minds of the religious of the Middle Ages that Christ was neither simply dead historically nor in his resurrection simply released from the world. In manifold representations, the Son of God remained on the earth: in the sacrament on the altar, in paintings in the church, as well as in those human beings who participated in a special way in his sanctity. His holiness could then still shine forth from the bones of those who had died, which in turn became reliquaries, and from other objects that were connected to those bones while they lived. In the case of Francis, such objects included not just his clothes but, as Celano also tells us, the rein he held while riding also contained wonder-working power that could aid a woman in labor to deliver her child happily and safely. Even the cord that held together Francis's habit is said to have worked a miracle: a man from Città della Pieve near Orvieto dipped the rope in water, or perhaps plucked out a few threads to make them wet, and used them to heal many people.[30]

Of course, tales like this are easily associated with the magical arts, and values are smuggled in that do damage to the texts and the experience of the Middle Ages. The separation between faith and magic is artificial and is to a large degree dogmatically charged. In the phenomena of our experience, it may be hard to establish clear theological points of connection. If we understand Christianity as something more than just a dogmatically organized set of norms, but instead approach it as lived religion, we can find space for the existence of Francis's cord that when wet dissolved and became a medicine for the sick. Such are all steps along the path that Francis climbed in the course of his earthly life, and in the unselfconscious way they are presented to us are entirely believable. Reality simply functioned differently in the eyes of people of the thirteenth century from the way twenty-first-century people imagine it, or want to see it, and this doesn't mean that the medieval imagination was mere fantasy. One can of course ask the question whether all people who came into contact with such an object experienced healing or whether the hopes of some were dashed. We can perhaps also doubt whether the rein or the medicinal drink exercised their power in supernatural or merely natural ways, prompting a psychological disposition. But this doesn't change anything in the world of Francis, for in the worldview of the day, these wonders simply happened. When Francis was rapidly canonized after his death, we might attribute this, as Jacques de Vitry did—with a sense of amazement—to the protection granted to him by the pope. But we have to acknowledge as well that his esteem among the people might lie in their encounter with his miracles, given their understanding of the nature of reality.[31]

This insight, that miracles are possible within certain plausibility structures, doesn't mean that we must believe each and every story of a miracle that we read. Naturally, some writers embroidered their accounts and applied literary conventions to shape their material. They produced some miracle books, one by Celano and one by Bonaventure as an appendix to his *Major Life*. These tales, as André Vauchez suggests, portray Francis as "a champion of Christian perfection," with more and more excessively fanciful details. At a minimum, they sought to work against any doubts concerning the miracles that Francis had done. Both begin by painting the greatest of the wonders, his stigmatization, where his body bore the marks of the wounds of Christ. And they knew of course that this was almost unbelievable. Celano ends his chapter on the stigmata with the question: "Who would not marvel at these things? Who would pretend anything different from what is preached about the stigmata as something wholly divine?" To ask a question like the latter had first of all the rhetorical goal of reassuring those who were already persuaded of Francis's sanctity, but it does something else too—it addresses the fact that there might have been legitimate doubt about the events. Even for medieval believers, it could not be assumed that everyone shared equally in the belief that every miracle was true.[32]

If there was doubt about the historical accuracy of the stigmata, given the strangeness of the occurrence, there were also other literary elements in the accounts that make us skeptical. On occasions the miracles were presented so didactically it is hard to imagine that they were merely historical events or efforts to portray an experience of reality. An example of this kind of writing can be found in that chapter of Celano's *Treatise on the Miracles* in which he described the resuscitation of the dead. Because Francis's saintliness unfolded in the course of his life, becoming more pronounced after his death, there are miracles both before and after he died. The first such resuscitation is one that Francis performed from beyond the grave. A noblewoman from Montemarano, near Benevento, known to venerate Francis, awoke from death and explained Francis's role in her coming back to life. Because of a serious and perhaps unconfessed sin, she had been sent to a dungeon-like prison, presumably purgatory. Francis had interceded for her and she was allowed to return to her life if she would confess her weighty sin to a priest. After she had done this and had received absolution, she died all of a sudden—or, more accurately, died again. Celano stressed with this story that "confession is a marvelous gift of God which ought to be wholeheartedly embraced by all," and then added another story to reinforce this one. While visiting a knight in Celano, Thomas's hometown, Francis announced that his host would soon die, so he exhorted him to make his confession. According to canon law, of course, Francis—not ordained— couldn't hear someone's confession, so the knight proceeded correctly by confessing to one of Francis's companions who was a priest before he died that night, as had been prophesied. This small detail about the correct form of confession underscores the overall intent of the passage: to teach people about obeying the requirements of the church, including the warning about confessing before death. The didactic intent of the narrative emerges from what is likely to be core elements of the account, with later refashioning of some of the detail. Or, to put it another way, this story represents a kind of literary production of wonder-stories that could only function as a coherent narrative because belief in miracles was possible, and that belief could be connected to Francis himself.[33]

In many such instances, it was closeness to Francis, a relationship in which strength and healing had been experienced, that most likely served as the proving ground for tales of wonders. Stories of people touching his clothes are an extension of simpler stories that even today would be readily accepted as the kinds of encounters that people living in another's proximity are likely to have. In Celano's *First Life*, he recounted the story of a brother named Riccerio who was scared that Francis didn't love him enough. Once when Riccerio returned home, he didn't have to let Francis know it was him, for Francis instinctively knew who it was, called him over, and said to him: "Let no temptation disturb you, son; let no thought exasperate you; for you are very dear to me. Know that among those who are especially dear to me you are worthy of my affection and intimacy." This narrative contains—quite literally—no wonder. It merely corresponds with what happens normally among people who know each other well. One has the sense that something is wrong and one can find just the right words of comfort.[34]

Stories like this are deliberately placed at the beginning of the accounts of miracles, and Celano sets them further within the context of a miraculous vision. In 1224, that is, during his lifetime, Francis was said to have appeared to Brother Monaldo in Arles, the provincial capital of Provence, filling those gathered with the Holy Spirit and offering them comfort by his presence. In this instance, even knowing the feelings of the brothers was understood to be a work of the Holy Spirit. Such a deep sense of his presence was understood miraculously, leading effortlessly to descriptions of other healings in which the focus remained on the circle of brothers. Celano goes on to describe how Francis healed a brother who was apparently suffering from epileptic fits, an ailment that was often attributed to demons and therefore was easily healed by making the sign of the cross. While this might be true, we should also remember to factor in the example of the apostles who exorcized demons in Acts 19:12 as a sign. The line between what was historically true for the earliest apostles and the literary construction of the apostolic life might be fluid, especially if an account presented Francis in the light of Jesus's own miracles—so, for example, when Francis healed a boy's lameness upon the request of his father and restored movement to someone suffering from gout. We might not be able to recount exactly what, when, or why something happened, but in the end that is not the real point anyway. He was experienced as a wonder-worker, which is something we shouldn't doubt, and indeed this is increasingly how he saw himself. His growing sense of self was doubtless fueled by his performance of these kinds of three-dimensional acts of communication, which were preached through deeds as well as words.[35]

The connection between his wonder-working deeds and his words shaped, in turn, the power of his words. He appeared to see himself more and more as a prophet who spoke with authority and could foretell the future. Two events related in the so-called *Legend of Perugia* that rely on eyewitness accounts show Francis's prophesying coming true. The most famous and most believable story involved his announcement to the crusaders in Damietta that they would soon face a devastating defeat, which they experienced not long after that. He appeared in stories like this as a man who was led by supernatural powers, and for his contemporaries these powers had a clear source: the Holy Spirit of God dwelt upon him and gave him power for his deeds and authority for his speech.[36]

Praise with the Creation

Francis's message was not just directed to other human beings. As we have seen so often, Francis had many peculiarities in the ways he thought and lived, notable among them how he approached all of creation, and in the earliest days of his conversion nature as a refuge was the starting point for such a posture. It functioned as an escape from the loathed bourgeois civilization and enabled experience of God's closeness in a completely different way. Just after he had split from his father, as Celano reports, Francis found himself running through a forest singing praises to God in French. It might be that the reference here to his praise in French merely pointed to words that others couldn't comprehend. Whatever the language, this episode is a reminder of how important it was for Francis to communicate with all of nature, not just with human beings. We will go into more detail later regarding his turn to God in prayer, but here we can at least acknowledge how prayer and nature formed a unique relationship. The attention he paid to nature is a distinctive feature of his piety, closely connected to his understanding of repentance. In chapter 5 of his *Admonitions,* he reflected on the greatness of human beings, who, according to Psalm 8, are just a little lower than God, and in the creation narrative of Genesis 1 are described as created in God's image. He deliberately used the Latin conceptual pairing of "imago" (picture) and "similitudo" (likeness) of God. And this very praise of humankind was then contrasted immediately with an accusation that we have failed to worship God. It was human beings who crucified Christ, not other creatures, not demons, meaning that humans must confess their sin and take up their own cross to follow Christ, for we in effect put him there. Francis regarded other creatures, which in the medieval worldview were different from rational human beings, lacking the capacity for reason, as innocent and upholding order in creation. This helps to explain why he fled to the woods after rejecting life in his family's home, in which gold rather than God was at the center. It wasn't just that it was safe to hide in the woods—they also represented order in a world where disorder ruled. Human reason and volition had led him to error, for which he was guilty, so Francis sought out those beings among which he could experience divine order again. According to Celano, such creatures became for him a reflection and expression of the Creator's wisdom, power, and goodness ("sapientia," "potentia," "bonitas"), even the image of his own goodness ("speculum bonitatis").[37]

Importantly, his attitude and behavior toward these creatures was likely just as transgressive as his posture toward society's human outsiders. Francis had once turned to the outcasts with exuberant spontaneity, and now he reached out to other creatures that had so often experienced the contempt of the world as well. Celano tells us he would pick up worms from the path and put them aside to make sure no one stepped on them. He made efforts to care for bees in winter by providing honey and the best wine so that they wouldn't die in the cold. He could spend a whole day praising God that such insects devoted themselves to his service in creation. Giving bees honey was tantamount to repairing an earlier injustice when human beings had taken it away from them. With these stories in mind, it is easy to see Francis as one of the earliest representatives of the ecological movement, as so many have done in recent decades, but we must be careful not to exaggerate his role or rip him out of his context. His positive approach to the creation was not entirely consistent. Soberly, the Franciscan scholar Sigismund Verhey reminds us that for Francis, "animals remain animals" (and remain working animals, to boot) that human beings can use. When Francis, for example, was away from Italy, the brothers decided that on non-fast days it was justifiable to eat meat that had been slaughtered by their followers, but upon hearing the news (from a messenger who arrived conveniently just as people had sat down to a meal of meat), Francis opposed the new rule. But we must note that his aim was not to encourage a vegetarian lifestyle, far from it. Of concern to him was the question whether anything could be added to their rule of life that appeared contrary to the wishes of the order's founder. In narrating this episode, Jordan began with the proposition that Francis enjoyed eating meat. It is only from the perspective of the modern world that there is a problem with Francis both expressing concern for the worms and the bees and his affirmation of a diet containing meat. In the end, Francis's chief concern was protection of order in the world, which implied that bees should have their honey, and humans should have their meat.[38]

Until the last few decades, Francis has been presented as a man whose values have been unappreciated. As the contemporary ecological movement has highlighted the impact of industrialization and consumer culture, so Francis pointed out that human beings disrupt creation rather than using their reason to nurture it. However, despite these significant parallels, there remain enormous differences between human beings of the thirteenth century and today. Alongside the obvious changes in the economic sphere and concomitant intrusions into the natural sphere, it is nature that functions as the framework to exercise Francis's critique of human beings in the first place. Nature, with humankind, cannot be understood without reference to God, who stands over both and who brings order to the cosmos, thereby giving it meaning. Whatever humans might do in violation of the creation, in the first instance such a violation is sin against the Creator. The world as a mirror of God was thus conceived sacramentally, as we have already had cause to mention in relation to the things Francis had touched. And in learned circles too, as Celano narrates, it was assumed that the creation was full of traces of the divine that God had imprinted within it. Indeed, this was a notion that the church father St. Augustine had bequeathed to medieval theology. In his book *On the Trinity,* he developed the idea that traces of the Trinity, the "vestigia trinitatis," testified to God in this world. Of course, Francis, who often spoke of how uneducated he was, knew as little about these philosophical and theological reflections as did those people who cut off swatches of fabric from his tunic in order to take home something of the sanctity of Francis or of Christ himself.[39]

But we don't capture the reality of medieval society either if we think that it was only the elites who upheld this kind of worldview. Scholars of the past might have included only the evidence of learned tracts in their attempts to reconstruct social norms, but we have come to understand that the reality was so much more complex. Not everyone today who speaks of the "superego" has read Sigmund Freud's original writings, nor has everyone who quotes John Rawls and his theory of justice actually read his works. When it comes to grand theories and concepts, there is often a trace of an idea in social self-understanding even when precise details are not familiar. We can safely assume that Francis believed God was present in all creatures, a belief that was not just invented by his biographers but was actually part of his own understanding of the world. He didn't need to have read Augustine or the Neoplatonists of antiquity to come to these conclusions. It was enough that he shared certain assumptions of his own day.[40]

The close relationship between Francis's piety and his philosophical reflection might be seen in this comment by Celano: "He spared lights, lamps, and candles, not wishing to extinguish their brightness with his hand, for he regarded them as a symbol of Eternal Light." God and Light: this was an inexhaustible theme of Neoplatonic philosophy, and was at the same time part of the way liturgical actions were perceived, in which candlelight played a significant role. He certainly understood the latter, though his comprehension of the former is unclear. It is easy to believe that he held the source of any light in high regard. We can thank Celano for providing us with such details in his *Second Life,* and they are further emphasized in other depictions of his cautious approach to the natural world, including also the inanimate world. Again according to Celano, he instructed the brothers when they cut down a tree not to remove it entirely from the ground, so that it might in time sprout anew.[41]

Francis's rich imagination needs to be taken into account when we read in Celano the famous story of Francis preaching to the birds. It appears in his *First Life* which, despite its hagiographical tendencies, is nonetheless trustworthy because of its early provenance. Of course it is true that the incidents of preaching to the birds, as well as other miracles concerning animals, are never described in the *Legend of the Three Companions*, but this is not as weighty a criticism as we might at first think, for those authors concentrate on the fate of the order itself after Francis's visit to Innocent III. If we do allow for the possibility that preaching to the birds bears some kernel of historical truth, it is because there is much in the account that significantly accords with the everyday life of Francis as it has come down to us.[42]

The story runs that Francis and several brothers were traveling through the valley of Spoleto. When they approached Bevagna, around twenty kilometers south of Assisi, Francis saw a large number of different kinds of birds and ran with accustomed spontaneity toward them. Though perhaps not expecting a reply, Francis addressed them "in his usual way," probably the greeting of peace that the brothers used to address other people wherever they went. In this extravagant action, he might have been playing a game with them, or the report might have been exaggerated. It was what happened next that is so remarkable, even if it was not especially supernatural. Despite Francis running toward them and addressing them, the birds remained still on the ground, as Celano reports. Then Francis delivered his sermon, from which Celano provides us an excerpt. Even if this story, based on an everyday kind of encounter with some animals, has been refashioned in a more hagiographic way, it nonetheless remains true that the birds' surprising stillness is miraculous. It isn't necessary to assume that we find Francis's very words in Celano's original text, but the basic tone of the incident is surely consistent with what we know elsewhere about Francis's relationship with other creatures: "My brothers, birds, you should praise your Creator very much and always love him; he gave you feathers to clothe you, wings so that you can fly, and whatever else was necessary for you. God made you noble among his creatures, and he gave you a home in the purity of the air; though you neither sow nor reap, he nevertheless protects and governs you without any solicitude on your part."[43]

Human creatures who acknowledge God's order in the world hear in this sermon allusions to the Sermon on the Mount with its praise of the birds of the air, for which God cares, though they never sow nor reap. Even if Francis's sermon is a fabrication, it is very close to what he believed.

It reflected his intensive connection to the creation, which in the end was a connection to God as well. Francis's sermon was not just an occasion to share information, nor was it an instance of communication between reasonable creatures. And even if in the course of the story we learn that the birds understood him, given that they flew away only after he had offered to make the sign of the cross over them and had given them permission to leave, the most decisive and historically suggestive feature is that Francis was drawing them into his own praise of God. Or perhaps we might state it slightly differently: Francis was encouraged in his praise of God as a consequence of his encounter with the birds, which represented the untouched and ordered natural world. The sermon contains not so much a reevaluation of the birds as a means for the preacher himself to reengage with the foundations of a Christian's faith, worship, and praise. According to Celano, this sermon was just the beginning of something that would occupy Francis continually, preaching to birds and other animals as well as to the inanimate creation. It sounds probable that he made every effort in the future to draw close to animals, a practice that characterized his later ministry, though this sermon might not have captured his precise words on that occasion.[44]

Celano's words probably belong to the tradition that allowed Francis's authentic and relaxed relationship with creation to be presented in ever more fanciful ways. This may have been partly true of his account of the sermon to the birds, but would apply even more to the extraordinarily influential collection of stories known as the *Fioretti*, the *Little Flowers of St Francis*, compiled in the fourteenth century, within which his preaching to the birds contained some extra details: after Francis had blessed them, they flew away to all four corners of the sky, and in so doing made the sign of the cross themselves. His praise of the creation was tightly connected to the cross, which was to become such an important part of the Franciscan way as the brothers took up their own cross to follow Christ. Theologically motivated changes to the first version of the story could have massive consequences within a few short years of its composition. Remarkably, in around 1230, Roger of Wendover retold the story for his own purposes. For him, it was not the stiff-necked Christians who were contrasted with the obedient birds, but instead Jews and Romans. And for Roger, Francis did not run spontaneously toward the birds but commanded with authority that they come to listen to him preach for half a day. It is extraordinary that so soon after his death in other places in Europe biographers were amplifying Francis's authority in this way. Others, in awe of his influence over the birds, began to write more fantastical accounts. Celano lists in his *Treatise on the Miracles* several variations of the story one after another, which cumulatively testify to Francis's authority over the animals and their deep love for him. For example, we learn about a pheasant that kept coming back to Francis after being released, and likewise about a hare that jumped into his lap instead of running back into nature. The theological meaning of encounters like this was more clearly in evidence in the story of Francis coming across a herd of sheep, which Francis greeted in his normal way but then heard them all bleating loudly in response. He spoke to the animals and they heard him too, just as Jesus Christ's voice as the Good Shepherd was recognized by the believing sheep in John 10:14. Francis's impact on animals stretched beyond his life, as was fitting for saints. Later, a student, disturbed by a swallow, commanded it "in the name of Saint Francis"—already dead—to allow itself to be caught, and at that moment it flew peacefully into his hands. All of this merely goes to show how later narrators enjoyed applying their imagination to the accounts while not minimizing their deep reverence for Francis. That the stories are not historical can be assumed. But they do point to that kernel of truth, Francis's uncommon connection to the natural world, that was demonstrated in his most famous poem, *The Canticle of Brother Sun*. We know for certain that this hymn was sung for we have a handwritten version of it from 1279 with musical notation, but how exactly the melody sounded, whether Francis composed it, whether it was written by someone else in his circle or is a later composition, we just don't know.[45]

The origins of this most famous canticle are described by Celano in his *Second Life,* where he drew a connection between its composition and a severe sickness Francis faced shortly before his death, though later biographers embroider the story still more. For example, material about Francis was collected together in the course of the thirteenth century under the title *Legend of Perugia*, which relates that Francis, when taken ill, lingered in 1224 in San Damiano, where the sisters of Clare took care of him. While this is not really contested, we find here the background for Francis's activity in writing several spiritual poems, the *Canticum fratris Solis,* or *The Canticle of Brother Sun,* among them. But given the late composition of the *Legend* and the easily understandable desire to highlight the sanctity of the community at San Damiano, we should not place too much weight on this particular account, and the short comment by Celano doesn't really provide much further support for identifying the actual date of composition.[46]

All we can say is that Francis composed the work sometime in his life, and likely toward its end, but we can't even say whether it was composed all at once. Even the late accounts don't make this clear, but we do know, according to the *Legend,* that Francis added an extra stanza (number 8) to the already completed song in which those who can forgive are to be praised. He added it around the time he mediated a serious disagreement between the bishop of Assisi and the town's mayor. And stanza 9, addressing "Sister Death," was added as he felt the pall of death approach. That the canticle gradually took shape is certainly consistent with the evidence of the text itself. The various perspectives within it, concerning nature or humankind, and the variations between how each line begins, point to a development of the text, which makes dating it even harder, probably impossible, especially since some of Francis's earliest followers argued that the poem had been drafted in several stages, perhaps drawing on similar arguments that we might use today.[47]

Yet despite lacking precise confirmation of the date of composition and notwithstanding its literary infelicities, there is still no doubt that this text gives us excellent access to Francis's world of belief. Directly and intensively, Francis expressed here his belief in creation, which took shape in the various stories about birds, hares, and sheep. The conviction that these stories should be judged as either true or false, historically reliable or literary fabrications, or in the case of the sermon to the birds fabulously fanciful, just won't do. The stories of the animals are one way that people in the Middle Ages expressed one notable feature of Francis's ministry. They attempted this not by recording precise historical details or outlining significant concepts but by presenting a narrative, which in the end might not be so different from ways we could build a case today. Occasionally, even in the twenty-first century, we might choose to characterize a given individual by telling a story about them, which may not be strictly true or might in part be exaggerated or embroidered. This kind of storytelling, moving beyond the unsullied report, is a respected feature of communication to spice up the account. We might want to read some kind of historical reconstruction or journalistic news that is an exacting and factual representation, but in truth this is not the only way of communicating. Perhaps it might help us to think better of the accounts of Francis if we compare them with contemporary filmmaking where real people are presented with dramatic license. Such films sharpen the portrayal of a person, perhaps more so than even medieval authors were prone to do. Historical research today can both thoroughly respect this approach and maintain a commitment to critical examination. With these observations behind us, we are finally in the happy position to expound *The Canticle of Brother Sun*, engaging with Francis in his own words, written in Middle Italian:

1. Most high, Almighty, good Lord,
yours are the praise, glory, honor, and every blessing.
To you alone, most High, they belong,
and no person is worthy to name you.

2. Be praised, my Lord, with all your works,
especially with Brother Sun,
to whom belongs the day and through whom you enlighten us.
He is beautiful and illuminates with glorious splendour:
bearing your image, Most High.

3. Be praised, my Lord, by Sister Moon and the stars;
you formed them in the heavens, clear and precious and beautiful.

4. Be praised, my Lord, by Brother Wind
and by air and clouds, in clear or any weather,
through which you give sustainability to your creatures.

5. Be praised, my Lord, by Sister Water,
who is so useful and humble and precious and modest.

6. Be praised, my Lord, by Brother Fire,
through whom you illuminate the night;
it is beautiful, and joyful, robust and powerful.

7. Be praised, my Lord, by our Sister, Mother Earth,
who sustains and governs us,
and brings forth varied fruits with colourful flowers and herbs.

8. Be praised, my Lord, by those who forgive because of your love
and bear sickness and distress.
Blessed are they who bear this in peace,
for they will be crowned by you, Most High.

9. Be praised, my Lord, by our Sister, carnal Death;
for no human can escape her with their life.
Woe to those, who die in mortal sin.
Blessed are they, whom she finds walking in your most holy will,
for the second death will do them no harm.

10. Praise and extol my Lord and give him thanks and serve him with utmost
humility.[48]

It is important to remember that this canticle is principally a song to God: "Be praised, my Lord" resounds throughout, followed by the Italian word *per,* here translated as "through." This underscores that the objects of creation are not themselves recipients of the praise, rather they join voices with Francis to offer praise, and are also a reason for that praise. Francis would also have known the Song of the Three in the book of Daniel (not included in later Protestant versions of the Scriptures), who praised God from the fiery furnace (Daniel 3), as well as the familiar Psalm 148, an Old Testament model of praise, in both of which the creation is addressed and exhorted to praise God. Francis imitated them without a second thought. Yet for Christians, the image of the sun has further resonance, here addressed as a brother, because the word *sun* in Italian, as in Latin *sole,* is grammatically a masculine noun, which allowed Francis to highlight the sibling characteristics of the various parts of the created order he names, which was not something he found a model for in other poetry but devised himself. His approach to the elements of the creation proceeded, then, from this grasp of their quasi-familial interrelationships, raising them to the status shared by human beings. In his *Praises of the Virtues,* which Francis likely did compose in the last years of his life, his obedience was described not just as submission to other people but to rapacious wild animals as well, "so that they can do what they like with him, as far as God allows them." The animals remain dangerous and threatening, yet that does not mean that they are the enemies of human beings.[49]

Human beings were for Francis deeply embedded in a diverse network of relationships with other creatures, which is plausible background for understanding how Francis could give thanks to the Creator through them. Like the account of the creation of the world in Genesis 1, he first turned his attention to the sun, and only then to the rest of the world and the four elements of air, water, fire, and earth. Of note is the fact that the animals, which played such an important role in other stories about Francis, have no place in the *Canticle*. They belong, of course, in that web of sibling-like relationships, but it is interesting that his biographers pay more attention to them than Francis does himself. We discover too that Francis in the *Canticle* emphasized the earth and addressed her both as sister and as mother, quite striking in a song that is focused on the sun, though we should be cautious here, as associations with prehistoric mother cults are out of the question for Francis. Much more likely, this form of address is an instance of the anthropocentric nature of the song with its concentration on human beings. Francis did not attempt to shake off his deep sense of connection with the world around him.[50]

In fact, the song climaxes with the role of humans in those stanzas that were added later, despite its emphasis on the earth in earlier verses. Human beings are not presented merely as the crown of the creation but also are acknowledged to have extra responsibility in the world to promote peace. Adding to the biblical background from Genesis 1, Psalm 148, and the Song of the Three, there are also New Testament roots for the *Canticle* that shape this song of praise, namely the Beatitudes, with which Jesus begins the Sermon on the Mount, and especially the line "Blessed are the peacemakers," which as we have seen impacted the core of Francis's preaching too. If he did indeed add this eighth stanza later, it might have served another purpose and corrected a glaring omission, for without it, there would have been no allusion to Christ in the whole *Canticle*. In a song like this, it would be unreasonable to expect a fulsome exposition of Francis's doctrinal system, but we might suggest nonetheless that for any Christian, Francis included, Christ can be assumed as the center of their beliefs. Indeed, several times each day in the various offices he prayed, Francis would have been called upon to consider Christ, who was for him the bedrock of his personal piety. But it is worth pointing out as well another perspective on Francis's Christological vagueness in this canticle. We should not expect here or anywhere else in Francis's writings to find a piety that draws attention to identification with Christ or being conformed to the image of Christ. His chief concern regarding Christ—highlighted here with reference to the Beatitudes—was to follow him in an apostolic way. At the beginning of the unauthorized *Rule of 1221*, he makes this very point.[51]

Indeed, the general nature of the stanza on peace hints toward the conclusion that it was not a direct consequence of conflict in Assisi that Francis wanted to address; rather, it came from the spiritual posture that he brought to the world to bear suffering and to promote peace. Noteworthy is the penultimate stanza, where death itself gratefully becomes our sister and is connected to a warning of Judgment Day. As mentioned earlier in relation to Francis's model sermon, Francis touches us tenderly with the *Canticle* but does not spare us the message about repentance and judgment. He warns us about dying in mortal sin, a veiled exhortation of the need for repentance; the ultimate spiritual goal was to confess mortal sin in order to avoid the second death, which according to Revelation 20:14 is eternal damnation. Francis, when traveling around the country to preach, did not avoid preaching about judgment. The humility that attended his lifestyle was deeply rooted in the fear of Judgment Day. Peace without deep repentance is just not possible. And for Francis, all this was profoundly embedded in his deep faith in God, praise for whom began and concluded the *Canticle*, and before whose face we feel unworthy and are driven to humility.

Finally, we see here something of eternal things too. With good reason, Thomas of Celano understood Francis's address to the creatures using sibling language as an anticipation of "the freedom of the glory of the children of God" of which Paul speaks in Romans 8:21. It was certainly part of his longing for human salvation that all the creation would be included. Along with humans, all creatures yearn for a better world in which corruption is quashed and life eternal is granted. Whether this is exactly how Francis conceived the future is uncertain, for in the *Canticle* (and elsewhere) he seems to separate sinful human beings from the creation, which is enduringly good and therefore not in need of redemption. Either way, humankind has to face the prospect of God's judgment, which is made clear when Francis speaks of the second death and when he preaches for repentance, with which his mission began. He is motivated by both love for life and fear of judgment and destruction. Again, we have to be careful of premature summaries of Francis's relevance to the contemporary world. Much of what he taught reminds us of Albert Schweitzer's motto "reverence for life." But still it was only part of Francis's entire message, which placed humankind under the permanent charge of transgression before the face of God.[52]

Longing for a Martyr's Death and the Conversion of Muslims

It isn't just Francis's sharp preaching of judgment that stands directly at odds with contemporary sensibilities. His efforts to win Muslims for Christ are also seen as radical in light of today's dialogue-oriented approach to interreligious encounters, and perhaps not just radical but strange, disruptive, and possibly damaging too. Again, the Francis who feels close to us might feel very distant if we seek to understand him on his own terms. Three times, according to Celano, Francis set out to convert Muslims. Behind this commitment was not only the need to convert unbelievers—as he saw Muslims—but also the longing for martyrdom. Indeed, as in so many instances in the life of Francis, this longing for the martyr's death has become such an essential element in the biographical accounts that one must genuinely ask the question whether references to martyrdom would be better explained in hagiographical terms, as Michael Cusato has suggested. Celano and the others wanted to demonstrate in this way Francis's perfect discipleship in following Christ, whose own life led ultimately to his death on the cross. It is simply impossible from Francis's writings to confidently ascribe to him a longing for martyrdom to build the case.[53]

However, we can imagine that the thought was not entirely absent from his imaginings. There is at least one way of establishing this possibility, by emphasizing the account of his journey to the Middle East, for it led him to his encounter with the sultan. Jordan of Giano, who was a contemporary of Francis, belonged to his order, lived in Italy, was a witness to this journey, and whose observations are at least as significant as the Three Companions', throws a bright light on this story in his *Chronicle*. He knew a great deal about events in the Middle East; for example, he reports that Francis had appointed Elias of Cortona as provincial in Syria, where the order was established with methodical structure. He also recounts an unusual episode in Spain in which five brothers suffered martyrdom. The *Legend,* being devoted to them, lists their names: Berald, Peter, Adiutus, Accursius, and Otho. However, as admiration for them spread, Francis tried to dampen such enthusiasm and to suppress the *Legend,* suggesting that no one should praise someone's suffering unless it was that person's alone. It was only then that he set out to the Middle East, and as Jordan recounts, this was a result of two factors: unwillingness to send individual brothers on such a dangerous mission and the possibility of jeopardizing his own reputation by remaining safe at home.[54]

If we give priority to Jordan's report, it has drastic consequences for the more traditional way of understanding the reasons for Francis's journey to Egypt. Celano tells us of three departures for the Muslim world, compared with the report of Jordan, who describes only one. However, the two accounts are easy enough to harmonize, for as we will soon see, in the first two of them (which Celano reports) Francis did not reach his destination, so Jordan merely presents the last, which did climax in Francis's meeting with Sultan al-Malik al-Kamil. Frequently in the story of Francis's life, we meet contradictions, so one should call to mind that Celano in his *First Life* recounts that some of the brothers set out in vain for Santiago de Compostela, which might have been one way of conceiving a path to the Muslim world. It is entirely possible too that the first two journeys, or at least attempts at the journeys, were fashioned out of material that had otherwise been forgotten, but that together were blended into the third journey to Egypt, which is well attested, giving them a purpose that was not obvious at the time. Indeed, the report of the first abortive attempt to reach Egypt is overlaid with many miraculous features. In Celano's account, Francis had set out by ship for Syria but only got as far as the east coast of the Adriatic, where he couldn't find any other ship to take him further east, so he decided to turn back. He approached the ship's crew to take him and another brother, who had accompanied him, back to Ancona, but the crew refused because they simply didn't have enough provisions on board. Undeterred, Francis hid himself as a stowaway until during a storm at sea (which had depleted the ship's reserves further), he emerged to feed the crew with the very little food he had smuggled in. As is evident, this story combines a number of incidents from the life of Jesus, for example, his journeys by ship and the stilling of the storm (Matthew 8:23–27 and parallel passages) with the story of Jesus multiplying the loaves (Matthew 14:13–21 and parallels). Julian of Speyer, the only other biographer to describe the thwarted first journey, makes explicit that the Lord helped the crew to remember Jesus through Francis: "And so, through him the Lord recalled to memory his miracles."

A life of discipleship in the pattern of Jesus has radically overlaid and reshaped the actual memory of the deeds of Francis himself.[55]

Despite the fact that both Julian and Celano agree upon the date of the journey, it may still be true that it did not actually take place. Francis was to have set out on the journey six years after his conversion, that is, in the year 1212. Celano, active in Germany for the order from 1221, must have known that in that very year the infamous and in many ways devastating Children's Crusade had set out from Germany and northern France. Perhaps it was also possible that he combined in his mind news of a sea voyage by Francis with reports of events north of the Alps. On the basis of such observations, it would not be unreasonable to assume that Francis had decided at this very juncture to set out for the Middle East, and he wouldn't be the only one whose attempt had been thwarted by the challenging travel conditions of the Middle Ages. But we still can't be certain, given that Celano recounts the episode in his *Treatise on the Miracles* and not in his *Second Life*.[56]

It is even more difficult to capture the details of the second voyage to the Muslim world, which Celano and Bonaventure (who follows Celano closely) recount. With Bernard, Francis set out for Morocco to the Emir el-Mumein (the Latin for the Arabic name is Miramamolinus), who was the head of the Muslims there, though if the account is reliable it was around 1213/14, and someone else bore the title at that very time, Mohammed-ben-Nasser, who was wounded in the battle of Las Navas de Tolosa in 1212 by Alfonso VIII of Castile and had to retreat to Morocco, one of the greatest victories of the Spanish in the reconquest of Spain as they sought to free the land from the Muslim invaders. If we were to synchronize events, perhaps Francis wanted to travel to Morocco in the aftermath of the victory, though it is hard to say. Celano provides some motivation when he says that Francis wanted to preach the Gospel to Mohammed-ben-Nasser and his people, and a danger implicit in this plan would be his death as a martyr. But even this trip came to nothing at the outset. According to Celano, through God's intervention Francis had taken ill in Spain and had returned home. This might well have happened, for the relatively detailed information that we have about Mohammed-ben-Nasser's retreat from Spain to Morocco might suggest that real memories are at play here, but the reason for turning back does give us cause for doubt. The idea that Francis would give up on the journey because he was sick had an earlier manifestation, for in Spoleto we learned that his military adventure was also cut short by sickness, and in this story too there were reasons for doubting the veracity of the story. The same motive is given in this later report, with God intervening to change his fate, and as Celano asserts, this for the sake of the whole community. Of course this is unquestionably possible. But it could have been different too.[57]

Perhaps Celano shared Jordan's insight. Perhaps the fate of the five brothers, martyred for their faith, had raised the question of why Francis himself had escaped a similar fate and had so long avoided these kinds of dangers, although since 1218 several brothers had undertaken a trip to the Middle East, albeit admittedly for different motives. It is quite likely that Celano had pieced together various episodes that he knew from Francis's life to tell the story of three times setting out and twice being thwarted through higher powers over which he had no control. Celano can fill in a gap in the narrative, which Jordan knew of as well, to defend Francis against any calumnies. And this fits in with the *Second Life,* where he doesn't mention the first two trips at all. The attacks on Francis's character were likely muted. Now the story would concern itself chiefly with his saintly miracles, not with his preparation for a martyr's death.[58]

What we know, and what is confirmed in the reports from other sources, is that Francis traveled to meet Sultan al-Malik al-Kamil in the year 1219. It is without doubt the best attested episode in Francis's entire life, as André Vauchez has shown. But less well recognized is the fact that Francis had not one but two significant encounters on that journey, to which Kathleen Warren has alerted us. Francis met both the sultan and the crusaders. Francis the peacemaker became, whether he liked it or not, part of the crusading movement, a tension that is really difficult to expound any further. It is hard to get past the sheer naiveté of Francis in his mission to the sultan, as later we might see naiveté in his relationship with the pope. He was able, for example, to provide a searing critique of early capitalism in Assisi but he seems to be blind to the power relationships of the church in the world of his day.[59]

Of course, at this stage in the early development of the crusading agenda, it would be inaccurate to reduce everything to the question of power alone. It is true that in calling the First Crusade in 1095, the then reigning pontiff Pope Urban II (r. 1088–99) was seeking an opportunity to assert himself in the face of the emperor, with whom he was still in conflict after the Investiture Controversy. But on the other hand, the enthusiasm that calling the crusade provoked can't be explained only with reference to political or social factors. It was more likely the belief that the way to the holy places had to remain open that motivated this "armed pilgrimage." In the age of Francis, there was a great mixture of motives inspiring the crusades, and against the will of the pope the most egregious misappropriation of the crusading ideal had emerged, for the knights of the Fourth Crusade between 1201 and 1204 had turned from the goal of liberating Jerusalem and instead had conquered the Christian city of Constantinople with some feeble political rationalization, ransacking, raping, and robbing the city over three days of hideous violence.[60]

Now it may be that Francis was unaware of these historical details, but it is still worthy of earnest reflection to imagine how a man who directed his brothers to offer the greeting of peace wherever they went could get mixed up in a crusading army. With caution, again, we need to consider the apparent contradiction inherent in his attitudes, so as to be aware of how we might be projecting our own attitudes back into the thirteenth century. Even a century earlier, just as the great mystic Bernard of Clairvaux had both preached tender sermons on the love of Christ for believers and had praised a new order of knights, the "nova militia," whipping up enthusiasm for the Second Crusade—so also the descendants of Francis had told stories of his support for the crusades. When asked by the sultan himself how he reconciled the ethics of the Sermon on the Mount and its call to peace with the invasion of Christian armies in Muslim lands, Francis quoted Matthew 5:29, "If your right eye causes you to sin, tear it out and throw it away," applying it to the Muslims who threatened to lead Christians away from their faith and so deliver them over to evil. This dialogue is as unreliable historically as many of the other reports of Francis's conversation with the sultan or his sermon in his presence, but it does represent the way that Franciscans of the second or third generation struggled with the content of their own proclamation in light of the war against Islam. The peace they preached was not of this world, which meant effectively that wars in this world could be reconciled with their spiritual commitments, a not implausible conclusion when we recall the other story in Celano's *Second Life*, in which Francis predicted a Christian defeat in the face of the Islamic forces in order to stymie any joining of battle with them. Even with this significant commentary, we still cannot detect any more general skeptical posture toward warfare. Francis did prophesy defeat in one given battle, which came true. It was on August 29, 1219, that the crusaders near Damietta stormed the Egyptian Mediterranean coast to engage the Islamic army, but thereby fell prey to their sophisticated tactics: the Arabs appeared to retreat, when all of a sudden they turned around and attacked the invaders as they fled. According to received estimates, around five thousand Christians were slaughtered and a thousand were taken prisoner. Francis was regarded among the crusaders as a prophet of doom, though a true prophet at that. A peacemaker he was not.[61]

This battle was part of the so-called Fifth Crusade, which was the context for the provocative meeting of Francis with both the knights of the crusades and the sultan. Proceeding via Egypt, this crusade was meant to secure the Holy Land for Christendom, and was energetically supported by the pope, whose authority in the field was exercised by the Spanish cardinal Pelagius (among others), who had arrived in Damietta in 1218 and who had angled after that to become the commander of the entire crusade. The siege wasn't quickly lifted, and it was in this period of standoff that Francis arrived in 1219: the mendicant among the knights, the prophet, the one always on a quest, the one whose mission was diverted.

After the battle of August 29, Francis did indeed proceed to meet the sultan, something attested by a direct eyewitness. That man was Jacques de Vitry, traveling with the crusading armies, who wrote home that Francis had fallen in with the knights and couldn't be persuaded not to enter the enemy camp to preach the Word of God there. We see Francis's persistent will to convert the Muslims to Jesus Christ, and perhaps as well his own desire for a martyr's death. He knew what could come to him in a foreign camp, for he had seen it himself when the crusaders, having accused eight Muslims of espionage, brought them into the camp and proceeded to cut off their noses, arms, lips, and ears. Whether as a sacrifice or as missionary, Francis's posture here revealed his awareness of the massive contrast between the great religions of Christianity and Islam. Even if Francis could not tally up any great success in his proselytising strivings, martyrdom was, ironically, also denied him. According to Jacques de Vitry, after hearing him preach, the sultan asked him to pray that he might receive knowledge to decide which religion was true. Jacques de Vitry expands on the account in his *Historia orientalis*, or *History of the Orient*, a sweeping historical overview that describes a remarkable and essentially plausible moment. In this version, Francis had not planned from the outset to enter the enemy camp but was moved spontaneously to take this dangerous step after he had a kind of visionary experience, something not unknown in his biography up to now. This story complements the account in the *Chronicle* of the French squire Ernoul, according to whom Francis and his companion—according to Bonaventure this was Brother Illuminatus—first asked Cardinal Pelagius for permission to take this step, bringing some shape to the narrative which, although unlikely to be quite as orderly as presented, was not very different from Francis's life overall.[62]

Once he had set out for the camp in Fariskar, south of Damietta, Francis was taken captive by some Arabic soldiers, according to Jacques de Vitry, but was spared on account of his proclamation "Christianus sum," or "I am a Christian." Well may we ask what language they used to communicate with one another. More plausible is the account of Jordan of Giano, who says that Francis called out "Sultan, sultan!"—words that would be the most easily understood by his Arabic interlocutors, and indeed were enough for Francis to be brought into the presence of the sultan. The conversation there must have been mediated through a translator, a "tarjuman" or dragoman, as the older reports convey. Jordan's report makes sense, not only because calling out the title of the sultan would be universally understood but also because it may have led to the misunderstanding that Francis was a spy, or at the very best serving in the role of emissary, which did cross the mind of the sultan later. In the light of the defeat of the Christians that the Muslims not long before had secured, it might be expected that the vanquished army would send someone to announce their surrender.[63]

The following scene has frequently been embellished. In the account of Jacques de Vitry, Francis is presented as preaching not just to the whole group of Arabs but especially to the sultan himself. Ernoul expands on this by saying that the sultan first called together his learned counselors to provide him with advice, though they refused to listen to Francis. There is no doubt that in Ernoul, Jacques de Vitry, and even in the sultan's request for prayer much has been fabricated. It is nonetheless possible that in his frequent exuberance, Francis tried to preach the Gospel to them, though it comes as no surprise to learn from all the reports that his sermon didn't have the desired effect. There were simply too many hurdles to jump for his message to be well received. The whole historical context didn't fit the proclamation he came to bring. It may just be, however, that after his arrest, as Jacques de Vitry describes it, Francis was dragged before the sultan not for him to listen to a sermon but to decide what they should do with the Christian. Ernoul's account sees the sultan's wise men demanding Francis's execution, which supports Jacques de Vitry's narrative. If Francis did indeed appear before the sultan, then it was most likely as a man accused who was threatened with torture and death, according to Celano, not because of his faith but because he had forced his way into the Arabs' camp. The question was whether Francis was an emissary or a deserter, which were probably the only two categories for understanding his arrival there. But because Francis was neither, and nor was he a violent attacker, they doubtless found it difficult to work out how to treat him.[64]

That the sultan stood there opposite Francis without a clue is not hard to picture. It is less likely that the sultan would have debated with him and probably is part of the story's embellishment through which Francis's profile and importance were magnified. Bonaventure later took up this thread and described Francis deep in conversation with the sultan, when Francis was said to have offered to the sultan a fire challenge. Francis was more than prepared with some representatives of Islam at his side to walk into a fiery furnace, so that when the sultan saw that he was uninjured, he should naturally promise to convert to Christianity. As powerful as this story has been, it is still legendary. Readers of the Bible will recognize at once associations with the prophet Elijah, who challenged the prophets of Baal on Mount Carmel to a fire challenge. In this episode, the victory would go to the God who could be moved to send down fire from heaven to consume the sacrifice (see 1 Kings 18:20–40). We are also reminded here of the three men who were thrown into the fiery furnace in the book of Daniel, whose song—as we have seen—played a significant role in the composition of Francis's *The Canticle of Brother Sun*. The point that Bonaventure made here was that the sultan reneged on the challenge out of fear that his people might rise up if he were to convert to Christianity. It appears that Francis, in this account, at least, was on the verge of witnessing a mass conversion of Muslims to the Christian faith.[65]

The reality, however, was a tad more banal. That Francis did preach the Gospel to Muslims for a time can be understood as something that happened while he was imprisoned for a couple of days before being led to the sultan. He was then quickly released, which probably had less to do with his sermon than with his harmless appearance. It wasn't the first time someone had thought Francis was mad. His demeanor, his forcing his way into the Arabs' camp, his presumed attempts to preach in Italian or Latin—all this no doubt gave the impression of someone who was of unsound mind. And even if we stop short of this interpretation, we would still have to admit that this ragged beggar was no threat to the sultan and it would make no sense even to keep him as a hostage. However, in the longer story, the Franciscans with their modest manners earned much goodwill, as Jacques de Vitry reports: the Arabs always listened attentively to the Friars Minor, he writes in the *Historia orientalis*, as long as they only preached the Gospel and did not speak against the prophet Muhammad, in which case the preachers would indeed be risking life and limb. Perhaps also running in Francis's favor was the fact that the sultan had not long before sent back to the crusaders a Frankish prisoner to offer an armistice, which he didn't want to jeopardize. Francis's appearance before the sultan was seen as rather more pathetic and piteous than impressive and threatening. He didn't find Francis offensive enough to make him a martyr.[66]

All in all, what remains of the story is, remarkably enough, a spontaneous act in which Francis entered an enemy camp, presumably tried to preach a sermon in an unknown language, faced some kind of trial regarding his fate before the sultan, whose responsibility it then was to decide whether Francis should live or die, and finally obtained his release on the basis of being no threat. One might also present this episode as something grotesque, as the appearance of a man who seemed unhinged, but we would thereby do Francis a disservice. Undoubtedly, his behavior showed a courage bordering on self-contempt, animated by a desire to face any danger for God's sake because of his sense of calling. This was almost the equivalent of a longing for martyrdom, and the attempt to preach was not so much about conversion in itself but more generally about confession of the Lord Jesus Christ, whom he was prepared to follow wherever he led given his identification as a Christian, as Jacques de Vitry makes clear. In his own eyes and according to his own subjective sense, this is exactly what he did before the Arabs and perhaps also before the sultan too, trusting that his actions counted for something before God. The elaborate narratives that were shaped directly after the event were intended to express Francis's understanding of himself, though for contemporary researchers they provide little to aid their attempts at historical reconstruction.

Much remains puzzling about Francis's encounter with the sultan. It was at least another expression of that stirring and simultaneously irritating spontaneity of Francis of Assisi, but perhaps he learned from this incident that spontaneity was not always necessary for the brothers to imitate, for he urged them to be more cautious. In the provisional and unauthorized *Rule* of the brotherhood written not long after the journey to Egypt in 1221, Francis gave to the community a series of instructions on how to engage with Muslims. Their missionaries should be patently aware of the dangers, so Francis quoted here from Jesus's commission of the apostles, "See, I am sending you out like sheep into the midst of wolves" (Matthew 10:16). Going to the Muslims was the most direct application of this text, which had played such a key role in Francis's life since his conversion, exactly because the text made a connection between mission and danger. And Francis spoke of two ways of going about their mission, of which proclamation of the Word of God was just one. On this path, the clear goal of the mission would lead to unbelievers being baptized, with the risk of martyrdom being part of the calculation. Whoever might go to the Saracens should know that the Son of Man would acknowledge them on the last day if they acknowledged him before others, as we read in Matthew 10:32. This is precisely Francis's approach to the connection between being prepared for martyrdom and proclamation of the Gospel, reminding us that we misinterpret the life of Francis if we see him primarily as a forerunner for peaceful exchange between religions, which is one way of approaching this encounter but perhaps not the most historically satisfying.[67]

There was certainly the possibility of a more peaceful and therefore less dangerous path that could maintain the same mission focus. Some would undertake their mission more discreetly, not denying Christ but, known for their humble way of living, establishing a ministry of presence, if you will; thus Jacques de Vitry in the above quotation described the Friars Minor in the Middle East as well liked. And in the end it was the Franciscan combination of witness through lips and lives that made them so successful. How Francis made his way back to Assisi, we just don't know. It could be that he got help from the crusaders in Acre. Whether he ever got to Jerusalem or other nearby holy sites (which later sources mention) against the express will of the pope, we can only guess. Though Francis did once later mention the holiness of the grave of Jesus in Jerusalem, this is still not enough to build on. Like so often in Francis's life, the tracks go cold, although the meeting with the sultan places his biography squarely under the searching light of world history.[68]

CHAPTER 5

Order

A Strange Alliance: Powerful Pope and Poor Beggar

O MUCH REPENTANCE, SO MUCH DENUNCIATION of the world. But no denunciation of the church, such a central component of the life of Francis. If we accept the events in the Middle East as we have described them here, they do not necessarily stand opposed to papal politics of power but are part and parcel of their expression. Francis pursued his own path, but it was still a path with and for the pope, for both were convinced of the need to engage the Muslims with the claims of Christendom, which meant of course reclaiming in their entirety the lands in which the holiest sites of Christendom—especially Jerusalem and Bethlehem, the sites of Christ's death and birth—were to be found. Against the advice of the Christian king of Jerusalem, John of Brienne, Cardinal Pelagius refused to accept al-Malik al-Kamil's offer of terms of peace regarding Jerusalem, for the crusaders sought not just a spiritual goal but more importantly a military victory through conquest and control, as was the case later with Frederick II as well. Of course, Francis had no part in such military considerations, which would have appeared strange to him. But it is also true that he did not stand against such stratagems, and indeed his own spontaneous naiveté effectively supported proceedings against the Muslim cause. This is the moderate conclusion of a scholar of Islam, Ahmed Mohamed Abdelkawy Sheir: "His overtures to al-Kamil could thus be seen as another form of the crusading mission to regain Jerusalem for Christianity."[1]

If we take this seriously, we must revise our approach to Francis. For so long, we have portrayed his idiosyncratic path as essentially a reflexive function of his own personal experience, though shared with friends. But now we need to set him within the story of the longer sustained developments within the church, within the power relationships of the papacy and their doctrinal provisions; indeed, we must examine how his fellowship became part of the church's structure and thereby grew increasingly conformed to its shape. The encounter with the sultan, as much as he might have regarded it as relatively unimportant, was nonetheless a clear example of Francis's desire to tread the world stage. He had done this once before when in 1209 he stood before the pope assuming a thankless side role, according to his own estimation, though his biographers have recounted the story differently. More and more, however, the encounter with Innocent demanded something of him. Though this might have been useful for his order, it also draws our attention to one of the most challenging problems in our understanding of Francis. We would perhaps prefer to see Francis on the side of the vulnerable, opposing the powerful, as one who had turned to the weakest of society, to those who had been excluded. But this portrayal sits at odds with his relationship with the medieval institution of the papacy, which had long since moved past its spiritual responsibilities to pursue a political role with increasing influence. There can be no doubt about Francis's close relationship with the popes of the period.

And it is not just the Franciscan sources that point to this conclusion. In a previously mentioned letter written from Genoa, Jacques de Vitry recounts his own close experience with Pope Honorius III (r. 1216–27), whose election in 1216 he had witnessed. He was shocked by the state of the Curia, whose members seemed interested only in worldly affairs. Jacques contrasts his experience of the Curia with the encouragement he had felt from the Friars Minor, describing their poor and modest lifestyle: "They are held in great esteem by the Lord Pope and the cardinals." This contemporary witness, a representative of the church's hierarchy himself, notes the tension between the papal court and the values of the brotherhood, and at the very same time reflects on the complementary roles they played: the church couldn't exist without Francis, nor the other way around.[2]

If we look at Honorius himself, during whose pontificate the events of Damietta played out, we can feel this tension in another way, especially in contrast with his predecessor in the chair of St. Peter, Innocent III, whom Francis, according to his biographers, knew earlier. Innocent was one of the most powerful—and truth be told one of the most ambitious—popes in history. Lothar von Segni was just thirty-seven when in 1198 he was elected pope, the third to take the name Innocent. Rather than seeing him as a theologian, we should approach him more as a highly educated lawyer, for he had studied Roman law and canon law in Bologna, one of the most important educational institutions of the Middle Ages. This was for a pope neither unusual nor unfortunate, for many of his responsibilities had more to do with legal administration than theology, even if during his attendance at the Fourth Lateran Council—named after the location of its meeting in the Lateran Palace and Basilica—he had much to contribute to its theological debates. But it must still be said that what a person studies has profound implications for the way that person views the world, so this young and ambitious man, now pope, maintained his interest in jurisprudential and political questions.[3]

But merely occupying the Petrine See wasn't enough to justify his authority. The demands of the office of the bishop of Rome might be understood in a different way. After much deliberation, the church had decided against the position of Cyprian (d. 258) that Jesus had given authority and leadership not to an individual but to the group of apostles. The church therefore set itself against the notion that this group was represented collegially by the five ancient patriarchs. Since the Council of Nicaea, the sees of Rome, Alexandria in Egypt, and Antioch in Syria had been preeminent, adding to their number in 451 Constantinople and Jerusalem. Further, a cursory glance at a map shows that Rome was the only one of these sees in the Western Roman Empire; the other four were situated in close proximity to each other in the Eastern Roman Empire, giving Rome a strategic advantage. Increasingly the Eternal City saw itself as preeminent. When the Western Roman Empire was extinguished in the fifth century, and with the rise of Islam since the seventh, the cities of Alexandria, Antioch, and Jerusalem found themselves under Muslim rule, giving further prestige and entitlement to Rome. And in contrast with Constantinople, Rome wanted to further validate its primacy, which symbolically was achieved in 1054, when delegates from the reforming popes in Rome placed their bull of anathema against the patriarch of Constantinople on the altar of the Hagia Sophia. In collective memory, this marked the moment when schism, the division of the churches of east and west, found its climax, though we have to beware of exaggeration, for the experience of Christians in the surrounding regions, whose sense of belonging to Rome and to Constantinople overlapped, was not as clear-cut as an anathema might suggest.

Nonetheless, as an expression of the developed identity of the primacy of Rome, this remained a high-water mark. Further, such reforming popes—taking their lead from Gregory VII (r. 1073–85) and his successors, shaped by Gregorian priorities—began to name themselves "vicarius Christi" (or "Vicar of Christ"), no longer "vicarius Petri," signaling a universal demand for preeminence, not just temporally but spiritually as well. It was no accident that this kind of claim by reforming popes refreshed the memory of earlier conflict with German emperors in the Investiture Controversy, in which major disagreements emerged concerning the right to appoint bishops, leading to attempts to rebalance power dynamics with Gregory VII's claim to be able to depose emperors themselves. All of this formed the background when Innocent III laid claims to the title "vicarius Christi" not just occasionally but as core to papal identity and entitlement. As a jurist, he had a keen sense of the inevitable consequences of styling the papacy in this way, including its impact on ways of interpreting the constitution of the ancient church. When the Fourth Lateran Council of 1215 named the five patriarchs of the early church—Rome, Constantinople, Alexandria, Antioch, and Jerusalem—it did so merely as a formal gesture. The assumptions lying behind this list had been discounted by Rome's assertion of priority, for above all these patriarchates stood the Roman church, which "through the Lord's disposition has a primacy of ordinary power over all other churches inasmuch as it is the mother and mistress of all Christ's faithful." This was nothing less than a papal claim over all the churches of the east. Now all questions of faith and doctrine would be adjudicated in Rome, with other churches expected to submit. The worldview of this highly educated pope was, without equivocation, hierarchical—such centralized leadership would enable the church to experience both unanimity and clarity in its rulings.[4]

This was not just a theological or canon law matter, however. Even though the course of the Fourth Crusade was probably not in the front of the pope's mind, the conduct of pilgrims on their way to the holy sites of Palestine probably was. The turn against Constantinople in 1204 had more to do with the interests of the mercantile class, and especially the Venetians, who hoped through conquest and plundering of the city on the Bosporus to secure their economic interests in the Mediterranean. But Pope Innocent was not going to let a good crisis get in the way of his ambitions. When the

Latin Empire, which now replaced the ancient Byzantine rule that traced its origins back to antiquity, assumed power in Constantinople and held onto it until 1261, it brought along with it a Latin patriarchate. More than a decade before the conclusion of the Fourth Lateran Council, the most important eastern patriarchate had been entirely subordinated to Rome.

But this was just a part of the political dance, which Innocent celebrated by virtue of his diplomatic acumen and his keen instinct for power. The circumstances played into his hands. Shortly before Innocent's election as pope, the German emperor Henry VI had died. Finding his successor was comparatively easy, insofar as his rule had extended to Sicily, which, through his marriage to Constance, the daughter of the Norman ruler Roger II (r. 1130–54), he could claim. Three years before his death, Henry had defeated all other claimants, so his wife ruled as regent on behalf of their two-year-old son, Frederick, who was later to become Emperor Frederick II (r. 1212/15–1250). He was first crowned king of Sicily in 1198, but his mother named Innocent in her will as her son's legal guardian—with immediate consequences, for she was to die in the very same year. Significantly, the pope was therefore a commissary, a ruler over Sicily, which popes had at least formally ruled over as a fiefdom since 1059. It is important to note that the kingdom of Sicily was not confined to the Mediterranean island of the same name, for its subjection to the patrimony of Peter, the papal states of central Italy, gave to this kingdom extensive authority over southern Italy.

But there were yet other complications. Henry VI had not yet succeeded in turning the Holy Roman Empire of the German nation into a hereditary crown—from the early Middle Ages the crown had been bestowed by election. To consider his son as his successor was a test case, for at first his plan to see his infant son assume the crown could not be guaranteed. Henry's brother, Philipp of Swabia (r. 1198–1208), claimed the crown first of all for the Staufen dynasty, but Otto IV (r. 1198/1208–18), from the Welf dynasty and the son of Henry the Lion, wanted the crown himself, opening old wounds from the twelfth century in Germany. Indeed, Otto had been elected and crowned, but Philipp nonetheless reached for both himself, so that now there were two kings claiming legitimate succession. Also, the pope had reason to exert his own power, for it was assumed in imperial constitutional law, the stages of which he saw as legally distinct, that only those duly elected and crowned as kings could thereafter by crowned by the pope as legitimate emperor. This brewing conflict provided Innocent with an unforeseen opportunity when he reserved his judgment concerning whom to crown. The learned jurist decided to use this propitious moment to legislate an outcome. In the bull *Venerabilem* of March 1202, Innocent gave to the German princes the right to elect their own king but reserved the right to examine the decision before conferring the imperial crown, which enabled him to play one side off against the other in determining who would accede to the imperial throne. Innocent raised the cost of imperial legitimacy through his own machinations at the same time that conflict raged between Otto IV and (until his murder in 1208) Philipp of Swabia. Innocent was playing the parties off against each other with aplomb.

This was clearly in evidence after the death of Philipp when Innocent crowned as German emperor Otto IV, who, as we have seen, traveled through Rivotorto on his way to Rome for his coronation by the pope. Soon enough Otto IV played politics and worked against the hegemony of the church in Italy, which the pope saw as egregious ingratitude so he sided again with Frederick II, crowning him twice as king, in 1212 and in 1215, in opposition to his Welf opponent, though papal pleasure in Frederick was short-lived. At least initially, Frederick's success was the pope's success, and other kings were likewise crowned. In 1204 Innocent crowned Peter II of Aragon in Rome, thereby furthering his claim to authority on the Iberian Peninsula. But the greatest success he scored was in England, whose monarch still laid claims to extensive territories on the European continent. King John of England, nicknamed John Lackland (r. 1199–1216) because of the military defeats that forced him back into his English territories, was as unlucky at home as abroad. As his newly elected archbishop of Canterbury, Stephen Langton (r. 1207–28), flexed his ecclesiastical muscles against the royal house, John refused to confirm his episcopal nomination, giving Innocent cause to place the entire kingdom under his interdict, a kind of ecclesiastical censure that prohibited the conduct of Sunday liturgies and sacramental observances. The difficulties emerging from such prohibitions in the medieval context are not hard to imagine, especially regarding questions of salvation. Under such conditions, John in the end could not continue to reign and had to subject himself to papal authority in 1213. He surrendered his kingdom to the successor of Peter and received it back as a fiefdom. That the pope protected him in other enduring conflicts proved to be of not much use. The barons decreed the Magna Carta Liberatum, or the Great Charter of Freedoms, in 1215, which had at its heart the limitation of royal power.

This did not concern the pope, for he had already established his authority comprehensively in several important countries of Europe.[5]

It was to this pope, the supreme pastor of the church, that the earliest hagiographers of Francis attributed a dream in which Francis, a small man, helped to keep the church from falling, the very church that exercised such power and controlled such wealth. And further, Thomas of Eccleston reports—though admittedly he alone recounted this—that the close relationship between Innocent and Francis was such that Francis was at Innocent's bedside when he died on July 16, 1216, in Perugia. The contrast between the two men is not evident only to modern observers, as Jacques de Vitry shows. Even Francis's contemporaries observed how remarkable their relationship was, particularly given that Francis's claim to follow in the apostles' steps had been attributed to "heretics" for some time earlier, and these believers had been excluded from the life of the church. They had fallen into conflict with their church and were thus named heretics, even though their disagreement did not necessarily consist of false doctrine. This is not the only reason why the label of heretic is problematic.[6]

The impetus for "heretical" movements generally emerged from feelings of dislocation, as was the case with Francis, though for him we must be clear that it was a different kind of experience altogether. His awareness of the contrast between his lifestyle as a merchant and the claims of the apostolic message in the New Testament was determinative, but for other movements, feelings of unease since the twelfth century were experienced by the laity when they contrasted the claims of bishops to be following in the apostles' footsteps to their actual lifestyle, which was so distant from what was known of the lives of the earliest followers of Christ. Francis's protest built on this movement and community among the laity, which had as its targets the church and its hierarchy.

Again the point was the text describing Jesus's commissioning of the apostles in Matthew 10, which had been so significant for Francis in 1208/9. Only one tunic, no shoes, no staff, no money: these were not characteristics of the bishops, who lived in prominent city palaces, whose families were often of the nobility, whose advantages they would not easily surrender for the sake of ecclesiastical office. The contrast was so stark that one might ask why Francis read this text and saw it as a challenge to his own lifestyle rather than as a critique of the leaders of the church of his day. But perhaps in another way it may not be so surprising. The text was from the Bible and was read in liturgical settings—and there were so many people who read it without drawing any subversive conclusions regarding the episcopacy that it may have seemed odd to do so. We are reminded that reading practices are also culturally conditioned. Just as today we read medieval texts and struggle to engage with their biblical allusions or their liturgical assumptions, so too for medieval readers what they took in may not always have been readily clear. And who is to say that there should be a strict one-on-one correspondence between the regulations for the apostles and for their successors? Popes and bishops did not uphold such a reading, and it appears that Francis did not either.

But there were just such critics in the medieval period whom today we might label as representatives of the movement known as "vita apostolica," an orientation to uphold the apostolic ideal. We can identify the origins of this movement during the period of the reform papacy in the eleventh century, with its rigorous demands emerging in Milan as a movement of the laity and lower clergy, who attacked the rich and noble bishops with sharp invective. And it didn't stop short of critiquing the pope either. We can thank John of Salisbury, later the bishop of Chartres, who reported that in the middle of the twelfth century Arnold (ca. 1155), a cleric from Brescia, had criticized not just the papal office but the man himself: "The pope himself was not what he professed to be—an apostolic man and shepherd of souls—but a man of blood who maintained his authority by fire and sword, a tormentor of churches and oppressor of the innocent, who did nothing in the world save gratify his lust and empty other men's coffers to fill his own." In this secondhand report, we note the scathing rhetoric Arnold applied to the pope, addressing not doctrinal deviation (though some would highlight this later) but his serious moral declension seen from a more rigorous perspective. Arnold may well have stood on the margins of the church in his day, but his critique and concern nonetheless found resonance among many.[7]

The most important movement shaped by the claims of the "vita apostolica" was centered on a merchant from Lyons named (perhaps) Peter Waldo (ca. 1140–ca. 1205). It is unclear whether his given name was actually Peter, for it might have been given to him later in deliberate contrast to papal claims to follow the apostle. Given his similar social background, further contrasts with Francis have been inevitable, not least his appeal to the "vita apostolica" not to render a judgment of the bishops of his era but instead to apply the call to poverty to himself and to his circle. It was only later that conflict arose with the bishops when he interpreted the commissioning of the apostles in Matthew 10 as also a duty to preach. The parallels with Francis, a man two generations younger, are further evidenced insofar as Waldo was also tolerated in his early ministry by Bishop Guichard of Pontigny (r. 1165–81). However, this kind of acceptance by the church stopped short at the feet of the pope, which marks the beginning of the difference between him and Francis. Pope Alexander III (r. 1159–81) was prepared at the Third Lateran Council in 1179 to officially recognize the life of poverty demanded by Waldo and those around him, but he refused to license him to preach. The details concerning the conflicts arising from this are not necessary here. Suffice to say that Waldo and his followers were excommunicated by Pope Lucius III (r. 1181–85) in 1184. At the time when Francis began to make his mark, Waldo's followers had either returned to the church or had radicalized further, and thus became in the eyes of the medieval church a heretical movement that in the time of the sixteenth-century Reformation found fellowship with Protestant churches.[8]

The Waldensians suffered greatly from suppression and persecution, which flowed out of the extreme measures being taken against the Cathars. Ironically, the word *Cathar* is itself derived from the Greek *katharoi,* meaning "pure." They too began as a movement aspiring to the "vita apostolica" but developed their religious outlook more quickly and comprehensively than the Waldensians, leading to clear dogmatic opposition to the medieval church. They espoused an increasingly dualistic worldview that exaggerated the contrast made by St. Paul between the church and the world. Indeed, the very same world that Francis comprehensively praised was thoroughly devalued by the Cathars. God represented for them the principle of good, linked to spiritual reality. Over and against the spiritual stood the material, which did not possess the same power as God but instead strove to oppose him. Their views bore significant resemblance to the ancient Gnostic religion of the Manichees, whose myths, long since condemned by the church, recounted the great battle between good and evil in the world as well as the fall of the angels, which brought humankind to its fatal position. This teaching had significant ethical consequences, which in some of their most rigorous moments could bear some resemblance to the doctrine of Francis, who is still occasionally set in relationship with them. But their motivation was significantly different, for the Cathars, arguing that the souls and spirits of human beings belong to the principle of good, whereas their bodies belong to the principle of evil, demanded that human beings distance themselves from material influences in order to turn to God. This required a massive commitment to the ascetic life. The inner circle of the Cathars, known as the "perfecti," prized sexual abstinence and refused anything that was the result of physical procreation—that is, all food from animals. Given that this lifestyle was attractive only to the few, other, less extreme adherents of the movement were known as the "credentes," the believers. Their radical lives and deviant doctrine meant that the movement was a more threatening challenge to the church than the Waldensians had been, so the reaction of the church was likewise more threatening. In a kind of prototypical crusade, both secular and spiritual authorities acted against the Cathars in 1177–81, and the thirteenth century witnessed an increasingly close alliance between differing political interests, leading to conflict with the Cathars in Languedoc in the south of France. In 1208, Innocent called for a crusade against the Albigensians, another name for the Cathars because of their location around the town of Albi. The contours of the conflict soon grew more complicated—transcending the apparently clear boundaries between the doctrinally correct church and the heretics—when the local nobility got involved, variously siding with different parties according to their own immediate needs and interests.[9]

If we leave aside for a moment the small north Italian group of the "humiliati," who had won papal recognition in 1201, it was concerns about heretics and rebels that formed the essential backdrop against which we must understand the significance of the movement to pursue poverty led by Francis at the beginning of the thirteenth century. His contemporaries were quick to recruit Francis as a weapon in their own war against the heretics, given his close relationship with the church. Celano, even in his *First Life*, recounts how the heretics would hide themselves when Francis came to town to preach, especially because he affirmed the true teaching of the Roman church and honored the nature of the priesthood. Julian of Speyer strives even more determinedly to portray Francis as the doctrinally pure opponent of the heretics: "He himself, a Catholic and totally apostolic man, especially recommended in his preaching that the faith of the Roman Church be inviolably maintained, and the order of priests be regarded with the highest reverence, because of the dignity of the Lord's Sacrament which is made present by the ministry of priests."[10]

One can hear in Julian's words an admonition to obedience: Francis urged submission to the church not in spite of but because of his apostolic credentials. What a contrast to the Waldensian and Cathar heretics! Stephen of Bourbon, a Dominican frontline opponent of the heretics, summarized this contrast with an anecdote: Francis was traveling in Lombardy when he came across a heretic, whom he couldn't quite place. He turned out to be a member of the Patarine sect or perhaps even a Manichee, which was another way of denoting the Cathars. As they were visiting a church at the time, he spoke to Francis about the priest of the parish in order to disparage the priest and stir up Francis, for the priest was living with his concubine and therefore had unclean hands. Francis wasn't baited so easily and resisted such anticlerical sentiment, and instead went to the priest, knelt before him, and assured him that even if this were true, the priest's hands would still be able to fulfill the purpose of the sacrament effectively. What Stephen outlined here through an anecdote was in effect a lesson in the "character indelebilis," the indelible power of the cleric. Through his ordination alone, he was empowered to dispense the sacramental mystery, no matter how he behaved, as St. Augustine had taught during his own debates with schismatic teachers in order to deny any outcome that could undermine assurance of salvation. If the misdeeds of the clergy invalidated the efficacy of the sacrament, and believers could not really know every detail of the clergyman's life to attest to his sanctity, then they could never really have assurance that their participation in the sacrament would truly offer salvation. But trusting in the efficacy of ordination, they could have assurance in the sacrament of the Mass. The moralizing tone of this story might suggest that it was a fictitious account, especially as Stephen of Bourbon tells a similar story in a different context without any sense of embarrassment. But on the other hand, it would be an exaggeration or even a distortion to infer from this account that such a defense of the priesthood was written back into Francis's story in order to make a statement about his heretical adversaries. Indeed, we are in the happy position that there are direct statements by Francis in his own writings, and not just these kinds of secondary accounts, that affirm his support for the office of the priest.[11]

That Francis stood opposed to the riches and lust for power in the church of his time with such incredible, perhaps even terrifying, naiveté goes almost without saying. But such naiveté was surely an expression of his experience of dislocation, though it was different from most of the other representatives of the "vita apostolica," for Christ's commissioning sermon to the disciples stood at the end of Francis's experience, not at its beginning. This commission didn't create his frustrations with the state of the church but clarified frustrations that had long been part of his experience. His sense of disorder did not begin in the cathedral of Assisi when he encountered the wealth of the bishop but had begun a long time before that in his own family home. It was the everyday Christianity of the merchants that disturbed him, not in the first instance the failings of apostolicity among the bishops that had proved such an offense to Arnold of Brescia and others. In fact, the opposite was true, and this can't be stressed enough. In a kind of origin story, every aspect of the trial circling around his wasteful use of his father's money drew Francis more and more into the powerful but also loving protection of the bishop of Assisi. This stage of his journey is distinctly different from everything that the Waldensians, Cathars, or others experienced, so it is hardly surprising that the conclusions he drew were also fundamentally different. His connection to the church was the result neither of naiveté nor of calculation but was instead the quite understandable result of the relationship of trust he had established in Assisi with his bishop.

And although in his later preaching he set out in a direction like the Waldensians that would test the limits of canon law, he did not push beyond its limits but expressed throughout his life a deep respect for the clergy and a desire for obedience. This is clearly seen in the emphasis given by Jacques de Vitry that the preaching of the Franciscans was always respectfully agreed upon with the leaders of the church, though it had nonetheless many other points of connection with the life and thought of Francis. Even in his *Testament,* Francis explained: "God inspired me, too, and still inspires me with such great faith in priests who live according to the laws of the holy Church of Rome, because of their dignity, that if they persecuted me, I should still be ready to turn to them for aid."[12]

This hint that Francis would run back to the priests in the face of persecution provides ample evidence of his acceptance of an ecclesiastical hierarchy providing shelter and protection in this world, which must be traced in his biography to the events that created deep attachment to Bishop Guido of Assisi. Unlike Arnold, who took an oppositional position, Francis blazed his path according to his apostolic vocation by and with the priesthood. And the path was well formed: life according to "the form of the holy Roman church" meant for Francis aligning himself with the norms, the canons, of the Roman church, in which he found assurance of a way of life that was at least not opposed to his apostolic way. One cannot stress this enough, for he saw the apostolic way as complementary to the church of his day, not in competition with it, as would be the case for the Cathars and the more radical Waldensians. And this is quite remarkable, as Francis did in so many other ways live and serve in tension with the accepted ecclesiastical norms of the period. Even the permission granted to him to preach as a layman was in breach of customary expectations, extended to him not merely by the local bishop—which was the case with Waldo—but in that memorable encounter with the pope himself. The difference between Waldo and Francis was in part explained by the difference between Alexander and Innocent too. Whereas the former permitted only the lifestyle of the Waldensians, not their preaching, the latter would stretch the interpretation of canon law by licensing Francis to preach, probably because his preaching was acceptable as a kind of admonition and not as an exposition of the Bible. It did not conform to the content or to the style of most contemporary sermons of his day. The change of form implied a change of content. Francis's sermons did not treat dogmatic questions narrowly defined and were therefore less prone to creating conflict than any proclamation of the Gospel would. In contrast to the juridical situation of the Waldensians, this arrangement made it possible to avoid any issues of canon law yet permitted lay preaching. Francis's ethical preaching, focused on the way Christian lives were to be conducted, was different from doctrinal sermons. This was the fork in the road that enabled Francis to remain connected to the church and not be declared a heretic.

However, there was yet another tension remaining that had to do with the official understanding of the clerical office: to what degree Christians had to obey their priests, "who live according to the laws of the holy Church of Rome." This could, on the one hand, refer to observance of liturgical regulations, as Francis impressed on the clergy in his *Letter to All Clerics*, likely an address that went through several different versions after its initial delivery around 1215. In its second version, Francis pointed to the "prescriptions of Mother Church" when he advised how to handle the Eucharist. First of all, priests must prepare their hearts when they approach the Eucharistic celebration, and only then concern themselves with appropriate places to celebrate the Lord's Supper and to think carefully about how to handle the leftover consecrated elements. This carefully composed instruction concerning correct administration raised a question that Francis wanted to put to the clergy who did not observe this regulation. He knew full well that being a member of the clerical class did not guarantee ethical behavior. Indeed, this divergence from acceptable norms had long been addressed in debates concerning the apostolic way and had often led to forms of anticlericalism. In his letter, he addressed similar concerns to the priests of his order. They were to be "of holy and pure intention" when they sacrificed the Mass, for they were to direct their thinking and feeling not toward other human beings but toward God.[13]

Francis was clearly laying before the priesthood an ethical standard to emulate, as the "vita apostolica" movement had already done. But this only appears to be in conflict with the doctrine of the "character indelebilis." Francis was certainly aware of the possibility that at this point he might depart from the officially sanctioned teaching of the church, as he was probably warned by theologically informed advisers. In the *Admonitions,* for example, we read an almost exact copy of the blessing to be pronounced on those who trust the clergy to live according to the form of the Roman church, and a curse on those who do not, though with a theological disclaimer: "Even if they fall into sin, no one should pass judgement on them, for God has reserved judgement on them to himself." This still isn't as drastic an evaluation as Stephen of Bourbon raises, but it is close enough.[14]

This clear evidence of Francis's espousal of the "character indelebilis," however, is not essential to establish the difference between his view of the priesthood and that of those upholding the "vita apostolica" who had distanced themselves from the church, or possibly who had been forced out of it. His own phrasing in his *Testament,* free of the need of any such dogmatic validation, emphasized the objective character of ordination and not its ethical entailments, which merely complemented it. In principle, the authority of the ordained priest remained unquestioned, and even the ethical norms of the priesthood were regulated by canon law. The priest's powers were established not by observance of the apostolic commission in Matthew 10, but rather through compliance with the Roman organization. This removed from the "vita apostolica" any hint of rebellious character that might have generated a tension with canon law or theological requirements. Further, Francis clarified what exactly obedience to the priesthood might have meant in one important sense: in his *Testament* he highlighted that he would not preach in anyone's parish against the will of the local pastor. Although at this time the order had already availed itself of the ministry of priests, he was resolute that this should not mean that those priests would distance themselves from the structures of the church. Francis was satisfied with conforming to the life of the church, which to an age that looks upon rebels with sympathy—especially if they belong to a past age—sounds boring. However, in the thirteenth century, this was the key to Francis's success. Only in this way could Francis find room within the church to express the apostolic way. He was no conformist, and he was not made to serve the agenda of the popes of his day. Yet he was the pious son of his church, and it would never have crossed his mind to revolt.

Francis knew, however, that others who followed him, or those whom he met in different contexts, could think differently on this matter. So he attempted to make clear that subordination to the priesthood did not consist merely in external subjection, it was an immediate consequence of the spirit of poverty he pursued. An impressive example of this position can be seen in his *Praises of the Virtues,* which we have discussed earlier in relation to his doctrine of creation. The *Praises* resemble features of *The Canticle of Brother Sun,* not least in the marked absence of reference to Christ, or at least to his work of salvation. Again, it is important to make clear that we can't deduce any systematic conclusions from occasional statements in Francis's works. His literary creations, either poems or songs, don't attempt to do more than expound one idea. In this case, it is the praise of virtues like wisdom, simplicity, poverty, humility, love, and obedience. Indeed, this chain of virtues stood in distinction from other schemes of virtue that were known in the Middle Ages, for instance, the triad of faith, hope, and love, which had profoundly shaped the Christian view of the world since the apostle Paul's exposition in 1 Corinthians 13. Or perhaps the pagan cardinal virtues of prudence, justice, fortitude, and temperance. Ideally, one might join these two sets to create a significant sequence of seven. But Francis refused to follow these schemes and did not avail himself completely of the evangelical counsels that shaped the ascetic life: he did name in his list poverty and obedience, but not chastity, which he obviously felt did not deserve such a prominent position among the virtues. In addition, he grouped the virtues together in an unusual way in three pairs: wisdom and simplicity (which were sisters in his song), humility and poverty, and obedience and love. Together, they formed a unity with their origin in God and in the ways they were to be lived out. To reject any one of them was to lose them all. They were individually aspects of the stream of virtue that flowed together out of the life of God. To praise the virtues was to recognize both their differing aspects and their ultimate unity, which functioned to displace sinning. This appears to be the meaning of the strange sentence Francis wrote: "In all the world there is not a man who can possess any one of you without first dying to himself."[15]

In a line like this, we are reminded of the New Testament's teaching about dying to sin (Romans 6:11) and within this dying to the world. What Francis really praised is the existence of virtues among brothers who shared a common rejection of the values of the world and had begun a new life of repentance, with virtues as the positive evidence of penance. At this stage of the argument, our interest is focused primarily on the nature of obedience, which as we have seen was a duty laid upon animals too, but principally "to everyone on earth." To submit to the authority of the priesthood was not named explicitly by Francis here, yet his qualification of abject subjugation is more than evident for spiritual reasons. Complete obedience in this reckoning included the mortification of "our lower nature," positioning the penitent in exactly that state made possible by the impact of the virtues. It is not only because Francis handled obedience so thoroughly that it is so central to Franciscan ethics, and it shouldn't surprise us that obedience was not only named in his *Testament* but was also taught in the *Rules* he gave to his order. These took definitive shape only in the last years of his life and assumed a more comprehensive structure for the order, which by this stage of its development included priests among its members. For this reason, in the so-called unofficial *Rule of 1221*, Francis drafted a regulation stipulating that the brothers were to receive the most important sacraments of penance and the Eucharist at the hands of a priest "of the order." Only in exceptional circumstances should they turn to other priests, by which Francis in no way implied that such a priest must be from the local town. And even if these regulations did not finally appear in the official *Rule of 1223*, they did nonetheless demonstrate the gravitas that Francis ascribed to the office of priest. There must have been brothers to whom this was not self-evident who could in all conscience have refused any ministry from priests or Francis's instructions would not have been necessary. Francis was seen in his own brotherhood as one of the moderates. He stood clearly on the side of the church and of its official sacraments. The heretics appeared profoundly strange to him.[16]

The Fourth Lateran Council and Its Prophet

In his *Letter to All Clerics,* Francis outlined in precise detail how to handle the Eucharistic elements, but these concerns were not merely the product of his own spirituality. In fact, his instructions follow almost word for word regulations produced by the Lateran Council itself. Indeed, this council of the church was perhaps the most consequential event during the pontificate of Innocent III, convened between November 11 and 30, 1215. Around eight hundred clergy were in attendance. It was characterized by attempts to bring increasing order to the church. On April 19, 1213, in his bull *Vineam Domini Sabaoth,* Innocent convoked the Fourth Lateran Council in order to make plans for a crusade as well as to promote "reform of the universal church." Agreement was achieved concerning both the crusade and the German crown. But the meeting also had the task of resolving important dogmatic issues facing the council. As has so often been the case, such theological issues were framed negatively: what to deny, or what to exclude. One of the condemnations in this council focused on the complicated matter of Joachim (d. 1202), abbot of the Cistercian monastery in Fiore in Calabria, who had rejected one of the theological statements of Peter Lombard (d. 1160) in his *Sentences.* This book was a compilation of theological insights from the early church fathers that Peter, later bishop of Paris, had brought together to serve as a kind of textbook for theological students, though Peter himself offered very little commentary on the texts he assembled. Since antiquity, Trinitarian belief had defined Christian faith as one God in three persons: Father, Son, and Holy Spirit. But Peter's description of God as a single entity (*res* in Latin) had disturbed Joachim as he studied Lombard's text, so he immediately replied with his own treatise, *On the Unity of the Trinity* (*De Unitate Trinitatis*). Unfortunately, this text has been lost to us, so we can only guess how Joachim argued his case against Peter. Essentially, we assume that Joachim read the language of "entity" and heard Peter speak of a fourth substance: not something that each of the three persons of the Trinity had in common in their interconnectedness, but something else again in which each of the three participated outside of themselves. At the Fourth Lateran Council, Joachim's ideas were presented, debated, and condemned. Of course, this had the immediate result of boosting the success of Lombard's textbook, helping to make it the standard textbook at the prestigious University of Paris for hundreds of years and guiding generations of students in practicing theological method.[17]

However, the decision of the council to condemn Joachim's teaching played out very differently from other condemnations of the church, for his ideas impacted theological reflection less immediately and more slowly. The combination of his understanding of the Trinity with his philosophy of history was profoundly influential and indeed grew in strength. He argued that history develops in three distinct phases in accordance with the three persons of the Godhead, reflected in three distinct forms of social organization on earth. First of all, the era of the Father was characterized by marriage, the era of the Son by the preeminence of unmarried clergy, and the era of the Holy Spirit by contemplative monastics who had turned their back on the things of this world. Indeed, many Franciscans later upheld this schema and saw in Francis a representative of this stage of history, combining it with the promise in Revelation 20 of the millennium, the thousand-year reign of God on earth. Though the Franciscan movement was in time torn apart by disagreements over this doctrine, in 1215 Francis and his companions were obviously not caught up in such debates. There is not even much evidence to support the claim that Francis attended the council at all, and even if he did, it appears that the questions Joachim's ideas raised did not impact him greatly, despite being part of the theological air he breathed. Joachim's condemnation resulted in a highly combustible mix of theological debates and ecclesiastical politics in the thirteenth century. But for the poor man of Assisi, whose preoccupation was simplicity joined to wisdom, speculative debates on the doctrine of the Trinity were as distant as far-reaching theological constructions of the nature of history.

Closer to Francis's world was the council's condemnation of the Cathars and the Waldensians. Against the former, the council insisted on the traditional doctrine of the Catholic faith, in which the one God who created the one world was affirmed, fatally critiquing any dualist tendencies among these heretics. With respect to the Waldensians, the council decided to excommunicate any who preached, publicly or privately, without official permission from the pope. This ruling is relevant to the story of Francis, for it indirectly attests to the fact that the preaching of Francis and his brothers must have been at some level approved, either by the bishop or the pope. No doubt Francis's meeting with Pope Innocent III in 1209 was pertinent to this outcome of the council, even if we are unsure of Francis's presence there.

But it was another ruling by the council that impacted him more acutely. In Canon 13, the council forbade the establishment of any further orders, or rather the establishment of any orders that required a new rule of life or constitution. In meetings with the pope or with Cardinal John of St. Paul, Francis made clear his decision to resist being merged with any previously existing order. Whether he and the brothers had already decided upon a particular structure for their order in 1215 is unclear, though it is highly likely that he had already begun adapting the simple *Rule* that he had previously presented to the pope into something more complex. On the other hand, it is important to point out that papal recognition in 1209 did not necessarily mean papal permission to create a newly structured order. Perhaps Francis just couldn't imagine that the ruling of the council was aimed at him or even applied to him at all. The ruling perhaps speaks more of the highly combustible religious context of his day, in which the founding of new orders or communities was so widespread that authorities believed they needed to restrict the practice more generally.[18]

Innocent, despite the vigorous and far-reaching debates of the council, clearly controlled its agenda, and he wanted not just to clarify processes on the edges of discussion but to regulate the life of the faithful, as we see in the proscription of new orders. This is most evident in the injunction that secret marriages—those neither authorized nor conducted by parents in the context of a legal framework—were to be banned. This didn't mean that such marriages were invalid, but it did imply that there should be a regular and legal pathway to the conduct of marriage in which the church should participate, although marriage was still not regarded at this time as a sacrament. According to the determinations of the council, the church's role in marriage, as it had been since the early Middle Ages, should be to proceed with the banns, that is, to announce in advance who was eligible to marry, and to offer the possibility of receiving objections to the marriage proceeding within a particular time frame.

Similarly, efforts to regulate the practice of confession in the life of the believer bit hard. At least once a year it was expected that adult penitent believers would offer their confession to their own parish priest. Exceptions were possible, but only on the recommendation of that self-same priest. This strengthened the parochial system of the church, though we should not be too quick to interpret this in terms of clerical control. Positively, even to our own day, it has led to a more adequate understanding of the seal of the confession for priests in many different denominations, even if the form of the seal has changed. According to the Lateran Council's conclusions, the priest who took the confession could in no instance betray the confidence of the penitent; if he did, he would be removed from his office and consigned for the rest of his life to a monastery. All this should make clear that confession was a matter between the person and God, mediated by the priest. This was not a strategy for social control for it was not a public exchange, but on the contrary helped to nurture Christian norms inwardly. Whoever confessed their sins once a year had ample time to reflect on how their life conformed to the demands of Christ. Of course we don't know precisely how rigorously these regulations were pursued, but their general direction nonetheless aligned well with the earliest concerns of Francis. His basic spiritual disposition was to reform the lives of Christian believers in response to the way he had experienced everyday Christianity in his family home.

With one basic difference: confession took its theological meaning from the dogmatic topic of the sacrament of penance. Confession was preceded by contrition of the heart and followed by acts of restitution. Francis, however, understood something different concerning penance. In his *Testament*, he reminded his followers that doing penance referred not to the sacramental event but to a way of life, which he and the brothers who gathered around him claimed for every facet of their life. Francis apparently did not see these views in contradiction, or if he felt some tension between them, he tried to resolve them. In the unofficial *Rule of 1221*, where Francis exhorted the brothers to submit to their parish priest, he explicitly mentioned the practice of penance and insisted that confession among the brothers must not replace sacramental confession to the priest. This touches on and indeed underlines a further aspect of life in the way of the cross, the classic mutual consolation that brothers and sisters in monastic contexts shared with each other and that itself was the root and foundation of sacramental confession. When Francis emphasized the importance of priestly confession, we can assume that there were members of the order who had reneged on this practice. Sets of rules are helpful for historians insofar as they suggest the existence of the very danger that the rules attempt to regulate. We also note here that at the end of his life, Francis was fully committed to the sacramental-priestly character of the church of his day and was not tempted to let his own understanding of penance do damage to the structures of which he was a part.[19]

One might be tempted to see Francis's position on penance as a concession or compromise with the cold hard realities of the church of his day, but when we turn to his view of the Lord's Supper, we witness something more extreme. The Fourth Lateran Council had reform of the Mass on its agenda, and its clear conclusions had implications for centuries to come. Essentially, each believer was instructed to take Communion at least once a year, at Easter. More substantive was the canon directed toward the heresy of the Cathars when it was affirmed that Jesus Christ's "body and blood are truly contained in the sacrament of the altar under the forms of bread and wine; the bread being changed into the body, the wine being changed into the blood of Christ ('transsubstantiatis') by divine power." Only 150 years after the monk Berengar of Tours (d. 1088) had explained with cuttingly sharp invective that it was impossible for the accidents (or outward and changeable form) of bread and wine to be maintained if the underlying substance of the elements were transformed into the body and blood of Christ, here at the Lateran Council the very same Aristotelian categories were being used to defend the contrary argument in its official text. Berengar had been condemned and was led to confess in 1059 that "the bread and wine which are placed on the altar are after consecration not only a sacrament but also the true body and blood of our Lord Jesus Christ, and with the senses not only sacramentally but in truth are taken and broken by the hands of the priests and crushed by the teeth of the faithful."[20]

Later Berengar was asked to repeat his confession because he had in the meantime tergiversated, but the judgment on his theological reflection did not ultimately resolve the intellectual issue. Even the council itself did not finally reflect on the matter beyond coining a new word, *transsubstantiare*, derived from the word *substantia*, meaning substance, to obviate the need for further explanation. Berengar's question of whether any kind of transformation could be possible had been avoided, and the council did not explain how such a process would concretely take place. The more comprehensive exposition of the doctrine of transubstantiation that grew out of the ruling of the Fourth Lateran Council and developed with more precision over the next two generations of thinkers had to wait for the magnificent systematic structure of the Dominican intellectual Thomas Aquinas (d. 1274) for its defense. But at the Lateran Council itself, not much more was said other than that Jesus Christ was indeed really and truly physically present in the Eucharistic elements.

This conception of the Eucharist lent, of course, a new dignity to the office of priest, as we have seen. It was through the manual actions of the priest that a transformation of the elements took place in every Mass. And even when it was acknowledged that the power was from God, the priest was still dignified by his encounter with Christ. Through him, the laity could experience Christ's particular presence here on earth and could actually touch their Lord physically and receive him bodily. In his letter to the entire order, which in the last years of Francis's life was now formally constituted, he could paint a picture of the importance of the priest's status: "Listen to this, my brothers: If it is right to honour the Blessed Virgin Mary because she bore him in her most holy womb; if St John the Baptist trembled and was afraid even to touch Christ's sacred head; if the tomb where he lay for only a short time is so venerated; how holy, and virtuous, and worthy should not a priest be; he touches Christ with his own hands, Christ who is to die now no more but enjoy eternal life and glory. . . . A priest receives him into his heart and mouth and offers him to others to be received."[21]

These lines make very clear that Francis was concerned not merely with the priests but at heart was concerned with the body of Christ, which had far-reaching consequences for the way the elements of the bread and the wine were to be handled, so we return to Francis's advice to the clergy and his warnings about carelessly handling the Eucharistic elements. If in the Eucharist we meet the Lord Jesus in the elements, the leftover elements then surely don't revert to being mere bread or wine. There arose therefore the need to reserve the elements after the Mass, and in the following centuries ever larger receptacles were built to house the remains. However, the regulations of the Lateran Council were more modest, though still clear. Canon 20 prescribed how leftover elements from the Eucharist were to be kept "in properly protected places provided with locks and keys." Francis's admonition concerning the misplacement of leftover consecrated elements reflected this regulation most seriously: "If the Body of our Lord Jesus Christ has been left abandoned somewhere contrary to all the laws, It should be removed and put in a place that is prepared properly for It, where It can be kept safe." This instruction may appear just a small detail in the story, but it does make clear how Francis—at least in some instances—was becoming a prophet in service of the decisions of the council.[22]

As is often the case with Francis, however, we can't remain content with simplistic interpretations. Francis had not taken all the regulations of the council into his own preaching: for example, fine distinctions espoused at the council in defending the doctrine of the Trinity remained foreign to him, nor was the council the chief cause of Francis's understanding and spiritual appreciation of the Lord's Supper. We see this chiefly in the more traditional vocabulary he used in reference to the Supper, which was different from the declarations of the council, though at least the admonition to keep the leftover sacramental elements secure may have been influenced by the precise determinations of the council. And added to deep reverence for the Lord's Supper at the council came new clarity, support, and impetus, not least because of its critique of other positions. In his *Admonitions,* Francis spoke quite critically of those who rejected the council's view of the Supper: "All those are damned who see the Sacrament of the Body of Christ which is consecrated on the altar in the form of bread and wine by the words of our Lord in the hands of the priest, and do not see or believe in spirit and in God that this is really the most holy Body and Blood of our Lord Jesus Christ."[23]

While this may not have been a literal quotation from the regulations of the council, it captured nonetheless its views with their background exclusion of the Cathars. Stress on the real presence in the sacrament had for Francis a significant spiritual meaning not precisely expressed in the council's resolutions, for he made clear in his letter to the order how Mary who was pregnant with Jesus was like the Holy Sepulchre in Jerusalem. This kind of comparison only made sense when we first grasp his understanding of the real presence of Christ in the sacrament of the altar as an instantiation of his earthly body, now with express connection not just to his death but to his resurrection as well. Berengar in his own day had been forced to promote this kind of identity too: the body of Christ that once was on the earth is identical with the body of Christ that now returns to the earth in every Mass. Surely that must have been a simply breathtaking notion for Francis and for many others. He taught more about his Eucharistic piety later in the same letter: "Kissing your feet with all the love I am capable of, I beg you to show the greatest possible reverence and honour for the most holy Body and Blood of our Lord Jesus Christ through whom all things, whether on the earth or in the heavens, have been brought to peace and reconciled with Almighty God."[24]

Francis's confession of the tight relationship between the elements of the Eucharist and the real presence of the Savior of the world can be seen elsewhere in his writings too, not just in the exhortation emphasizing the purity of the priesthood. Whoever would receive the Eucharist should do so with inward and fitting self-awareness: the faithful should recognize the difference between the Holy Communion and other meals, and so decide not to eat unworthily, nor to receive it "without faith or proper devotion." Francis's wording might not have been as carefully expressed as we might wish, but in the context of the Lateran Council his meaning was in no doubt. Unworthy was the one who had not undertaken the sacrament of penance before participating in the sacrament of the altar, as the council warned. But unworthy eating on the other hand still did not benefit recipients even if they were themselves worthy by virtue of their penance, since it failed to honor the presence of Christ in the meal. The warning, applied to both scenarios, could have massive consequences if unheeded, as we learned previously in the judgment sermon of Francis. Whoever would take the Supper of the Lord without possessing the Spirit of God was inviting judgment onto themselves, according to 1 Corinthians 11:29. This was not the case just for unbelievers but also for those who claimed to be Christians without being integrated into the fellowship of the Spirit—presumably another veiled reference to the heretics. More positively, such warnings culminated at the sacrament of the altar in a kind of Christ-focused piety with which Francis approached the meal. Following in the way of Christ and receiving the presence of Christ in the sacrament set the contours for this kind of spirituality. Both belonged together for Francis—life under the cross and the gift of Christ in the manger at Bethlehem—and both were new at every celebration of the Mass. In this way, Francis combined in his profound song of praise the presence of Christ on the altar as the ultimate entailment of the condescension of God to humankind:

> Our whole being should be seized with fear, the whole world should tremble and heaven rejoice, when Christ the Son of the Living God is present on the altar in the hands of the priest. What wonderful majesty! What stupendous condescension! O sublime humility! O humble sublimity! That the Lord of the whole universe, God and the Son of God, should humble himself like this and hide under the form of a little bread, for our salvation. Look at God's condescension, my brothers, and pour out your hearts before him. Humble yourselves that you may be exalted by him. Keep nothing for yourselves, so that he who has given himself wholly to you may receive you wholly.[25]

Put boldly, the Eucharist was the ultimate goal of the incarnation. For Francis, it was only at the Eucharist that Christ was bodily visible, as he wrote in his *Testament*. To stress the visibility of Christ in the plain host may sound strange, but Francis would explain further that when Jesus was on the earth, many people had failed to recognize God too, but they should have believed nonetheless. In just this way, believers should trust in the presence of God in the bread. If we understand the Eucharist in this way, as the condescension of Christ into lowliness, one does not have to ponder long how Francis's Eucharistic theology aligned with his understanding of the apostolic life. Both were, as the last lines of the admonition teach, an expression of humility in following Christ. The sacramental presence of Christ on the altar and following Christ in the peripatetic lifestyle of the first poor apostles were two sides of the same coin, which thus shaped the discipleship of Francis: a life under the cross and a life lived in the light of the incarnation. It was in this way that the Eucharist played such a central role in the edification of the fellowship. Francis insisted that even in a monastery where several priests resided only one public Mass should be celebrated, not private ones. It was not the sacramental act of an individual priest before God that was determinative of the community but rather the corporate encounter with Jesus Christ in the Eucharistic celebration. But this should be done daily, as the *Admonitions* promote.[26]

The presence of Christ was linked in a special way with the Eucharist but extended far beyond this sacramental act. Occasionally in Francis's own writings, we glimpse how the sanctity of the Lord's Supper was transferred to other things that stood in some kind of relationship with it. Consequently, one could see representations of Christ everywhere. To these ends, around 1220 Francis drafted a letter to the leading brothers, the "custodes," in which he exhorted them, as he had previously done in his address to the clergy, to handle the Eucharistic elements carefully, and including here as well instruction concerning reverence for "his holy name and the writings which contain his words, those words which consecrate his body." This formulation bears some resemblance to the Words of Institution of the Lord's Supper, through the means of which transubstantiation was achieved: "This is my body" and "This is my blood" can be found in Matthew 26:26–28 and its parallel texts in the other synoptic Gospels. These words could be found since late antiquity written on small tablets as an aid to memory for the celebrant. Such objects were often part of the inventory of the altar, and very possibly were handled carelessly as well. If these tablets were located in proximity to the elements of the Eucharist, we might have found an explanation for Francis's explicit mention of the name of God in this context. It appears that this instruction relates to some notes inscribed with the name of God or other depictions worthy of reverence. They arose perhaps in the context of vows or attempts to denounce the influence of evil spirits, which might be kept away through voicing holy names, although such techniques had lost their meaning. Their misuse was apparently a significant concern for Francis, for even in his late *Testament* he vowed to remove such jottings of the holy name wherever he came across them in inappropriate places and to put them back into appropriate settings. This way of Christ making himself present was different from his presence in the Eucharist and provides further explanation of Francis's theology. Christ, or God himself, could make himself present in the world in so many different ways and was not bound to sacramental actions. Indeed, Christ's presence in the cross of San Damiano, which the biographies report, was yet another expression of just such a spiritual understanding. And even if the call of Christ from the cross was merely a literary device to explain the beginnings of his path of repentance, it may still be possible to see that this crucifix had a special role to play in Francis's sense of vocation by virtue of this fundamental spiritual posture and therefore hints that there is more than a kernel of historic truth in this story.[27]

All this is to say that Francis quite clearly appears to be a significant example of the piety of representation of his day, for he believed that in certain relics of the saints the presence of God was made accessible. How widespread this view was—indeed, how misapplied this belief might also have been—is suggested in resolution 62 of the Fourth Lateran Council: "From the fact that some expose for sale and exhibit promiscuously the relics of saints, great injury is sustained by the Christian religion. That this may not occur hereafter, we ordain in the present decree that in the future old relics may not be exhibited outside of a vessel or exposed for sale. And let no one presume to venerate publicly new ones unless they have been approved by the Roman pontiff. In the future prelates shall not permit those who come to their churches 'causa venerationis' [for the sake of veneration] to be deceived by worthless fabrications or false documents as has been done in many places for the sake of gain."[28]

It is interesting to note that it was not first the moderns who concluded that relics might in some circumstances be an opportunity for spiritual fraudulence. Awareness of this phenomenon as a problem existed in the thirteenth century. But underneath the exasperating issue of fleecing the flock or fabrication of sites for veneration a pious posture can be spotted that for various reasons encouraged the belief it was entirely possible in some locations to draw near to something holy, or indeed to take it with you. Such a relic was the reflection of the presence of God here on earth and was, though certainly a material form, nonetheless something more than material—just like the consecrated elements of the Eucharist were, although in a different way. These relics were made holy not through the verbal or manual actions of the priest but rather through their attested connection to a holy person who had so lived on earth that Christ was unusually present in them.

Francis was fully engaged with the veneration of relics, as troublesome as this is to much of contemporary piety. In the early accounts, such veneration did not appear to play a significant role, but this might be explained by the fact that the goal of these accounts was to suppress the veneration of his own remains. It was more likely to be expressed when his own miracles were presented as his veneration of relics. Whether the story that Francis decided to take care of the relics from a completely abandoned church is true, as Celano relates in his second *Life* and Bonaventure happily recounts, remains unclear. In Celano's account, Francis recovered the objects and then entrusted them to the brothers, who reneged on caring for them. So God himself restored them to their previous glorious state. While the story may sound like a pious invention meant to encourage the veneration of these relics, a story full of wonders invented after the fact, whether by Celano or by someone else who then passed it on to him, the main point cannot be obscured: awe of relics was doubtless a powerful cultural practice.[29]

It is perhaps more difficult to investigate another, more infamous feature of medieval piety, the sale of indulgences. That the reputation of indulgences has been so sullied can in large part be traced back to the ministry of Martin Luther, who vehemently and comprehensively turned against this practice. Of course, Luther was not the first critic of indulgences, and Pope Innocent III and the Lateran Council were fully aware of the excesses attending this issue, but a flourishing trade in indulgences with all its commercial implications still existed. The council nonetheless ordered a time limit to the application of an indulgence, not more "than one year be granted, whether it be dedicated by one bishop only or by many, and on the anniversary of the dedication the remission granted for penances enjoined is not to exceed forty days." It must be recognized, however, that Innocent and the fathers of the council did not retract their offer of a plenary indulgence for all those who participated in a crusade. The principle of the practice of indulgence remained.[30]

Theologically, indulgences were closely connected to the practice of penance. Since the early Middle Ages, spiritual penalties had been applied after confessing sin as a way of making restitution for the damage done. These penalties could be reduced if the good deeds of others were in excess of their own needs and could then be applied to another. The word *indulgence* simply means "reduction." If someone was required to pray the Lord's Prayer a certain number of times as penalty for his or her sin, that person could request a monk to pray those prayers on the supplicant's behalf. In God's sight, this would be the same as if the offender had prayed them him- or herself. This was one of the simplest kinds of indulgence. The whole practice was particularly attractive if the penalty imposed by the priest wasn't possible to discharge in this lifetime alone. The alternative was to discharge remaining penalties after death in purgatory. The character and justification of the concept of purgatory were not well established at the beginning of the thirteenth century, but the longing to receive indulgences was by contrast very developed, as the resolution of the Lateran Council made clear. Often indulgences were attached to a particular place, so pilgrimages offered a way of securing the grace of indulgence too. One of the most important pilgrimage destinations in the thirteenth century was the Portiuncula near Assisi, where the grace of indulgence could be transferred to others, as was the case for many other pilgrimage destinations. To come full circle and return to the theme of the Reformation, it is of more than antiquarian interest to note that indulgences secured at the Portiuncula could be applied to those on pilgrimage to the Castle Church in Wittenberg (a great repository of relics), on the door of which on October 31, 1517, Luther is alleged to have nailed his ninety-five theses in protest at the sale of indulgences.

It is easy to suggest that securing indulgences through pilgrimage to the Portiuncula was in some way connected to Francis's own sanctity and his close connection with this church, which was granted new status after his death in 1226. However, a whole string of accounts from the thirteenth century present things differently, making Francis himself the direct instigator of the Portiuncula indulgence. Beginning with Crescentius of Jesi, a call was put out by the minister general of the order to collect testimonies to Francis's memory. Another call went out in 1276 by Jerome Massi of Ascoli. Among the accounts received from witnesses, one report by Pietro Zalfani (found in a codex from around 1300), who was apparently present at the consecration of the church of the Portiuncula, states that Francis dramatically assured anyone visiting the church of immediate indulgence. From the same codex, Benedict of Arezzo, from 1217 provincial of the Marches of Ancona who introduced himself as one the earliest followers of Francis, related that he had heard a report from another brother that Francis had beseeched Pope Honorius in Perugia to grant an indulgence to the Portiuncula, which was then bestowed.

Though we might choose not to place too much weight on these accounts, the fact that they mention a papal visit to Perugia in 1216 is worth further reflection. But the fact that the story of the pope's granting Francis's request of the Portiuncula indulgence is first told some fifty years after Francis's death gives us pause, as does the fact that the other stories were set at a distance from Francis's life and in the case of Benedict was only provided secondhand. If we proceed with caution, given our source-critical commitments, we would have to conclude that the Portiuncula indulgence was first granted and instituted after the death of Francis, though this shouldn't mean that we assume Francis was skeptical of the value of indulgences. It is not problematic to say that Francis was a man of his time and lived in light of the assumptions of his day regarding piety.

Another Father? Hugolino of Ostia and the Constitution of the Order

Francis's orientation to the structures of the church and to its norms of behavior, as we have seen, is not easy to explain. This posture was present from the beginning of his renewal movement when he benefited from the help offered to him by Bishop Guido, and it seemed only to increase in the course of his ministry. If it was the case that Francis deliberately propagated the canons of the Fourth Lateran Council, then we can affirm his growing appreciation of the church and its authority, which presumably had been latent in his life from the outset. From a true member of the church, he grew to be a man wholly dedicated to its service. No longer was he merely hoping for some measure of approval from the church for his new way of life. Now he could be both fully committed to the apostolic way of life and to the concerns of the church, which may not have been part of his initial aspirations for the order. Without any formal office, he had become an important figure in the church's structure, embodying both the authenticity of apostolic simplicity and loyalty to the pope and council. His was an eminent rejoinder to the position of those heretics who argued that uniting both paths was just not possible.

With increasing connection to ecclesiastical concerns came the need for clarity about the organizational structure of his own order. On his first meeting with Innocent III, Francis had discussed with him why he didn't want to fold his order into a previously existing monastic structure. The outcome was a form of life that was extraordinarily brief and barely adequate in the light of canon law. In time Francis developed this early rule into what we have already commented upon in several places, the so-called unofficial *Rule* (in Latin the *Regula non bullata*) and the official *Rule* (the *Regula bullata*). The obvious difference between them is expressed in their titles: the first had no formal legal status without papal recognition in a bull, while the second had been awarded such status. But here ends any sense of certainty concerning them. The uncertainties are of course less likely to attach to the official *Rule,* which was proclaimed on November 29, 1223, within the lifetime of Francis in the bull by Pope Honorius III known as *Solet annuere.*

However, the kind of certainties attending this *Rule* were lacking for the unofficial *Rule.* The traditional account of its origins rests on unstable footings, according to which the rule "has its origins in the simple form of life which Francis brought to Pope Innocent III for his approval in 1209 or 1210" and "it developed in light of the experience of the brothers, the teaching of the Church, especially the decrees of the Fourth Lateran Council, and the teachings of Francis himself. The final stage of its composition occurred at the Chapter of 1221, the last Pentecost Chapter at which all the brothers gathered together." This description combined two quite different declarations from the sources. The Three Companions first of all reported that Francis had over the years drafted several rules. This makes it sound like each of them was a completed text and has set Franciscan scholars off in search of fragmentary texts that might have served as discrete rules to establish the roots of the movement. One such text they claim to have found in several manuscript versions in a large collection, some of which are only preserved in translation. That these vary is not, however, a good enough reason to conclude that they are not based on one final earlier version, as is frequently the case with medieval texts. However, it is also the case that we have no evidence for a final earlier version ever being decided upon. The most direct evidence we have for a date doesn't make things easier, for in the prologue Innocent III is identified as still living. Since he died in 1216, this would make for a very early date for the work's composition. In fact, in another place in the *Rule*, a papal bull of September 22, 1220, is explicitly referenced, which is difficult to square with the other date. If there is any chance to reconcile these conflicting dates, the best we can do is suggest that the text developed slowly over a number of years, with the mention of Innocent a leftover detail from an earlier document, probably referring to the beginnings of the drafting of the *Rule* in 1209. In the end, the overwhelming interpretation of the origins of the *Rule* affirms that the text of the so-called *Regula non bullata* was the result of redactional work that expanded, completed, and corrected the text.[31]

David Flood has carefully reconstructed the process of composition, showing that authorship of the text of the unofficial *Rule* can be attributed not just to Francis but to a whole cadre of other brothers who worked alongside him. Jordan of Giano, for instance, also acknowledged that Brother Caesar of Speyer added Bible quotations to "adorn" earlier drafts. These were responses to Francis's direct requests, but there are also hints of resistance to his plans. He had the intention in preparing the *Rule* to carefully include the words of institution that had been transcribed onto the small tablets, as this reference in the *Legend of Perugia* suggests: "Out of respect for the most holy Body and Blood of our Lord Jesus Christ, he wanted to include in the rule that if the brothers found writings with the name of the Lord on them or words of the ritual of the most holy Sacrament carelessly abandoned in an unsuitable place, they were to collect them and put them aside." However, the Franciscan ministers, likely the gathering of the chapter of the movement, argued against the plan. Unrelated to the question of whether the description of this resolution actually held true, the account does give us an impression of how the development of the text was understood from the perspective of the early fourteenth century, providing further confirmation of conclusions we have reached concerning the changes that the text underwent.[32]

With this insight into the gradual development of the text, we still have not resolved the questions of whether that Pentecost meeting of the chapter produced a definitive text, and whether this text was then rejected by the pope. This would have fascinating implications for our understanding of Francis's relationship with the curia, as it would make abundantly clear its contentious nature and how dependent Francis was on the pope. There is, however, no clear evidence of just such a final draft. Accepting this proposition is bound to the suggestion that the final addition to the text must have taken place at the earliest in 1220, as we learn through several accounts of a major gathering of all members of the order in Assisi in 1221. It is significant to note that in no report of that meeting can we find evidence of the resolution of the rule, not even by Jordan of Giano, who provides the most thorough account of the meeting, leaving aside for the moment the *Fioretti* and its legendary origins. And Jordan had good personal reason to do so, for it was at this meeting of the chapter that he finally decided to move to Germany, more coerced than willingly. We just can't conclude from reports that the chapter of 1221 finalized any rule. Nor is it possible to conclude that any text that might have emerged from this chapter would necessarily be what has come to be known as the unofficial *Rule.* If we begin with the assumption that this text grew and developed as it passed though many different hands, and that we can observe both a variety of handwritings and a more formal independent edition of the text in the *Fragmenta alterius regulae non bullatae,* the questions just get larger, leading Kajetan Eßer to conclude that the older fragments of the rule "are the basis upon which the manuscript tradition of today's text of the Regula non bullata lies." The complex set of circumstances surrounding the development of the rule's text provides a way into the question that is distinct from the search for an officially authorized text. Taking Flood's investigations into account, it could be that there were several versions of a rule, with the late *Regula non bullata* just one of many, with no one text having any kind of priority or better legal authority than any other until the ultimate *Rule* was officially approved in 1223. That the unofficial *Rule* appears to have had some prominence among the brothers is the result not of any formal acclamation but instead is the result of its widespread usage. Indeed, the Spiritual Franciscans, espousing more radical streams of the Franciscan movement, were the ones who especially handed down this rule, and who after the death of Francis were determined to fight any growing laxity among the brothers. They especially found in this text, along with the *Testament* of their founder, a welcome alternative to the official *Rule* of the order.[33]

With this kind of approach to the text-critical questions, some concerns have been relieved, including the proposition that Francis had ingloriously failed to persuade the pope though he had produced a text resolved by the community. The various rules that the Companions mention are therefore likely to be just new approaches in writing to explain the nature of the growing order. Other witnesses might have concluded differently, however. For example, John of Perugia knew just two rules: the one of 1209, which was just too short, and the one of 1223 officially recognized by the pope, described as the "other one." Everything else that lay between these two firm dates were drafts of various kinds. They diverged from each other and perhaps also competed with one another too. What must be conceded is that the text known to us as the *Regula non bullata* is part of a lively debate about the origins of the order between 1209 and 1223, nothing more, but still quite a lot, for just such a developing text responsive to the vicissitudes of history might give us more insight into Franciscan spirituality than any set text could.[34]

This is especially true when we compare it with the official *Rule of 1223*, which bears without doubt the mark of Francis, for he himself says in his *Testament* that he was its author. But in the same place he recognized as well the contribution of Hugolino of Ostia, the later pope Gregory IX (r. 1227–41), who in the bull *Quo elongati* of September 28, 1230, acknowledged the part he played in drawing together a rule from a collection of spiritual reflections to create the structure for an order. Francis described him in these words: "his lordship the Bishop of Ostia, who is the superior, protector, and corrector of the whole Order." In doing so, he effectively outlined a new way of understanding the relationship between the papacy and the brotherhood after the publication of the *Regula bullata*. Indeed, this relationship would outlast both of them and secure the order permanently under papal authority.[35]

It would also be true to say that Hugolino was the hinge between papal sovereignty and the developing order, and indeed, as Francis suggested in the title he gave him, it went both ways. He protected Francis and those of his movement, but he also made sure that their path continued to conform to the dictates of the church. As both Thomas of Celano and John of Perugia point out, it was Francis himself around the year 1220 who besought

Honorius III to appoint Hugolino as "Father and Lord" of the community. Perhaps it was even the case that they had known each other for a while by this time, for Celano mentions a meeting between them in Florence, which is likely to have taken place in the year 1217. This appears to have been an incidental encounter, and perhaps not the first meeting between them. How exactly they came to meet remains unclear, as does the initiator of their collaboration. According to the account of the Three Companions, it is possible to imagine some kind of mutuality in their movements. After the death in 1214 or 1215 of Cardinal John of St. Paul, who seems to have continued to feel responsible for the order even after 1209, Hugolino turned his attention to the brotherhood around Francis, who had heard of his good reputation and traveled to visit him with a few other brothers to ask for his support, which the cardinal duly guaranteed. Their relationship solidified, perhaps as a result of the order's increasing need of protection, given difficult conditions in several dioceses, for "the friars suffered many tribulations at the hands of both the clergy and the laity." John of Perugia named Hungary, Germany, and other regions north of the Alps as places where the brothers were threatened. On top of this, Francis faced internal challenges, which he struggled to contain or resolve. We can assume that one of the reasons for this was Francis's journey to the Middle East, which took place in the same year as Hugolino's appointment and led to chaos at home. For example, changes to the regulations for fasting were made in this period by those deputized by him to lead in his absence, Matthew of Narni and Gregory of Naples, and Francis discovered on his return that he could no longer assert his authority over them, requiring the assistance of Hugolino.[36]

This constellation of events nonetheless benefited all the players. Hugolino could see the strategic lay of the land more clearly than the then pope, recognizing how the church might profit from Francis's influence, though he was no neutral bystander in the growth of the order. Raoul Manselli summarizes his role plainly: "The Franciscan sources otherwise agree, with different shadings, in giving weight and importance to Ugolino [sic]. They also concur by not attributing any intervention to him of any magnitude." The integration of the brotherhood and its many members from the movement for the "via apostolica" into the church carried Hugolino's signature, yet its integration was also its domestication. Irrespective of the reservations concerning any new order expressed by the Fourth Lateran Council, a new order emerged anyway, which from within the church could authentically espouse a call to poverty without turning against her. In the end, this would prove successful only because Hugolino appeared to combine an acute sense of ecclesiastical political realities with a deep spiritual closeness to Francis, though we must be careful here. Celano's *Life*, whose recollections came to influence other sources, was commissioned and in part written by Hugolino, now crowned Gregory IX. It records, no doubt to his satisfaction, reports about the pope by the pope. So it is his very own portrait that we read of in Celano. Even in his own lifetime, Hugolino revered Francis as an apostle of Christ, kneeling before him and kissing his hands. In the symbolic style of communication practiced in the Middle Ages, to do so would have been a severe condescension on the part of a bishop. In reality, however, his acts of humility might have been perceived differently, though they were still considerable gestures for a highly regarded clergyman.[37]

After Hugolino became protector of the order, the Companions report how he would be greeted by the brothers when he attended annual meetings of the chapter: they would run toward him and when they got close, he would dismount from his horse and walk the remainder of the way with the brothers to the Portiuncula. His symbolic superiority was subsumed by his spiritual equality, though not much more can be said, for Celano's expansive descriptions do begin to sound like the pope's vision of himself retroactively superimposed onto the narrative, having in the meantime declared Francis a saint, hoping thereby to bask in the glory of his reflected holiness. And this could be applied in the other direction too as he received the veneration that Francis offered, akin to the love of a son for his father. What a delightful notion: a decade after forsaking his parental home and perhaps never visiting it again, at last Francis could say that he did at least have a spiritual father. Yet his relationship with Hugolino was probably more formal than with a father, shaped as it was by Francis's subordination to the cardinal and to his regulations, which required obedience from his priests. Both Celano and John of Perugia mention the sincere but ultimately still official form of address that Francis used in his letters to Hugolino, none of which, unfortunately, are extant. He does use "father" as a form of address for Hugolino, though we shouldn't interpret this in an emotional or pastoral context but rather as a sign of submission to a hierarchical order: "To the venerable father in Christ, the bishop of the whole world." Even the title that Francis gave to him in his *Testament*, "Protector and Improver," didn't particularly acknowledge any real familial intimacy, as much as Celano might have intimated this. Both terms might merely represent the very practical needs of protection and improvement required of the young community.[38]

The Three Companions reported precisely on how necessary protection proved to be. After acceding to the role of protector of the order, Hugolino wrote to several prelates instructing them that "it would be far better . . . if the friars were invited to dwell and to preach in the different provinces; and that those in authority should help and advise them." Understanding the background, it doesn't take much to imagine the kinds of conflict that might have stood behind Hugolino's intervention. It appears that the brothers had been caught up in anti-Waldensian sentiment, and had experienced unmerited episcopal discipline too. The problem was unauthorized preaching, authorization for which was soon to issue directly from the pope through his cardinal.[39]

When it came to improvement and rebuke, on the other hand, Hugolino in his capacity as highest supervisor of the order was prepared to take concrete action within the fellowship to assert correct order and doctrine. If a priest of the order was not conducting the Mass in the right way or was not doctrinally faithful ("non essent catholici"), the other brothers were bound to deliver that priest over to their cardinal-protector. This was outlined by Francis in his *Testament* and thereby made it abundantly clear just what Hugolino's responsibilities were: vigilance regarding heretics. First of all, he was to protect against unjust accusations of heresy from outside the order, but he also had the task of purifying the order from false teaching within. In proceeding against heresy, concern was also expressed to create a constitutional framework shaping the order's life. In essence, then, it was Hugolino's signature that authorized the *Regula bullata*. In one particular case, we can sharply observe how both respect for the concerns of Francis and clear rebuke of him were expressed. Sometime between 1217 and 1223, Francis wrote a letter to the minister of the order, a representative of the leadership team, as it were, who had expressed to Francis his concerns about how to relate to some brothers who had fallen into sin. Francis was so disturbed by the question that he suggested adding an extensive paragraph to the rule or, more precisely, announced: "We shall make one chapter out of all the chapters in the Rule that speak of mortal sin." From the seven verses that the section consists of in modern versions, not one complete sentence is taken up directly in 1223 for the official *Rule*—and this despite Francis having suggested to the minister a tactical plan to take his writing to the meeting of the chapter himself to secure its enforcement.[40]

Francis's authority alone would not be enough to include this regulation in the final *Rule*. Of course, from a legal perspective, Hugolino's status was much more influential. Whatever the content of the collection of rules in the *Regula non bullata* that Francis had handed over to Hugolino, it might have appeared as a rule to someone not legally trained, and it certainly was closer to being a rule than the "rule" of 1209 would have been. But from the perspective of an experienced cardinal, the work probably appeared like a hodgepodge of ideas, regulations mixed with a sample sermon and a prayer. All this looked more like random spiritual instructions than anything that was legally actionable. The official *Rule*, on the other hand, was quite different in character. First of all, entry into the community was clearly regulated, which accorded with the spirit of Hugolino. If in the unofficial *Rule* someone seeking entry into the community was informed by the minister of the basic ideas governing the community's life, in the official *Rule*, by contrast, that same person would be tested concerning the content of the Catholic faith and the sacraments of the church. This was just as regulated as making sure that upon entry into the order one was not leaving behind a wife. These kinds of brief and goal-specific regulations created the need for clear leadership of the order as well, at the head of which now stood a minister general. Under his authority, the order was divided up geographically into provinces, over each of which a provincial minister was appointed. Under him, leadership was devolved to "smaller areas" under the supervision of "custodes," or "superiors." We can see how this worked with a well-known example. Thomas of Celano was himself a custos for the region incorporating Mainz, Worms, Cologne, and Speyer. North of the Alps, such areas were likely to be larger than in Italy, which was the case for dioceses too, but either way we get a clear impression of the extent of the responsibilities given to a custos. Strangely, there is no mention in the *Rule* of who was responsible for the lowest level of the life of the brotherhood, the individual houses, which were overseen by the guardians.[41]

Of great importance for the whole structure of the order was the notion that the brotherhood should not be understood in a hierarchical way. Instead, it was to be seen as a community of service, flagged by the word *minister*, essential to each position's description. But it was still the case that the strictness of the order was valued as a contribution to its effectiveness.

In earlier forms of the rule, it had been the case that an individual brother did not have to obey his superior when to do so went against his conscience, but in the official *Rule of 1223* it was only to be at the leadership level as a group that resistance might be offered, when the provincial minister and the custodes together might exercise their prerogative to remove a general minister. The formalization of the structure of the order as well as the language of the text can be understood in various ways. First of all, it expresses some measure of normalization. The brotherhood in 1223 had indeed become a fully fledged order. The early spontaneity of Francis is no longer to be seen, spontaneity being a characteristic that belongs to certain moments or certain people, not to movements. Hugolino's restructuring of the order contributed significantly to the fact that the community Francis had formed now could survive without him. Indeed, when later as pope Hugolino made Francis a saint, he further boosted its chances of survival. The legacy of Francis was secure, but he himself retreated increasingly from its concerns.[42]

CHAPTER 6

Retreat

The Dangers of the World

T IS NOT ONLY BECAUSE OF THE CHALLENGES relating to sources that the biography of Francis is difficult to assemble. Within the story itself, there are several gaps, especially if one is looking for external events that shaped the man. After he abandoned his parental home, converted, and gathered his first supporters, we know very little about individual events of his life. Of course, his meetings with Pope Innocent and with Sultan al-Malik al-Kamil stand out and can be dated precisely, but apart from these, although the biographies offer quite a bit of material, the ordering of events with dates remains difficult and speculative. His sermon to the birds, if it has any historical context, can't be dated at all, and *The Canticle of Brother Sun* only very approximately.

However, any life, but especially the life of a religious person, does not consist merely of external events. Just as important, perhaps more so, are internal attitudes. Of course, at this point we are warned in the canons of modern history writing about investigating the interior life of a subject because sources don't give us access to the soul. This is an insight into history as well as an insight that is profoundly theological too: in the end the deepest part of a human being is indeed accessible only to God. But it is true nonetheless that what appears on the outside is an expression of the heart within. We can therefore at least investigate how Francis's early biographers understood his religious convictions, and when we note his own words, allow them to be understood in the way he himself intended.

The quest to grasp Francis's spirituality must also be undertaken with a certain sense of reserve, but like all other aspects of his biography it is not completely hopeless. We might have to acknowledge and respect some limitations, but after all is said and done, we can learn to appreciate his piety given our access to his preaching, in which he worked to persuade, to convert, and to move others to change. We need to be honest, though, regarding the ambiguous picture that emerges from his preaching. Peace and judgment belonged together for him; the devil and God were both determinative of his worldview. Next to the Francis who hit a beautiful note in *The Canticle of Brother Sun,* or who supports contemporary attitudes regarding ecological sustainability, stands the preacher of repentance. His message of peace can't be heard without reference to judgment, a judgment that—perhaps especially—applies to those who believed differently than he did.

Mirrored to some degree in such theological statements, we can glean elements of psychological ambivalence that derive ultimately from the earliest years of his life. At the beginning of his spiritual quest stood his sense of dislocation, his own antipathy toward his background and family. To say no to his father was the beginning of a much greater confrontation with the world, an early critique of a Christianity both superficial and vapid. When Francis retreated to the Portiuncula, he first encountered the Gospel when he heard read the account of Jesus commissioning his apostles, a narrative that offered him a sense of certainty and clarity. Of course, this is not to say that any lingering unease with his spiritual background magically disappeared. He could praise the creation, but this did not mean for him that the world was all good. Great themes from the biblical tradition continued to move him, for the world is much more than the description of a particular place or a particular structure. Jesus Christ said, "My kingdom is not of this world" (John 18:36), suggesting that the Christian tradition evaluated the world negatively as something opposed to God, so Francis—though not the first to have difficulties understanding this—attempted to bring this conviction together with belief in the good creation of God.

But one thing was clear: it was human beings who had done the most to disrupt the good equilibrium of the world. Indeed, his preaching repentance reinforced this very point, disclosing human sin and moving those listening to make a change. Given his own background, it is not surprising that his preaching of repentance took particular aim at economic interests and values, though we shouldn't expect to hear analysis of commercial realities in Italian cities of his period or critique of the system in which a merchant might make personal profit. These would assume insights that only later could be understood as central to capitalist economies. Simply, for Francis rejection of the economic forms of his day increasingly meant rejection of money.[1]

While there is evidence that at the beginning of the brotherhood's life Bernard was responsible for keeping a common purse, and that on one occasion Francis availed himself of some money to pacify Silvester, who felt affronted that some of their money had been redirected from church repair to care of the poor, the story later disappears from the record and is replaced with sharp invective. The presence of money in the community's early phase can be explained through the details of Bernard's conversion story: following the account of the rich young man in Matthew 19, he sold his possessions and exchanged them for money as a first sign of his transformation. The verse "Go, sell your possessions" (Matthew 19:21) can be found frequently in those drafts that were collected as the *Regula non bullata*. However, in this text, the verse is connected with sharp regulations that are hard to square with the pragmatic consideration of how to exchange goods for money in the first place, causing a deep-seated fear of any literal contact with money at all: "So all the friars, no matter where they are or where they go, are forbidden to take or accept money in any way or under any form, or have it accepted for them, for clothing or books, or as wages, or in any other necessity, except to provide for the urgent needs of those who are ill. We should have no more use or regard for money in any of its forms than for dust."[2]

As much as it might sound like the opposite, the money that Francis was talking about here did not possess in his eyes any negative power in and of itself; otherwise Francis could not make the exception to use it for the care of sick brothers. To assign money to the realm of something opposed to God, as it might be understood from that verse in the Sermon on the Mount—"You cannot serve God and mammon" (Matthew 6:24; Luke 16:13)—was not Francis's conclusion. In fact, this verse never appeared in Francis's own writings, and even his first biographers never quoted it. It was Bonaventure who made the connection in his sermons about Francis. When the brothers made money taboo, it was not because they believed that money had any intrinsic power but because of its capacity to lead human beings astray. Instead, malice and greed were the terms Francis connected to money in the unofficial *Rule*, based on Luke 12:15, which warned of letting money draw us into the worries of this life. His use of another biblical text is especially important to note. He clearly cited Luke 21:34, "Be on guard so that your hearts are not weighed down with dissipation and drunkenness and the worries of this life," but expressly did not actually include the words "dissipation and drunkenness," instead adding a deliberate warning about the world's cares. It could barely be expressed any more clearly where the dangers of this world lurk for Francis. It is not the lust for pleasure that is likely to lead the brothers astray—worries concerning money are more likely to rule in their hearts.[3]

In this way, Francis illuminated brightly what he regarded as the true issue of economic life facing north Italian merchants in the thirteenth century. It was the worries of this world, worries that had so preoccupied him as a merchant's son and had absorbed his family such that they no longer spoke to him, that had to be avoided at all costs. The temptation of money was the work of the devil. Of course Francis could never have imagined that centuries later the German poet Johann Wolfgang von Goethe, in his play *Faust*, would introduce us to a young woman who lusts after jewelry that had been provided for her in her bedchamber by the devil himself. But in the same scene, centuries of experience later, we hear the echo of the same awareness warned of by Francis, that money is the devil's tool because it rewards our efforts to seek our own advantage instead of the common good. It appeared so dangerous to Francis that brothers who misused coinage were to be excluded from the community or directed to do penance. An example of someone who kept the common purse and misused their responsibility was Judas, who now appeared all of a sudden in the text of the *Rule*, though up to now no one had been bothered enough by the parallel to connect it to Bernard. But astonishingly, by the year 1223 we see how the fellowship had been radicalized and brought back to first principles when the official *Rule* was accepted, for the section on money was distinctly more concise than in the drafts, and accordingly in substance it clearly still contained a ban on the acceptance of money and coins except for emergencies to care for the sick.[4]

This intensification of attitudes from drafts of the unofficial *Rule* toward the completed official *Rule* corresponds with increasing clarity concerning the hallmark of the movement. If at the outset the brothers had pursued different kinds of work, by and by they devoted themselves to begging. Perhaps they took their lead from the experiences Francis had known in his life as a dropout, or in the following period when he began to supplement his income with other kinds of work. Both the unofficial and the official *Rule* recognize the value of work and of begging. The quotation above from the unofficial *Rule* considered the possibility that any prohibition of money could undermine the necessity of earning an income if necessary. Even the official *Rule* included its own regulation concerning the "modus laborandi," the way of work: one should labor responsibly and with respect. Besides its value in providing for the means of existence, namely nature's harvest, work could also function as an encouragement to self-mastery and a contribution against the vice of idleness. Expectations of work were complicated under these conditions. Managing any emerging conflicts in the community was likely to have been better served by the details and layers of the unofficial *Rule*, as the final version of the official one (which had more of a legal cast) was more general in order to encompass a variety of possible circumstances. In the unofficial *Rule*, by contrast, many occupations were expressly ruled out, especially chamberlains and cellar masters—occupations that were connected to business and commerce or to alcohol use or abuse.[5]

Further, for many brothers, artisanal work may have been increasingly preferable to the sophisticated responsibilities of a scribe, which would assume a high standard of education—in Francis's *Testament,* he expressly wished that more brothers would learn a trade as a way of avoiding the growing practice of begging. Here too the point was to take precautionary action. Francis and his counselors stated in the unofficial *Rule* that a trade might be pursued if it did not interfere with one's salvation and if it could be carried out with honor. When we attempt to read and understand legal texts, we notice immediately that they are an indication of one kind of problem but also a provocation to another. Put in another way, a stonemason was right to try to work out why erecting a palace for a nobleman was acceptable but constructing a building for a merchant to use as his business was not. The delight in details betrays the fact that in the fifteen or so years since the foundation of the brotherhood, a whole set of hurdles had been identified, but there was no easy way of resolving them. Even the fact that the workman's tools were legitimate possessions and therefore did not contravene the vow of poverty had to be regulated somehow. Rules like this were an example of how the coexistence of begging with certain kinds of work, as emerged in the early phase of the brotherhood, had not been adequately resolved in organizational terms during the life of Francis himself.[6]

In the brotherhood, questions concerning both begging and working were expressions of great importance relative to issues of poverty. Even Francis's nickname *poverello* betrays how closely he was identified with poverty. Celano reports in his *Second Life* that the brothers once debated which virtue was most likely to bring them closest to a friendship with Christ, to which Francis responded, "Know, my sons, that poverty is the special way to salvation; its fruit is manifold, but it is really well known only to a few." Of course, this is a token of the impact of his whole life story, for Francis himself did not lay as much emphasis on poverty as the highest virtue as is often imagined. Given the close association that history has placed on the relationship between Francis and poverty, we might be surprised to learn that there is very little in his own writings about it. Of course, his community was shaped from the first by its commitment to poverty—indeed, radical poverty—but this was not the core of the Franciscan message, which was defined instead around the apostolic lifestyle in general. Christ's commission that had provoked Francis's conversion contained clear instructions concerning poverty, but it was Bernard's conversion that placed the poor in the center of the movement, and this then reinforced the solidarity of the brotherhood. There was little discussion of poverty, illustrated above by the matter of a common purse. As long as a life of poverty was taken for granted, it didn't need to be discussed. It was only with the possibility of money being misused that more attention had to be directed toward its role in the movement. For Francis, the question of money wasn't a topic that needed to be considered because its place in the brotherhood was simply assumed. Nowhere did he express himself so comprehensively concerning money as in his *Rules,* since such legal texts were classically the place to regulate what was allowed and what not.[7]

When Francis contributed to the theme of poverty, he didn't suggest exactly what to renounce but instead what inner posture to assume. In the Sermon on the Mount, Jesus says, "Blessed are the poor in spirit" (Matthew 5:3), and Luke provides an alternative: "Blessed are you who are poor" (Luke 6:20). When Francis in his *Admonitions* wrote of poverty, he chose not to use Luke's version—which picks up on social realities—but, importantly, cites Matthew instead. In the most literal sense of the word, poverty was for Francis first and foremost something spiritual, drawing the connection from the Latin "paupertas spiritu," which of course for Christians triggers awareness of the Holy Spirit, through whom God is present to believers. If we consider again later debates within the order concerning the role of material poverty, we would have to say that they miss the boat entirely. Physical poverty in Francis's mind is a consequence of spiritual poverty, even though this does not fit precisely into the narrative of his life. At the outset, it was the spontaneous rejection of material goods that both launched his life of poverty and created significant conflict with his father, and it was only after this that theological and biblical meaning was applied to this incident, though poverty does provide some insight into the shape of Francis's inner world.

The spiritual poverty of which Francis spoke in the *Admonitions* is best understood not against the backdrop of social dynamics in the thirteenth century but in relation to the piety of those who follow the Lord Jesus Christ by humbling themselves to the extreme. A life devoted to Christ involves giving up all self-praise or self-pride, and therefore the only thing worthy of praise in us is either our weakness, according to the writings of St. Paul (see 2 Corinthians 12:5), or our readiness to carry the cross of Christ in this life. Poverty of spirit is an expression of carrying one's own cross, for "a person is really poor in spirit when he hates himself and loves those who strike him in the face." The *Admonitions* are a useful summary of Francis's emphasis that a posture of poverty of spirit provides deeper foundations than efforts concerning external pious practices like prayers or attendance at the Mass. In this way, the whole person was challenged as Christians distanced themselves from their deeply sinful ego, though such renunciations should in no way distract from doing good—rather the opposite. From the most internalized humility emerged the most earnest expression of discipleship in following Christ through both "words and example." Our lives, then, express permanent control of our selfish affections and contempt for all that is worldly, which then comes to light in external poverty and a new relationship with others. We must refuse envy and thereby fulfill Christ's instruction to love our enemy, which Francis interpreted in a very particular way as not to be controlled by the hurt that has been done to us, but rather to express compassion for the sinners who hurt us in the first place. This is exactly the attitude of Jesus, who when dying on the cross forgave those who sinned against him, "for they do not know what they are doing" (Luke 23:34).[8]

But none of these actions can be reckoned as merit for us. Francis warned of self-glory, and he impressed upon others that anything good a Christian can do is attributable to God alone, who works through us. This tension between the command to make a difference in the world and the consciousness that whatever we do, God receives the thanks is expressed elegantly by Francis in his correspondence with the brothers of the order. At the beginning of the letter, he wrote, "This is the very reason he has sent you all over the world, so that by word and deed you might bear witness to his message and convince everyone that there is no other almighty God besides him." Yet at the end of the same letter, in his prayer we read his confession that we might "make our way to you, Most High, by your grace alone." This kind of theology of grace, typical of medieval piety, is often misunderstood. Some might hear here an admonition to obedience, which equates with a demand for self-redemption, or "works righteousness," as a later polemical phrase suggests. Francis suggested the opposite: deep insight into human sinfulness and human limitations on the one hand, and deep trust in God's grace on the other. All this is mediated by the cross, which demonstrates the grace of God and motivates our obedience.[9]

Now, with this explanation behind us, it is easier to see how poverty should be understood as part of the Franciscan way of life. It is part of a whole series of virtues, as we saw in our discussion of *The Praises of the Virtues,* and is not even the first. Here as well, poverty was to be understood as something spiritual in the first instance, which "puts to shame all greed, avarice, and all the anxieties of this life." And in the Latin, reference to the "worries of the world" takes us back to an earlier exposition of Francis's view of the dangers and consequences of money. Although Francis did see poverty as primarily something spiritual, this did not mean that his understanding of poverty must entirely be disengaged from economic or social realities, just given its rightful place in his world—and this in part to make sure that religiously minded social reformers from Assisi, prone to ecstatic expression, were not so hasty in their interpretation of his views. Given that his protest had begun with the egregious consumption of the rich in his sights, his own transformation necessarily had to begin from within. Just such an awareness resonated with the praise of poverty, which Francis included in the final version of the *Rule,* now firmly connected with the promise of reward in the hereafter: "This is the pinnacle of the most exalted poverty, and it is this, my dearest brothers, that has made you heirs and kings of the kingdom of heaven, poor in temporal things but rich in virtue. This should be your portion, because it leads to the land of the living."[10]

Grateful and loving discipleship of Christ was apparently insufficient motivation for a life of poverty because heavenly reward had now been named as an added incentive, although those who listened to his message from the beginning had already heard how these rewards were a stark alternative to the threats of eternal hellfire. Perhaps in the end it was not the substance of his preaching that had changed, merely its tone. He had come to experience ever more painfully that the pursuit of poverty was just not as self-evident as it had been in those first years after he had begun his life of penitence. In his *Testament*, he had to impress on his readers' consciousness the role of poverty, which was in eclipse: "The friars must be very careful not to accept churches or poor dwellings for themselves, or anything else built for them, unless they are in harmony with the poverty which we have promised in the Rule." Poverty had become a problem. And it took up a lot more oxygen in debates among the Franciscans themselves.[11]

With these debates in mind, it has been easy to overlook how Francis's rejection of the world and refusal to own property spilled over into other dimensions of life. Again, we find a Francis who has less to offer modern inquirers—at least at first blush—than we might expect of someone renowned as a critic of money and wealth. But then again, perhaps not. There is yet something else that for moderns is relegated to one of the darker corners of Christian history: "We must hate our lower nature with its vices and sins; by living a worldly life, it would deprive us of the love of our Lord Jesus Christ and of eternal life, dragging us down with it into hell." In the light of such forceful statements, it is easy to think that Francis belonged irretrievably to the stream of Christian tradition that, leaning on the apostle Paul's argument in Romans 7, contended that it was the human body that was the chief carrier of sin and of everything opposed to Christ. That the body with its desires was more closely ordered in a theological sense to the world than to the Spirit of God was for Francis completely self-evident, as it would have been to most people of his day. However, there were just a few of his contemporaries who saw things differently. At the same moment that Francis experienced the definitive confirmation of his calling in his experience of the commissioning sermon of Christ, north of the Alps a contemporary, Gottfried of Strasbourg (d. 1215), was writing about the enchanting power of love in a courtly epic. Here, Tristan and Isolde, the main characters, are irresistibly attracted to each other through a shared drink, and so transgress all social barriers until they find themselves in a grotto—reminding them of a church but not of the sufferings of Christ—in which they celebrate human love.[12]

As so often in history, things that feel like they shouldn't fit together in the same moment do just that. It is not just irony that sees a love-obsessed German poet set in the context of an Italian friar who lacks a sense of body positivity. It is as hard to capture national stereotypes as it is to capture reality expressed at a given moment through local and concrete examples. It is not enough to say, with a slap on the back and a tepid apology, that a person like Francis was "just a man of his time." Of course he was a child of his age, and of course he made his own the view that the body continually leads the soul away from God. But it is also true that we simply can't know if every story that reflected this position actually happened. Nevertheless, they are still vividly associated with Francis. Celano recounts in his *Second Life* that the devil sent "the enticement of the flesh" and "a most severe temptation of lust." To escape these trials, Francis flagellated his flesh, but when this proved of no avail, he threw himself naked into the deep snow of his garden. He then made snowballs, which he saw as symbols of the transitory nature of family and household, which disappear just as quickly. But we must assume that these are fabrications, given the context Celano reports at the end of the story—that one of the brothers had secretly been able to observe these events because the light of the moon was so bright that night, and that part of the story had taken place indoors anyway! And the additional fact that Francis had sworn this brother to secrecy until his death also sounds like an attempt to explain why this story had for so long been unknown, although it would have been a powerful example of the nature of the ascetic life.[13]

And this is exactly what it remained: an example of what Francis's followers could make of his instructions for ascetic living when they read in his *Admonitions* this strange addition to the beatitudes from Jesus's Sermon on the Mount: "Everyone has his own enemy in his power and this enemy is his lower nature which leads him into sin. Blessed the religious who keeps this enemy a prisoner under his control and protects himself against it." That such self-mastery might have been achieved as Celano describes it—even if the story about snow is contrived, for there is never much snow in Assisi—through kinds of self-punishment like whips and other forms of torture is certainly possible. Francis's body was often in poor health, so it is unlikely he spared it such rigors. And why would he anyway if his body was his enemy, a plaything in the hands of the devil? The areas of life in which human beings classically experienced desires and longings were those of food and sex, both of which could then be regulated through the practice of fasting. While Francis did appear to have a comparatively more relaxed attitude to fasting, his attitude toward women was more like his extreme response to money, in both instances motivated by fear of temptation.[14]

His biographers like to present Francis as a model for disciplined fasting. Both Celano and the Three Companions tell us how Francis mixed ash into his meals either to ruin the taste of the food or to make the food go further and to minimize its nutritional value. Even these stories are embroidered. For example, when in the course of his itinerating he was invited to dine with noble families, he would eat a little for the sake of the Gospel, because the commissioning narrative in Luke refers to eating when invited into someone's home (Luke 10:8). But then he would hide the rest of the food in his lap and pretend to be eating in order not to give offense. And the Three Companions also make clear that Francis didn't want to draw attention to his abstinence, but this may well be part of a literary construction, for there does not appear to be any substantial accounts of such abstinence underlying their narrative. This may have been a deliberate accommodation to a kind of game played by their contemporary Elizabeth of Hungary, making it historically quite plausible. But it might be explained as well by the mere fact that Francis didn't take fasting as seriously as others who came after him. Even the regulations in the unofficial *Rule* don't seem to prescribe more than just an extension to the traditional periods of fasting in Advent and around Easter as well as Fridays, which are the sixth day of the week if Sunday is the first: "All the friars without exception must fast from the feast of All Saints [November 1] until Christmas, and from Epiphany [January 6], when our Lord began his fast, until Easter. The friars are not bound by the Rule to fast at other times, except on Friday." The official *Rule* further watered down this regulation, making fasting from Epiphany voluntary, so only the general period of fasting for forty days on weekdays before Easter was mandated.[15]

Francis was apparently not known as a saint who fasted. Fear of the body was expressed in a different domain for him, in relation to sexuality. Fornication was severely punished and led to expulsion from the order, but this was hardly unusual for the time. The term was applied to any sex not legitimized by marriage, and to his way of thinking this meant chiefly sexual intercourse with a woman, either outside the order or with a woman in Clare's community. Francis's own perception of women was shaped by his deep-seated anxiety of sexual desire. Women were for him a constant provocation to sin. His ambivalence toward women was palpable. Remarkably, he could on the one hand loosen the way the sexes had been understood, so that in some settlements he might divide the brothers into two groups, the mothers and the sons. The external physical sex of a person did not determine social roles, with a further possible biblical justification: the life of a mother was to be modeled on the life of Martha (Luke 10:38–42), and the life of their sons modeled on the life of her sister Mary, likewise a woman. Insofar as Francis used the example of women in leadership who didn't aspire to rule over others as models, he is a distant precursor for contemporary theories about the construction of gender. However, when it came to questions of sexuality, or even just the possibility of sexuality, he diverged wildly from contemporary notions of the relationship between the sexes. Indeed, we can easily imagine that in his relationship with Clare he learned to think of a woman not primarily from the perspective of gender, nor of sexual desire, but chiefly as a companion in the path of discipleship. But overall this still didn't mean that Francis esteemed women much at all. According to Celano, Francis was quoted as saying contemptuously: "What business should a Friar Minor have to transact with a woman, except when she piously asks for holy penance or for advice concerning a better life?"[16]

Given the context of this quotation in Celano's *Second Life* and Francis's very technical usage of the term "Friar Minor," we can perhaps assume that Francis did not literally make this statement, but the sentence can't be far from statements that do have historical support. His support for the autonomy of women around him was only achievable through making sexual feelings taboo and repressing them. We must of course be careful here not to excerpt a part of a rule and overlay it with biographical intent, but even Celano, who is not normally suspicious of insinuations, believed that Francis's reserve toward women was so extreme that it should not be interpreted as care and concern but as fear and fright. What must have been in his own day quite impressive for us instead suggests that Francis, for personal reasons of embarrassment in his avoidance of women, was prone to exaggerated reactions. This biographical background becomes clear when we consider that in the instructions relating to women, none of the brothers could welcome a woman into the life of obedience, that is, to the order. And this wouldn't have been comprehensible were it not for the fact that he first of all bound Clare to the way of penitence but then released her to go her own way. We notice particularly that this regulation appeared in the same paragraph that mandated quite generally how men were to protect themselves from "the sight or company of women, when it is evil" and indeed from any engagement with them. The foundation of this approach was, like much in the ministry of Francis, found in the Sermon on the Mount when Jesus offers this admonition: "Everyone who looks at a woman with lust has already committed adultery with her in his heart" (Matthew 5:28). Where in the teaching of Jesus the emphasis lay on the internal spiritual posture, not so much the external actions, in Francis's teaching this became a new and restrictive set of rules, established with more clarity in the official *Rule*. All suspicious meetings and discussions with women were to be avoided and men were not even to set foot in the sisters' monasteries unless one had been given express permission to do so.[17]

It should be noted that these kinds of strict regulations reflected more than just Francis's own experiences. In the early phase of the brotherhood, when there was still so much that remained unclarified, many dilemmas presented themselves, in part the result of the brothers pursuing homelessness on their travels. This was especially clear in the work of John of Perugia. In his account, many people with whom the brothers sought lodging were afraid of theft, and many young women fled when they saw the brothers from a distance arriving in town. John's explanation focused on the fear of falling into the same kind as madness as the brothers, but by concentrating on the reaction of the women he surely implied other reasons for fear and caution. From the outside, the brothers—despite some form of papal recognition—still constituted a vague and disorderly community that in several major ways deviated from social norms. Having so obviously reneged on sexual norms, they lost yet another way of expressing solidarity with the world around them. Indeed, the sharp edges of the instructions regarding fornication suggest that such worries were not without foundation either. Francis himself followed these developments with care, perhaps even with dismay, and processed them in his own way. Sexuality for Francis did not belong in the realm of the goodness of the creation, which otherwise he could praise so eloquently, but instead was something dangerous that the devil could exploit, and so was to be avoided at all costs.[18]

Contemplation

Francis learned this too: it was in vain to flee the world if there was no direction in which to flee. Of course he was profoundly shaped by the circumstances of his external life, being sent into the world to all people and to all creatures. But the power for this was rooted in his intensive relationship with God, Christ, the angels, and the saints. And when he prayed, all these things were of even more importance to him. But we can't investigate the heart of the person praying—we can examine only the prayers themselves. Celano reports that Francis, when asked how we should pray, pointed to the Lord's Prayer as Jesus had done, but also taught about Christ and his atoning death on the cross. And even if a conversation like this never took place, his response was typical of his thinking, for in his *Letter to All the Faithful* he made the same point, admonishing others to pray the prayer the Lord gave us. Besides more general instructions to pray the Liturgy of the Hours, Francis valued and expounded the Lord's Prayer in particular. With a mixture of explanations that he had come across, and in his own words as well, he expanded the individual petitions of the Lord's Prayer, applying them to the particular context of his own community. In reading this meditative interpretation of the Lord's Prayer in the light of the afore-mentioned admonition to use this prayer continually, it becomes clear how much Francis exerted himself at every moment to live for God. Even the request for our daily bread had for him an essentially spiritual meaning: it is Jesus Christ whom we must receive daily, whether he comes to us in the concrete form of the Eucharist, in pious memory, or in the practical path of discipleship. And Christ's mother, Mary, couldn't be separated from Francis's worship of Christ in the first instance either.[19]

That Mary and Christ belonged together was especially evident in the office of the passion of the Lord that Francis at some unknown time had put together for the clergy of the order. It consisted chiefly of verses from the Psalter. Christ was named here, but the main concern of the liturgy was not Christ but Mary. In this office, it was customary for the clergy to alternate lines of prayers, of which a call to venerate Mary was an essential part: "Holy Virgin Mary, among all the women of the world there is none like you; you are the daughter and handmaid of the most high King and Father of heaven; you are the mother of our most holy Lord Jesus Christ; you are the spouse of the Holy Spirit. Pray for us, with St Michael the archangel and all the powers of heaven and all the saints, to your most holy and beloved Son, our Lord and Master. Glory be to the Father, etc." We also have from a different text a prayer to Mary composed by Francis, in essence an expanded version of the greeting Ave Maria, in which the bearer of God, Mary, the *theotokos* or the holy Mother of God, was tightly bound to the Trinity. Here she was blessed together with the Son and the Holy Spirit by God the Father, and so became the dwelling place of God on earth, his palace, his servant, and his mother. Consequently, Mary was also bound up with the illumination of the hearts of the faithful by virtue of the Holy Spirit. It is perhaps too difficult to say exactly what dogmatic role Mary played in the thought of Francis, but that he turned to her in particular moments is evident in this prayer, even if we can't precisely date it in Francis's life.[20]

This veneration of Mary accompanied Francis through his entire life. Shortly before his death, he promised in Italian in a word of admonition that he wrote to Clare and her sisters concerning life eternal beyond the grave: "Each one [of you] will be crowned queen in heaven with the Virgin Mary." It is just impossible to imagine Francis without his veneration of the Virgin, for she was simply a counterpart to his veneration of Christ. The office shows that for Francis the sufferings of Christ were a significant and sustained theme in his spirituality. He wanted both to praise him and to follow him. This is attested by a prayer Francis learned as a young believer that—as he wrote in his *Testament*—was given to him by God in the first place: "We adore you, Lord Jesus Christ, here and in all your churches in the whole world, and we bless you, because by your holy cross you have redeemed the world."[21]

Praise of Christ who redeems through the cross can be found in other places too. In Francis's *Admonitions,* a collection of varying instructions from different periods of his life, one such line is worth noting as an entry point to the spirituality of the period of composition. Francis exhorted his readers to pay attention to the "good Shepherd": "To save his sheep he endured the agony of the cross." And it is only in the cross that a brother can boast, not in his own achievements, an interesting belief that reminds us that in worshipping Christ we become more aware of the distance we experience from the Savior. This gives us cause to reflect in the light of later interpretative layers on how we should be cautious and not allow the role of the cross in his thought to be overplayed. Indeed, the Franciscan academic Oktavian Schmucki has expressed it soberly in this way: "Not once in his *Officium*

Passionis does the suffering of Christ stand exclusively and dominantly in the foreground." The passion of the Christ was part of a larger understanding of piety focused on the person of Christ. The theological belief in the incarnation of Christ, God taking human flesh, was also part of the package of piety, which was of course connected to Mary as well.[22]

Indeed, the beginning of the *Letter to All the Faithful* brought together the most varied biblical traditions concerning Christ. From John's Gospel, Francis took up the language of Christ as the Word of God but integrated it into Luke's infancy narrative: "Our Lord Jesus Christ is the glorious Word of the Father, so holy and exalted, whose coming the Father made known by St Gabriel the Archangel to the glorious and blessed Virgin Mary, in whose womb he took on our weak human nature." Significantly for Francis, the meaning of the incarnation of Christ had taken deep cultural root in annual Christmas celebrations, which Celano recounts in his *First Life*, according to which Francis invented the three-dimensional nativity scene that we now commonly see placed under a Christmas tree. Or more modestly: in the year 1223, we have an account of the first time a Christmas scene was staged. According to Celano, Francis inquired of someone in Greccio, a town in the vicinity of Rieti, about a hundred kilometers north of Rome, where he might enact the humble birth of Jesus Christ "before our bodily eyes." At this point, John, the man whom Francis had spoken to, fetched a hay box and some hay as well as an ox and a donkey, though these creatures never make an appearance in the biblical narrative. Then on Christmas Day an otherwise unnamed priest celebrated the Mass over the crib, with crowds in attendance, all of which made abundantly clear that the nativity scene was not first erected under a tree, a practice that came much later. The scene didn't consist just of a manger, a concrete expression of the representation, but the whole Christmas story was presented in a graphic and tangible form. Indeed, this style of teaching matched Francis's own method of preaching, which was not just about the words chosen but built on gestures, actions, and the whole performance. It is also true that this kind of teaching tool was much less spontaneous than other approaches that Francis might have used normally. The inclusion of an ox and a donkey indicates that Francis was not trying to reproduce the text of the Gospels directly. It appears that he had before his eyes a pictorial representation of the nativity he had seen somewhere, perhaps a painting, that he would now transform into a living three-dimensional story and integrate into a liturgical setting.[23]

We must admit that there are elements in Celano's story that give rise to some skepticism, for they appear in an account stating that the materials used for the celebration are subsequently turned into relics (for example, the hay wasn't just given to the animals to eat but was later used to cure sickness in both animals and humans, especially pregnant women). Perhaps most suspiciously of all, Celano informs us that the spot where the nativity was erected in Greccio was later the site of a church. That it was founded exactly in the year 1228 suggests it functioned as a contemporary recommendation for a newly minted site of veneration, given Francis's own recent canonization in the same year and that according to Celano the altar in the self-same church was also dedicated to Francis. Such legends easily serve as the basis for a new sanctuary and provoke historians to approach the narrative with a pinch of salt, for such accounts are often invented or at least embroidered.[24]

But nonetheless, let us not dismiss the beautiful story of the nativity scene in Greccio too hastily. Celano wasn't able to narrate the whole without drawing attention to two infringements of the law that it is unlikely he would have fabricated. The first breach focused on the account that Francis purportedly read the Gospel in the Mass—this was the responsibility of the deacon, which from all we know Francis was not. It seems unlikely that Celano would resort to this if it were not to fill a gap in a story he knew to be true, otherwise he would have only validated one fabrication by creating another. Instead, he could have simply decided not to mention from the outset Francis's role as deacon in reading from the Scriptures. But perhaps more difficult to explain (Celano did not even attempt to) would be the fact that in celebrating the Mass in this location, the priest was not conducting the liturgy on a consecrated altar. We would have to imagine, then, that the unnamed priest was using a portable altar that had been consecrated to this use to avoid a massive transgression of canon law. So if we think the whole story is invented, these details could easily have been removed to make its entirety more believable. All these problems would have been unnecessary and even senseless to invent, suggesting that the narrative of the nativity in Greccio as a performative Christmas sermon likely has a historical core. The Christmas scene is above all a confirmation of the spiritual importance that the birth of Jesus had for Francis.[25]

As much as the account of the nativity scene lent a haptic dimension to salvation history, Francis's relationship with God was often not so concrete. For this we find evidence in a prayer Francis not only composed but wrote down. To this day, it is reverently protected as a relic in Assisi. It shows signs of use and of age, but there is almost no other object that transports us so intimately back to Francis himself. On the origins of the note we need to listen to Brother Leo, to whom it belonged:

> Blessed Francis two years before his death kept a Lent [a forty-day retreat] in the place of Mount LaVerna in honor of the Blessed Virgin Mary, the Mother of God, and of the blessed Michael the Archangel, from the Feast of the Assumption of the holy Virgin Mary until the September Feast of Saint Michael. And the hand of the Lord was laid upon him. After the vision and words of the Seraph and the impression of the Stigmata of Christ in his body he composed these praises written on the other side of this sheet and wrote them in his own hand, giving thanks to God for the kindness bestowed on him.

We will get to the question of Francis's vision and stigmata in due course, but in the meantime, the mention here of words of praise is important, leading to diligent editorial work and the partial reconstruction of this barely legible text. The words of praise contain elements of the dogmatic Christian tradition, for example, confession of the Trinity or God's omnipotence. But above all the text is concerned with the way that God can be grasped in his reflection through a variety of characteristics. Almost like a liturgical litany, there is in the text the repeated phrase "You are"—good or beautiful, life eternal or patience. Much is attributed to God, and in the context of Francis's life it will come as no surprise that in this phrasing we sense a kind of spontaneity, too, by which Francis pursued a chain of thoughts held together by association, climaxing in God's praise. Directly after God is characterized as joy ("Gaudium"), he is then connected to happiness ("Laetitia"). God is twice addressed as "our hope" ("spes nostra"), once in a list of positive feelings, once in the triad of the theological virtues of faith, love, and hope according to 1 Corinthians 13. A variety of ways of organizing the patterns are suggested, but in the end the importance lay not in the strict order of the concept.[26]

This text was not composed merely to carry meaning eight hundred years later. It emerged, as Leo suggests, from a very particular situation, and the blessing had value for Francis beyond the internal sequence of the prayer. This is exactly this point—that all forms of worship of God appear equally valid—that allows us to learn more about Francis's piety than any finely polished tract might offer. One who continually described God in new and different ways but at the same time stressed how God is one shows us through the multitude of terms that in the end the terms themselves are not what really counts in trying to capture the deepest experience of God. Put like this, we are on the verge of defining what Christian mysticism is all about.[27]

Indeed, we can say by way of summary that Francis in certain features of his spirituality picked up basic forms of mysticism. Perhaps this explains why he proved so irritating to so many of his contemporaries. A mystical posture can place an individual at a distance from the concerns of this world, which to some degree helps explain how to manage the confession of one's own sin. If sinning equates with too close a relationship with the world, then mysticism leads to a position that demonstrates no further need of the world. Pitched against Francis's break with his family and his past, mysticism might just have been the most understandable expression of spirituality for him ultimately to espouse. In the twenty-seventh of the *Admonitions,* we find an amazing sentence that summarized this position. Through careful lexicographic analysis, Jan Hoeberichts has called into question whether Francis wrote this text at all or whether it belonged to the monastic tradition more widely. But even if this contested theory were true, the fact that this admonition has entered the list and that the manuscripts point to its integral relationship with the other admonitions, we can say without doubt that he made it his own spiritually, even if he didn't write it himself.

> Where there is Love and Wisdom, there is neither Fear nor Ignorance.
> Where there is Patience and Humility, there is neither Anger nor Annoyance.
> Where there is Poverty and Joy, there is neither Cupidity nor Avarice.
> Where there is Peace and Contemplation, there is neither Care nor
>   Restlessness.
> Where there is Fear of God to guard the dwelling, there no enemy can enter.
> Where there is Mercy and Prudence, there is neither Excess nor Harshness.[28]

If praising God brings together all the divine attributes and orders them in relation to one another, then this text lists the various human attributes that reflect full submission to God's leading. The qualities named in the first few lines are entirely focused on God: love belongs to him, as does humility;

poverty refers to the spiritual poverty of which we have already spoken and that is in itself an expression of humility before God. Peace is that kind of peace after which Augustine, the early church father, strove when he said, "You made us for yourself and our hearts find no peace until they rest in you." And all these flow in the second to last line into the fear of the Lord, which is praised in Proverbs 9:10: "The fear of the Lord is the beginning of wisdom." Linguistically, the two uses of the word *fear* are identical, even though one in this poem is rejected and one is accepted. But this distinction can be made: it is not fear of circumstances or the pressures of the world that should direct our path, but only the fear of God, which most accurately today would be translated as reverence.[29]

This kind of anthropology, of which the least we can say is that Francis made it his own in this text, reflects the deep inner peace Francis had achieved, which he found not within but outside himself in God, enabling him to serve his neighbor with "misericordia," or mercy. Of particular significance is the way the poem ends, warning against overreaction in one direction or the other. And if we remember the early years of Francis, perhaps we can sense in these lines some kind of self-correction, a gentle critique of his own exuberance in that period, when his own actions were barely controlled—but perhaps also for that reason they were so impressive.

It would not be too much to say that Francis aspired to be the kind of balanced person who in such a dramatic way is presented before our eyes in the *Admonitions,* a balance that might easily be mistaken for an ancient philosophy idealized among the Stoics. But we shouldn't forget that for Francis, it was God who is the foundation of this kind of ideal, a God who can't be recognized as the result of human effort, an assumption common to both Francis and to most mystics too. All human knowledge would be of no avail in coming to know God, for "the Father dwells in light inaccessible and that God is spirit and . . . no one at any time has seen God" as the first admonition puts it. This warning is a combination of biblical quotations (1 Timothy 6:16, John 4:24, John 1:28), but together they provide a vision that has become central to the mystical tradition. Tracing its origins to the most important theologian of the mystical tradition, Pseudo-Dionysius the Areopagite (ca. 500), this tradition affirms that God is light, and therefore concludes that he can't be seen or recognized by human beings because light blinds as much as it illuminates. It appears that Francis shared these assumptions, though God is not entirely hidden, for in Christ God has made himself known. Again, for Francis, the incarnation was pivotal. It can be no coincidence that Francis paid particular attention to the prologue in John's Gospel (John 1:1–18), which speaks with such powerful images of the Word of God, who was with God and who came to this world by taking human flesh in Jesus Christ. But for Francis the enormous gap between the events of the incarnation and his own world was bridged by the Eucharist, where Christ again becomes visible, an idea that has already become familiar to us.[30]

The meaning of and emphasis placed upon Christ becoming visible again in the Eucharist in the form of the host make more sense with the background of the mystical spirituality of hiddenness, which was so encompassing for Francis. In physically eating the Eucharist a spiritual union with Christ is made possible: "And so it is really the Spirit of God who dwells in his faithful who receive the most holy Body and Blood of our Lord." When Francis stressed the physical presence of Christ in the Eucharistic elements, something shared with the proclamation of the Fourth Lateran Council, he did so not as an end in itself but as a means of explaining a spiritual event, enabling and deepening the meaning of Communion while not undermining the notion of really and truly eating and drinking the body and blood of Christ under the elements of bread and wine. If we were to further characterize this type of Christian mysticism, we would describe it as a church-sacramental mysticism: God's unknowability, the impossibility of putting his nature into words, does not for Francis end up, as it has done with other mystics, in distance from or critique of the church. Rather, it climaxes through the ministrations of the priest in the most important spiritual act of all, the Eucharist. It is here that the mystical experience of the Lord finds its fulfillment in the fellowship of Christians called to participate together in the Eucharist. Adding to his admonition to pursue humility, in the *Letter to All the Faithful* Francis promised that those who accept his admonition will experience the Spirit of God coming to rest on them and making his home among them. The presence of God would thereby create a new family: "They will be children of your Father in heaven, whose work they do. It is they who are the brides, the brothers and the mothers of our Lord Jesus Christ. A person is his bride when his faithful soul is united with Jesus Christ by the Holy Spirit; we are his brothers when we do the will of his Father who is in heaven, and we are mothers to him when we enthrone him in our hearts and souls by love with a pure and sincere conscience."[31]

That God is born in the soul of the believer, that the believing soul is brought into a nuptial relationship of love with Christ—these are tropes that are known in mystical spirituality and whose whole point was to establish the closest possible relationship between the Christian and Christ. They are pictures that try to capture the mystery of our union but in doing so sit uncomfortably with other images and create paradoxes: brothers—or, better, siblings (for women were included too)—were simultaneously groom and mother, which implies that a one-on-one correspondence was not the outcome sought—as we have seen already in discussion of the hermitages. Francis was swept along by the most intimate fusion of believers with one another and with God. This letter was directed to all Christians, but the promises Francis made are probably more readily applied to the community of the brothers or the sisters who had taken the path of penitence. It is worth noting too that his relationship with this religious community wasn't always as positive as such mystical notions might suggest.

The Scraps Thrown Away: The End of Leadership in the Order

If we tried to outline precisely the relationship between Francis and his order, we would have to say that the order soon outgrew the man. Indeed, "the Franciscans" may be in common usage to describe the order, but this doesn't officially appear in its title. We have seen already that at the outset Francis did not plan to found an order. His conversation with Cardinal John of St. Paul was not about expending effort to organize anything, not least integrating his movement into any traditional structure. He wanted his community to be something different, something looser, and as is so often the case with reform-minded initiatives, the point of his movement was to pursue not a certain form but particular content—a focus on Jesus Christ— which he tried to capture, as we have mentioned, in the original *Rule*. We can safely proceed, then, with the assumption that Francis exercised some kind of leadership function even before there was a title for him, which in the *Rules* would then be defined as the "minister-general" ("generalis minister"). He was to be a minister, a servant, as the official *Rule of 1223* defined it. And this was no doubt the way Francis understood his task too. But this kind of explanation doesn't in the end get us very far, for administration of the order didn't suit his gifts or his interests. In his *Chronicle,* Jordan of Giano described two tasks that any leader of an order had to fulfill: to accept new members and to comfort ("consolare") the brothers, which effectively meant pastoral care, despite the difficulty in defining the term exactly. This was where Francis could make his greatest contribution.[32]

His authority in the order was not as weak as the terms *minister* or *servant* might suggest. In his *Admonitions,* Francis wrote that he expected the brothers of the order not only to renounce the world and their possessions but, importantly, each should also give "himself up completely to obedience in the hands of his superior," though we have already seen how such obedience had its limits in the soul or the conscience of those who were subordinate, at least in liminal cases. The normal rule was clear that a subordinate had to submit his own will to the one set over him, even when an alternative seemed like a better option. In this way, the order demonstrated a clear command structure. That Francis was generally not keen to resort to this approach to authority we can observe in a memorable piece of writing. As noted in the blessing for Brother Leo, it has been assumed that this letter to Leo was also in his own hand. Hypotheses like this might rest on unstable foundations, but the text we have of the letter certainly goes back to Francis, even if he was not the actual scribe. We must still decide if the piece, directed to Leo, expresses goodwill or reflects certain tensions between them:

Brother Leo, send greetings and peace to your Brother Francis.

As a mother to her child, I speak to you, my son. In this one word, this one piece of advice, I want to sum up all that we said on our journey, and, in case hereafter you still find it necessary to come to me for advice, I want to say this to you: In whatever way you think you will best please our Lord God and follow in his footsteps and in poverty, take that way with the Lord God's blessing and my obedience. And if you find it necessary for your peace of soul or your own consolation and you want to come to me, Leo, then come.[33]

The actual manuscript of the text is not clear, and even scholarly scientific reconstructions have not produced an indisputable version of the text, which in the end was not merely the result of Francis's difficulties with Latin. One does have to proceed with caution in any interpretation of this letter. Perhaps we should understand the letter as Francis pushing

Leo away, advising him not to visit so often. But on the other hand, more positively, perhaps this letter gives us some clues about how the movement functioned to foster freedom among the brothers. Perhaps Leo was to decide for himself how to lead a life of poverty, and so the letter functions to encourage individual discernment in the way that someone might express their obedience to Francis, who is here deliberately narrowing his role to focus on pastoral care for his brother. It is surely significant that of all the possible metaphors to describe the relationship between these two men, the relationship of father to son is not chosen; instead the picture (as in the instructions for hermitages) is of a mother giving advice, not giving orders. We don't know exactly when Francis wrote to Leo, but whenever it was, the letter expressed an understanding of leadership that corresponded with the nonhierarchical character of the beginnings of the movement. And it is probably no surprise that we learn of this kind of leadership in a letter from one individual to another.

Francis's strengths were especially to be seen in his encounters with individuals. His spontaneity could be seen in the way he shook someone's hand or gave them a kiss, and his targeted words, as in this letter—despite later difficulties in interpretation—would certainly have meant something to Leo. But understanding how to lead the fellowship as it grew into a large movement proved too difficult for Francis. In fact, his experience with the brotherhood was not unlike other movements that trace their story from some kind of charismatic origins. Enthusiasm at the outset is not necessarily enough to bind a movement together for the long haul. Francis had to face the fact that the movement he had called together at the start had become too big to ignore the need for external structures. The various *Rules* came together in their ultimate form in the official *Rule of 1223*. Of course, this was just the visible expression of patterns that had been shaping the brothers' common life for some time. Once they had all been able to fit together in a barn in Rivotorto, but within a very short period they had had to confront the truth that their followers were spread throughout Italy and beyond. This expansion was a sign of success, but success brought with it its own challenges. An agreement across hundreds of kilometers was just not possible without the application of much effort. It wouldn't be hyperbolic to claim that the movement faced a crisis of growth—a crisis for the order as much as for Francis himself. The creation of the order might well have appeared to those coming later as a magnificent achievement, lasting for centuries, but truth be told: Francis was in over his head.

From the very beginning, the Portiuncula was the hub of all communication for the movement, and Francis had managed to create some kind of organizational structure around it. He determined that a chapter should convene twice a year, once at Michaelmas on September 29, and once at Pentecost in the spring, and both were to take place at the Portiuncula, as the Three Companions tell us, though the task the brothers set for themselves, to discuss "how to observe the rule more perfectly," might suggest some maturity in the movement, as might their desire to form the brothers into provinces for the sake of their mission. How the first meetings went, we can't really say. Some contemporary commentators were inclined to see the origins of the chapter early in Francis's biography, perhaps around 1213, but there isn't much support for this date. It is, however, quite uncontroversial to say that meetings of the chapter were expected in the year 1216. In his letter from Genoa, Jacques de Vitry mentions that the brothers would assemble each year to announce papal decrees. As he lists only one annual date for the meeting, it appears that the institution was still just in its infancy. Given the reference to papal determinations, it would be reasonable to conclude that this was referring to the regulations of the Fourth Lateran Council. Indeed, perhaps the council's discussions prompted the brotherhood to begin meeting in the first place, in order to implement the decrees in their fledgling movement.[34]

Jacques de Vitry takes for granted that the brothers who met for their chapter had come from all around Italy, and that after the chapter was finished, they scattered back to their homes. But it wouldn't be long before their movement spread even further. In his *Chronicle,* Jordan of Giano wrote that after the chapter of 1219 was over, the brothers were sent back to France, Germany, Hungary, Spain, and other provinces of Italy. It seems clear that by this stage the young movement had achieved an international organization with corresponding growth, though the challenge of long journeys to attend the annual meeting was a distinct downside. Perhaps according to this account, the organization had been in existence still earlier than Jordan had reported, for Jacques explains quite surprisingly that the year of the meeting was the tenth anniversary of Francis's conversion. Given that he dated the beginning of Francis's repentance as 1207 and also dates the year 1209 as the third year of his conversion, the facts don't quite fit together. The tenth year of Francis's change of mind would otherwise be 1216 or at the latest 1217, which on the other hand does fit with the details given by the Three Companions, though their reckoning is not entirely opaque either: they recounted that ministers were sent out into the provinces eleven years after the beginning of the "religio." If we were to translate this word as "order" or "community," as would most often be the case, then we can surmise that it was referring to the beginnings of the order in 1209 when it was sanctioned by Innocent, which would make the first meeting of the chapter something like 1220. Perhaps it is best, then, to assume that the Companions are referring not to the beginning of the order but to the beginning of Francis's life of repentance, meaning that we are back to believing that the first chapter meeting took place in 1217, which would match the details as we have them in Jordan's account.[35]

When we put all these observations together, we can conclude with just a little caution that regular meetings of the chapter began at the latest in 1216, perhaps a tad earlier, but assumed their legal status from this date, and that by 1217 a nationwide organization of the fellowship had been established. Jordan reports, based chiefly (it appears) on anecdotes, just how difficult some of these intercultural encounters were, given poor understanding of other languages and the limited knowledge of Latin by anyone other than the elite. So the story goes that a group of around sixty men, led by a certain John of Penna, set out for Germany, answering the question put to them wherever they went of whether they needed bed and board with a firm "ja" (as the Latin text literally states), meaning "yes." The result was that they found what they were looking for, so they persisted in answering every question they were asked in Germany with "yes"—including, unfortunately, the question put to them of whether they were heretics. Not surprisingly, this drew serious consequences with some measure of persecution, and according to Jordan meant that it was difficult for the Franciscans early on to get a foothold in Germany. Of course, this story may have been exaggerated, but it suggests nonetheless how complicated their mission may have been as they moved beyond their Italian home base. It is true that even their experiences may have been misinterpreted elsewhere: going barefoot in northern Italy is something very different from doing the same in Germany. Asceticism proved to be more observable and therefore more impactful in some places compared with others.[36]

Although their journeys had now become longer and more onerous—imagine for a moment what it would mean to cross the Alps—the meetings of the chapter were kept up, even if the ministers from regions beyond the sea and beyond the Alps were now given permission to attend just once every three years. The most famous meeting of the chapter was held in 1221, not least because of its sheer size, which must have been quite impressive. Several thousand brothers are said to have met together at the Portiuncula during Pentecost in 1221 (May 30), with Jordan of Giano estimating in his *Chronicle* around three thousand, and Thomas of Eccleston following Bonaventure in estimating five thousand. Even if the figures are inflated, they express that the number of delegates was in no way restricted but incorporated a great number of members of the quickly growing order. Included in this large number was Cardinal Rainer of Viterbo and other bishops. There were in fact so many that the brothers had difficulties finding accommodation in the small area immediately surrounding the Portiuncula, so it was just as well that many of them made huts with straw roofs ("umbracula"), leading to the meeting's nickname the Chapter of Mats. The whole event was both a celebration of the size and universality of the new community and a commemoration to welcome home Francis their founder after his journey to the Middle East. It had become clear that the small community, which in its corporate memory originally consisted of just twelve people who traveled together to Rome, had now become a mass movement. Of course this brought challenges—which everyone except Francis saw. It was possibly this meeting where it was decided to no longer include all the brothers as members of the chapter, but henceforward to invite only the ministers.[37]

It will come as no surprise that it was during this period of the movement's rapid growth that we see Francis withdrawing from active leadership. During his voyage to Egypt, Francis had already tested how the community might fare without his direct involvement. Unavoidably, his stay in Damietta meant a long period of absence from the Portiuncula and indeed from Italy. So Francis in the interim—according to Jordan's account—set up two "vicarii," or two representatives or substitutes, in his place. Between them they were assigned different tasks: Matthew of Narni would remain at the Portiuncula and take responsibility for admitting new members to the order. Gregory of Naples would take on the task of providing pastoral care for all the order in Italy. Unfortunately, he would later get himself into trouble, with Jordan reporting that in the meeting of the chapter both Francis's delegates enacted new regulations concerning fasting that Francis, upon his return, decided to waive. These difficulties no doubt contributed to the reason why in early records the incident did not get as much attention as it did in later writing. Around ten years after the original *Rule* had been awarded official status by Pope Innocent III, Francis had handed on responsibility for the order to others, which meant that the tasks had so multiplied that any absence of the founder—now viewed effectively as the minister-general of the order—required a replacement. Months of absence, it appeared, were now unthinkable. But the opposite was also true: Francis did not see himself as irreplaceable, as so many leaders have done and still do today. The journey to meet the sultan was more important to him than leadership of the order. And here we observe just how much Francis had already distanced himself emotionally from the order's day-to-day running. Perhaps we can even see what led to this state of affairs by examining other regulations. For example, in the unofficial *Rule of 1221* it becomes evident that there was not a common mind among the brothers in several important matters, especially when we recall the text from Acts 4:32 that describes the earliest Christian community in Jerusalem as being of "one heart and soul." Instead, there were daily disagreements. Apparently, it was necessary in the rule to require the brothers whenever they met to honor each other "without murmuring." This is one of the few regulations that is actually more precise and contains more detail in the official *Rule*: "And this is my advice, my counsel, and my earnest plea to my friars in our Lord Jesus Christ that, when they travel about the world, they should not be quarrelsome or take part in disputes with words."[38]

How Francis could imagine his order without disagreement can be seen in his "Letter to a Minister," who was apparently overwhelmed by his responsibilities. Francis admonished him strenuously, "There should be no friar in the whole world who has fallen into sin, no matter how far he has fallen, who will ever fail to find your forgiveness for the asking, if he will only look into your eyes." When pushed, the minister was to pursue compassion, even when the person standing in opposition to him didn't want to reach out for reconciliation. Indeed, the whole order of the community should be determined by sacrifice and thoughtfulness, not by doggedly pursuing the enforcement of law. But even including an instruction like this betrays the real situation of a community that had lost its cohesion. Very basic assumptions about life in a community needed to be guarded, and the rules themselves were doubtless a product of tedious balancing of interests and compromises with the reality of life, which probably only in part reflected what Francis really worked for among the brothers. And of course, his original goal had not been the formation of a larger community anyway. He had sought an alternative to the world he knew, along with the closeness of the Lord, but in the context of a community quickly getting out of control, he no longer found either.[39]

So, upon his return from Egypt, despite the only partial success of his experiment with vicars, he quickly set course to pass on the leadership of the order to others. His immediate successor in leadership was to be one of the brothers who had accompanied him from the very first, Peter of Catania. The handover took place during the chapter immediately after his return in 1220, and this exact year points to a further implication to the change of staff, for Hugolino at the same time became protector of the order. Peter of Catania thereby got extra support, or perhaps even supervision. According to Celano's account in his *Second Life,* Francis handed over responsibility before all the brothers of the chapter with these words: "From now on I am dead to you. But see, here is Brother Peter of Catania, whom I and all of you shall obey," promising the new minister-general obedience and deference. Of course, we run up against the same questions concerning the original sources here too, for this text could also function to alert later generations that even the widely venerated Francis did not pull back from pledging complete obedience to the new leader. As we will soon see, we could possibly come to a different conclusion in examining his *Testament,* and so see Celano's report as somehow dressed up. But even if everything happened just as described, there is still one issue in relation to the handover of authority that needs to be resolved. To this day it is possible for a predecessor to make trouble for successors through the sheer force of his presence. Francis was the founder of the order, and, at least in most accounts, he was the uncontested example whom others chose to follow, for we must not forget that he had privileged access to the pope as well as to Hugolino of Ostia, who remained responsible for the order. Any successor to Francis wouldn't have much room to play with, especially if Francis remained on the scene. Indeed, these very kinds of issues can be viewed through the titles that the new man at the top was awarded. In the *Legenda Perusina,* which recounted the same event, Francis submitted to a minister-general of the order, which was to be the way Peter of Catania was to be addressed. In other places, we come across the title "vicarius," meaning a mere representative, which would imply that Francis formally maintained authority in the order. The former is actually the correct title, but it didn't matter much, for Peter of Catania was not long in the job. On March 11, 1221, he died, having been minister-general for just less than a year.[40]

In reality, the leadership fell back to Francis. But if Jordan of Giano is correct, it appears that appointment of Peter's successor was more of a symbolic act. During that convening of the famous Chapter of Mats on May 30, 1221, the day of Pentecost, Francis had been so weakened by illness that he couldn't even manage to speak. So he got Elias of Cortona, a leader who had previously served as provincial minister in Syria, to speak some words on his behalf. He went beyond what was required to stress that he was not claiming leadership by virtue of his own authority: Francis sat at his feet and tugged at his habit. At this point, Elias leaned over toward Francis, listened to what he had to say, and then announced, "Brothers, thus says the brother." He was nothing more than Francis's mouthpiece, and certainly not the new minister-general.[41]

When on November 29, 1223, Pope Honorius III proclaimed the new and official *Rule,* it was still Francis who appeared to hold the office. In the rule's prologue, he expressly promised the pope his obedience, and the brothers were urged to be obedient to him. Sometime later, roughly between 1224 and 1226, he expressly described Elias as the minister-general, and this in a letter to the whole order, which just aggravated the tension further. Brother Francis described himself here as "the least of your servants, worthless and sinful," "an unworthy creature of the Lord God." Earnest humility accompanied his self-presentation here, but this humility was more form than content, more pious attitude than practical expression, for what followed was a series of imperatives—certainly a string of imperatives that took their lead from Jesus Christ, the true commander of faith, but imperatives nonetheless, beginning with the opening words of the sermon Peter gave on the day of Pentecost: "Men of Judea and all who live in Jerusalem, let this be known to you, and listen to what I say" (Acts 2:14). Christian history is full of attempts to express humility in the shape of the exercise of power, and his letter to the order suggests that Francis was not free of the temptation either. As much as he would repeatedly "ask" or "admonish," and as it were metaphorically kiss the feet of his listeners, in every line we observe Francis still trying to determine the course of the brotherhood. The authority he claimed was of course the authority of Christ and of the apostles, but it was also authority that stood in competition with that of the minister-general, who—if the official *Rule* had begun to take effect by this date—had been chosen by the meeting of the chapter. Francis had not. Those who understood the letter could be under no misapprehensions: "And so I beseech the Minister General, my superior, to see that the Rule is observed inviolably by all."[42]

Francis had said in the *Admonitions* that he would still obey his superior even if a different path proved preferable to him. But stating this publicly, in a letter deliberately addressed to the brothers of the fellowship, represented an undermining of the authority of the minister-general. Charismatic claims to leadership and formalized structures of leadership are not easy to marry, and Elias here had been discredited by someone who appeared untouchable, certainly not an enviable position to be in. This very kind of obstruction is easily understood when we acknowledge the frustrations the founder of the order must have felt. The appeal of the young son of the cloth merchant had once drawn many into his orbit, but now the realities of the community were increasingly at odds with its developing vision, and Francis was probably right. It wasn't he who had lost his ideals; the brothers had driven them out. From today's perspective, we might confidently say that this kind of dynamic is inevitable as an organization solidifies its structures. For Francis, it was indeed a most dramatic turn of events.[43]

Perhaps something of Francis's disappointment is captured in a fanciful way in the *Little Flowers*, with its historical core potentially seen in the text Francis dictated to Leo, which he had subsequently written down, the account of *True and Perfect Joy*. In this document, Francis was thinking through various possibilities of what might constitute pure joy, but he rejected them all: joy would not be complete if all Parisian masters joined the order, nor would it be complete if all prelates or leaders of the world were to join—no, not even the conversion of all Muslims would secure that kind of joy. It would prove its worth only if joy abounded even if he were to be ejected from his order, making humility the most important virtue. Significantly, there is a further story in which patience is tested. In this imaginary story, Francis arrived at the house of the brothers in Assisi, but the gatekeeper denied him entry, chastised him as an uneducated brother, and sent him to a hospital in the city. All this was of course as much fiction as the possibility that the king of England would join the order. But it was nonetheless a fiction whose foundation lay in a deep estrangement from his brothers. In his last years, Francis had become lonely. Even in his own order, he could find no end to his search and no reassurance in his troubles.[44]

Stigmatized: Between Wonders and Pious Deception

The loneliness Francis experienced was surely a part of the way of life he had chosen. Indeed, even the minister to whom he had once dedicated a letter had considered withdrawing from the community to become a hermit. At that time, Francis had been successful in dissuading him, but now Francis was himself increasingly drawn to the eremitical way of life. In one sense, this was a retreat to the beginnings of the movement when he wore the robes of a hermit. That Francis should long for those earlier days at the very moment when life was becoming more difficult was noted as well by Julian of Speyer: "He wished to turn back again to his early simplicity, abjectly to serve the lepers anew, and remove himself from human contact to the most remote places." One thing we can be clear about: he did indeed withdraw, though not by himself, as Celano emphasizes in the *Second Life*. Francis denied taking a brother as an assistant, though this did not mean that he was without company. He merely expected that in each place where he sojourned brothers might accompany him to the next location as they chose. This was not inconsistent with the status of being a hermit, nor with the rules of a hermitage. Among the brothers, there were apparently many who sought out the life of a hermit, so Francis determined to provide a rule for them too, outlining that hermits might live in groups of three or four. Of these, two would serve as "mothers" to the group, responsible for engaging with the outside world and so fulfill a role like that of Martha, while their "sons" devoted themselves entirely to contemplation. Their lives were thus shaped by ongoing prayer to God and silence in relation to other human beings, though they could speak for a time with the "mothers" after *terce*, the office held at the third hour, or with their superiors if they were present. It does appear that Francis from time to time lived as a hermit too, without technically committing himself to an eremitic rule. His period of fasting in 1224, according to Leo from August 15 to September 29, was effectively a kind of eremitic life, which he spent in La Verna, a rock elevation in the Apennines about one hundred kilometers northwest of Assisi, and this was not the first time he had done so. Indeed, Celano used the word *eremitorium* to describe its function, and Leo made clear that it was here that Francis received both the vision of the seraph who spoke to him and the stigmata as well—that is, the imprint of the wounds of Christ on his own body. Celano did not, it must be stressed, claim to be an eyewitness of these events.

This would be to make it all too simple, but what he came to understand from the Assisi "chartula," the parchment in Francis's own hand with prayers praising God on one side and on the other a prayer of blessing on Leo, was enough to make plausible the case for stigmatization, given Leo's closeness to Francis.[45]

However, concerning Francis's stigmata, the first person to give a report was not Leo but in all probability Elias of Cortona, the general-minister of the order and a close companion of Francis, though their relationship may not have been entirely happy. In the only extant version of a circular letter (and a late reproduction at that), a copy of which was sent to the province of Francia, Elias shared with the brothers that Francis, on October 3, 1226, had died. This letter is famous for its description of the dead body of Francis:

> And I now make known to you a great joy and a new thing among miracles. From the beginning of the world no such sign has been heard of, except in the Son of God, who is Christ. Not long before his death our brother and father appeared as one crucified, bearing in his body five wounds which are the very Stigmata of Christ. For his hands and his feet had as it were the holes of nails, pierced through on both sides, remaining as wounds and having the blackness of nails. His side also seemed to be pierced, and often bled.
>
> While the spirit still lived in him his appearance was not respected but rather despised, and there was no part of him but had undergone great suffering. From the tightening of the nerves his limbs had become rigid, as are those of a dead man; but after his death his appearance became most beautiful, shining with a wonderful light and giving joy to all who saw it. And his limbs which had been stiff became perfectly loose, so that they could be moved about according to the position in which he was lying, like those of some charming boy.[46]

The historian Richard Trexler has shown, however, that this text has been misunderstood, including even the date of its composition. The connection between the announcement of Francis's death and the description of the stigmata in the same text has led to the assumption that Elias saw the stigmata on the dead body of Francis. However, this is not exactly what Elias reports when we examine more closely the grammatical construction of the letter: while the description of the stigmata is in the past tense, Elias wrote about the corpse in the present tense, without mentioning the stigmata at all. Instead, Elias's point is substantially different, arguing that during his lifetime Francis's body had suffered terribly, bearing the ugly marks of tortured flagellation while conforming to the passion of Christ, with all his muscles contracted, but now after his death his body appeared relaxed, beautiful, and indeed resplendent. If we accept Trexler's persuasive philological argument, we would have to conclude that the absence of marks of Francis's suffering would mean the absence of the stigmata as well, meaning that they were an ephemeral phenomenon "not long before his death."[47]

In summary, along this line of reasoning, the stigmata should be understood differently from the way Celano and the Three Companions have presented the evidence to us, for in their presentation they stressed how the stigmata were visible on the dead body of Francis. Celano wasn't present at the death of Francis so he can't have seen the corpse. His report could be derived from the report of others but is more likely to be a determined embellishment of Elias's own announcement, which he wants to set right. In his account, many people came to see the corpse and to marvel at what they saw, which was not merely the holes in his limbs where nails had once been. He does use the same vocabulary as Elias, namely, "puncture" to refer to the holes, but Celano added further detail, describing how one could see not just the holes but the actual nails as well, "themselves formed out of his flesh and retaining the blackness of iron." As if this was not dramatic enough, Celano noted that Francis's appearance was like representations of Christ's crucifixion, with the heads of the nails visible in the palms of Francis's hands and on the upper surface of his feet, and in both cases the sharp points of the nails were visible on the other side emerging from the flesh.[48]

Even among Francis's contemporaries, Celano's influential depiction of the corpse of Francis was not without an alternative. The English Benedictine monk Roger of Wendover reported in around 1230 that the wounds of Christ were visible on the body of Francis up to fourteen days before his death, with crowds of people coming to Assisi to witness them. Francis interpreted them to the crowds as signs of Christ, though they disappeared upon his death. Roger might well have been distant from the location of Francis's death, but he did write close to the date of his death—just two years after Celano—providing a thirteenth-century interpretation of Elias's letter that aligns with Trexler's analysis. His linguistically important insights, suggesting the appearance of Francis's stigmata in life but not in death, are suggestive, perhaps even persuasive for our narrative. In the end, though, it was Celano's account of the stigmata that has powerfully shaped Francis's legacy, perhaps because of its literary characteristics and despite a problem it engendered: interpreting the phrase "not long before his death" not as two weeks—as Roger did—but as two years. It is Celano whom we must thank—alongside Leo—for the recurrence in art of Francis receiving the stigmata in La Verna two years before he "gave his soul back to heaven." Given that Francis carried the stigmata, according to Celano, for two years before his death and then after it as well, it is incumbent on Celano to explain how they remained concealed for such a long period of time.[49]

In the *First Life*, the only person apart from the happy Elias who is named as being an eyewitness of the stigmata is Rufinus, who once inadvertently touched the wound on the side of Francis while rubbing him down, likely to remove dirt from his chest, at which point Francis screamed with pain. It isn't hard to imagine that this story was likely a fabrication, or at least stood on shaky ground. The center of memory is Rufinus touching the wound, which, having read the account of Elias, he would understand to be the wound on Francis's side imitating Christ's own wound. Perception and interpretation clearly diverge here, though for Celano the story remained very important, and he repeated it in his *Second Life* without naming Rufinus as a source and added other brothers who either by happenstance or through cunning saw Francis's wounds while he was still alive, though the multiplication of witnesses is not especially trustworthy. Celano appears to be trying to shore up his account, which is further attested when we compare the changes he made between his *Brief Life* and the *First Life*. The few people who are said to have seen the wounds in the latter are in contrast with the many who saw them in the former. And it is not difficult to speculate on the reason for the changes, which Celano actually named in his *Second Life*: "Even the exposed location of his members did not permit it to remain concealed." Expressed more simply: Franciscans would always find it hard to conceal their hands and their feet, given their dress, though Celano also adds that Francis chose to wear socks to cover the wounds, or, when others asked to kiss his hand, would offer just his fingertips or cover his hands with his sleeve. Celano offers increasingly convoluted explanations alongside nameless witnesses in his attempts to defend the lack of visibility of Francis's stigmata. It would have sufficed to report in the *First Life* that Francis tried to cover the wounds.[50]

It is quite clear that Celano wanted to persuade doubters, who existed even in the Middle Ages. Questioning the veracity of miraculous events is not something only modern critics pursue. In his *Treatise on the Miracles,* Celano recounted in detail the story of the stigmata directly after the founding of the order, when he introduced the cleric Roger of Potenza in Apulia. Having just prayed before a picture of the newly canonized saint, suddenly he was plagued by doubts: "Was it really true that a saint might be glorified through a wonder like this, or was it just pious mocking by his followers? Perhaps it was faked, perhaps an invention, a feigned deception by the most daring brothers. It exceeds all human good sense and lies far from every judgement of reason!"[51]

Such reflections serve to prove that if one confuses medieval belief with gullibility one has misunderstood. Neither doubts nor searching questions based in reason were unknown. Of course, reality was approached with different assumptions and a different framework for understanding. And in this instance, Roger was shown to be wrong when God miraculously gave to him a wound on his hand that could be healed only through the intercession of St. Francis. But the fact that just such evidence was required to change his mind is significant, as was its placement in the narrative, connected to Celano's account of the wounds of Francis on the one hand, and the number of witnesses called on the other. The awkward introduction of the several witnesses, let alone their possible fabrication—Elias's evidence aside—suggests how precarious was the claim that Francis's stigmata appeared two years before his death. Even the notion that Leo affirmed the appearance of the stigmata during Francis's time in La Verna doesn't help much, for Leo was not a direct witness to the events, as much as we might wish him to be; he presented his case in dependence on Celano's literary construction.[52]

The connection between the vision of the seraph and the appearance of the stigmata, which Leo held together, also had its origins in the account of Celano. For much of modern scholarship, these two occurrences are understood to be two different occasions, though Celano and the Three Companions place them together in one episode, which for the Companions took place on the day of the Feast of the Exaltation of the Cross, September 14, 1224. On this occasion, Francis was said to have experienced a "visio Dei," a vision of God. It remains unclear whether this is to be understood grammatically as an objective genitive—that is, a vision of God himself like Ezekiel saw in Ezekiel 1—or whether a subjective genitive is to be preferred—that is, a vision given *by* God but not directly *of* God. Of course, it is perfectly possible that both are implied, for what Francis saw was a mixture of a man hanging on a cross bearing (according to the Three Companions) the characteristics of Jesus, as well as a seraph, a kind of angel, who had six wings, like the prophet Isaiah saw around the throne of God in Isaiah 6. It is worth noting that the details of the vision don't precisely match Isaiah's description of the wings, for Francis also saw elements of the vision of Ezekiel's chariot, around which the beings displayed just four wings, not six. Celano's account reads: "Two of the wings were extended above his head, two were extended as if for flight, and two were wrapped around the whole body." But we shouldn't be too surprised if details were adapted from the biblical text. On the contrary: visionary experiences often take up common knowledge and refashion it for new purposes.[53]

The historicity of the account of the vision finds extra support from the fact that it is quickly put into the service of the narrative of the stigmata. To invent an incident with such precise details as its dating in this context would be quite odd, for its meaning was self-evident even without combining it with the account of the stigmata. We can safely assume that the seraphic vision did indeed occur in September 1224, its meaning not entirely derived from the physical marks of Christ that appeared on Francis's body. Indeed, this interpretation is suggested by the biblical texts themselves. Isaiah's vision of the throne of God in the temple as well as Ezekiel's vision of the chariot of God both make possible a vision of God, though in the case of Francis the throne had become the cross of Christ, and the "appearance of the likeness of the glory of the Lord" (Ezekiel 1:28), which for Isaiah more directly spoke of the Lord himself (Isaiah 6:1), is understood by Francis to be the crucified one. In other words, Francis's vision was most literally a self-revelation of God in Jesus Christ, which had profoundly shaken him, as reflected in his own poetic expression of the incident. According to Leo, Francis's *Praises of God* were composed in La Verna, and if the dating of Celano and the *Legend of Perugia* is correct, Francis composed his *Canticle of Brother Sun* just a little later. It is perhaps the case that the period immediately after the vision was the most productive literary phase of Francis's life in which he, a restless exile in this world, learned to praise God and his creation.

However, his experience with the seraph wasn't only positive. In his presentation of the arrival of the brothers in England, Thomas of Eccleston recorded some further facts which, according to his account, go back to Leo and Rufinus. In his telling, Francis experienced not just a vision but heard Christ speak, promising that the Friars Minor would exist until the end of the world. However, Christ was also reported as saying something that Francis was never to repeat. According to Thomas, the seraph had apparently "treated him harshly." The whole incident didn't so much honor Francis as join together fear and fascination, as often in the tales of the saints. With these words Francis appeared not close to the example of Christ but distant from him, and Thomas further presented the vision of the seraph without any connection to receiving the stigmata.[54]

So we come to an impasse, at which point the seraphic vision no longer adds much further to our understanding of the stigmata. This in turn means that the theory of Oktavian Schmucki—that the stigmata are a psychosomatic consequence of the vision—doesn't hold water. He maintains that the supernatural origins of the Franciscan view of history lie in the vision, but then reaches for natural processes to advance the story, physical and psychological processes that easily conform to twenty-first-century insights. But without due understanding of the context of such an impressive event, his theory becomes even harder to maintain, especially after he has himself acknowledged that identification between Francis's and Christ's sufferings played no central role in Francis's piety. Instead, Schmucki's narrative concerned following Christ obediently, not conforming to Christ, which would be something quite different. If we take seriously the notion that we can know more about Francis's internal rather than external biography, at this point we are able to say only this: what we know about Francis's spiritual life, a conception of piety that is to be clearly distinguished from the much more intense and mystical piety focused on the passion embraced by the Cistercians, doesn't necessarily suggest a psychic identification with Christ that has physical ramifications.[55]

These considerations might just as easily be applied to a commonly preferred insight among more recent scholarship, which sees the wounds of Christ experienced in the body of Francis as the result of a stigmatization that Francis in some ecstatic state inflicted on himself. Indeed, in this period there were several examples of self-crucifixions. In Oxford in 1222, just four years before Elias's letter concerning the stigmata of Francis, a man was punished by the authorities for having inflicted on himself the five wounds of Christ. Something similar happened in Huy in France, and it was Jacques de Vitry, no less, who paid such great attention to the Franciscans who reported the fact. These instances are striking and might confirm the thesis of Christoph Daxelmüller that Francis was responsible for his wounds, not with the intention of deceiving but as a consequence of mystical rapture in imitation of the drama of the passion. These kinds of reflection draw their strength from their connection to the nature of piety from the medieval period: Francis is contextualized. But context might have the opposite effect too under closer investigation, for we see that Francis's passion piety is more reserved than his contemporaries', giving us cause for suspicion, even if his spontaneity makes it difficult to rule it out.[56]

We return to the question of the date of the stigmata's appearance. Daxelmüller and Helmut Feld chiefly follow Celano and share the problems his account prompts: even if the wounds were self-inflicted, how might they have remained unnoticed for two years, or how might they have remained unhealed? Daxelmüller resorts to the theory that the nails accidentally bent and couldn't be pulled out, leaving gaping wounds over those two years, an explanation that feels as contrived as the one provided by Celano. Even given Elias's reference to the stigmata's appearance "not long before his death," it would seem improbable that a man as sick and near to death as Francis over a number of months could imagine inflicting such painful torture on himself, let alone the immense physical exertion it would take to carry out the act, and the fact that in his last months he was cared for with great devotion by friends who watched over him constantly. Finally, if self-stigmatizing were widespread, there is no reason why it should be kept secret, as Elias seems compelled to do, though he felt free to describe the vision. Of course, these acts were sometimes connected to heretical ideas, like the case in Oxford, but in other instances, like that of Marie of Oignies (d. 1213), we get no sense of theological error—Jacques de Vitry, her spiritual companion, recounts that her self-inflicted injuries reflected her extraordinary spiritual journey. However, in her case, we can't be sure if her wounds pictured the wounds of Christ, though her story is to be read within the broader context of her day, as Paul Bösch correctly avers: "Stigmata, which are intended to show a similarity with the Son of God . . . are judged as blasphemy by the church and are punished strictly. However they are tolerated and perhaps even interpreted as signs of holiness when they . . . are acknowledged to be an expression of suffering with the crucified Jesus." In short, self-inflicted stigmata would not necessarily be condemned by the church, and as a consequence would need neither to be hushed up nor hidden.[57]

We return, then, one more time to the letter of Elias, with the interpretation of Trexler as our conversation partner. With reference to Elias's words, we might suggest that the theory of self-stigmatization places too much weight on the physical phenomenon itself. And the theory of self-stigmatization doesn't actually explain very well why Elias placed so much emphasis on the change to Francis's body after his death, in which case one would have to assume that the wounds had healed in the course of his life and that a second stage of his transformation came with the relaxation of the muscles and tendons of his body, which according to Elias was connected to the end of the signs of the passion on his body. It might just be easier to understand from his account that the stigmata were an ephemeral and temporary phenomenon, which in Elias's words appeared like a vision but then disappeared just as quickly.[58]

It must also be said, however, that for Elias the meaning of the stigmata was not incidental. It was clear for him that the stigmata were not of human but of divine origin, given his use of the word *miraculum* and his introduction, which spoke of his message of great joy, alluding to a biblical text that at the beginning of the twenty-first century still has some currency: Elias is referring to the appearance of the angels to the shepherds in the Christmas story, proclaiming their jubilant message, which points not to any instance of human stigmatization but to God's intervention in human history. He also used the language of "appearance" to refer to Francis being like the crucified one, which in the Latin New Testament ("apparuit") is subsequently used to describe the miraculous appearance of the resurrected Christ (Luke 24:34), his being made contemporary to his world. How all this happens was not explained. Elias gave no physical description or explanation at all—unlike Celano later—but rather did the opposite. Elias wrote of his hands and feet having "as it were the holes of nails." He is not claiming to have seen a physical transformation but to have received a vision of Francis bearing the marks of Christ on his living body just before his death, and he attributes the vision to a miracle of God that only he witnessed. Perhaps we can explain the whole event in this way: Francis's body as it neared death bore some fresh marks on the skin that might have appeared similar to the wounds of Christ, but in the medieval world, where visions were accepted as means of God's self-expression, such a naturalistic explanation was not adequate to understand the event. Elias's witness to the stigmata of Francis doesn't sit easily with the more prominent models of modern research, for example, supernatural causation, deception, psychosomatic illness, or self-stigmatization. Elias saw the wounds instead as visionary reality.[59]

Elias's chief presuppositions for understanding the stigmata were biblical, so we need to introduce another category of interpretation: mental-spiritual context. There had been no precedent in Christian history through which to understand the nature of stigmatization, but contemporary attention to biblical texts as well as to developing medieval theology and spirituality pointed to new resources for understanding. For example, when Francis positioned himself as in some sense on a par with the apostles, of which those around him were fully cognizant, he paved the way for a new understanding of his relationship with Christ himself and of being conformed to his image. After all, the apostle Paul had written metaphorically, "I carry the marks of Jesus branded on my body" (Galatians 6:17). It was just this verse that Elias cited in the description of Francis's stigmata. Carolyn Muessig has pointed out the rich interpretative history this verse has enjoyed since late antiquity, in which the marks had often been used to refer to imitation of the apostles, if not yet a Christ-shaped spirituality. With this background in mind, whether referring to the wounds in a physical sense or in relation to their appearance in a vision—as the term *apparuit* might suggest—Elias might well have wanted to convey that not long before Francis's death (that is, shortly before it), he saw on the body of the Umbrian apostle several wounds, which then promptly disappeared from his spiritual sight. In the stigmata, following in the footsteps of the apostles and the experience of bearing wounds like Christ might merge.[60]

This in all likelihood was the beginning of the story about the physical marks of Christ on the body of Francis. And theologically, this story reinforced the notion of Francis's conformity to Christ in his discipleship, which probably had its own origins in the voice Francis heard speaking from the cross in San Damiano in the first place. Beginning with the call to follow the model of the apostles, Francis, like Paul, was to bear the stigmata of Christ. Further, harkening back to the Christmas proclamation, Elias went on in his circular letter to proclaim the meaning of the stigmata was to make of Francis an "alter Christus," a second Christ. As the Companions state, "Through the tenderness of his compassion he was transformed into a living crucifix." Following Christ had led to transformation by him.[61]

The End

Elias did not merely report on the stigmata. He recalled as well the battered and tortured body of Francis. Throughout his life, Francis had been plagued by sicknesses. Even handing over leadership of the order had not been for spiritual reasons alone. Many accounts of the transition of leadership mention his illnesses. At forty years of age, his body was simply exhausted. He has asked too much of his body, or others had expected too much of him. Perhaps his early experience incarcerated as a prisoner of war had contributed to his weaknesses, or maybe the strenuous adventure to the Middle East exacerbated his pains. Most of all, the Franciscan lifestyle had exacted a heavy burden on his body. Sickness was a constant theme in his later years. Celano frequently references his ailments without specificity, but there are some notable exceptions: his liver infection, an enduring eye disease, probably chronic conjunctivitis that he contracted in Egypt, and perhaps he came down with malaria in the Middle East as well.[62]

We must also not exclude the long period of fasting at La Verna, and perhaps the impact of the vision of the seraph so shook him that it instigated a new health concern. The *Legend of Perugia* recounts that two years before his death in 1224, the period in which *The Canticle of Brother Sun* was composed, Francis had to spend more than fifty days in San Damiano under the care of Clare and her sisters. It was at this time as well that Elias of Cortona exhorted Francis to see a specialist eye doctor, which Francis had long refused to do, in part perhaps motivated by his longing for death. Further, the admonition of Elias of Cortona expressly mentioned Thomas of Celano at exactly the point in the narrative when Francis had already received the stigmata. Taking these hints together, we can safely assume this period of illness occurred in the fall of 1224, immediately after his stay in La Verna. His stay in San Damiano, then, would have been a time of healing from both his sickness and his eye surgery, which Francis finally relented to undergo, the consequences of which were apparently excruciating. Celano's report is gruesome in the details: a glowing hot iron cauterized his face from his cheek to his eyebrow. From that day to his death, Francis wore a bandage around his head to cover the scars.[63]

Celano describes exactingly the disease that flared up in the spring of 1226. Francis was undergoing treatment for his eye in Siena when he experienced severe stomach pains, perhaps the result of an injury or at least debilitating weakness, which resulted in him coughing up blood. After this incident, he regained his energy and was able to set out again, traveling to Le Celle near Cortona, though not without experiencing swelling of his belly and feet, perhaps caused by water retention, itself a consequence of his stomach gradually failing. There was now no doubt for Francis that he was preparing for death. It was likely at this point that he dictated a text he named "my testament." Because he owned nothing, this last piece of writing was not going to concern the transfer of possessions—instead, one more time, Francis undertook to explain the nature of his mission.[64]

At the end of his life, Francis experienced significant tension with his pragmatically oriented successor in the order, Elias. Consuming all Francis's remaining energy, this tension became active competition between these two men, their two models of leadership, and two justifications of authority. This context helps us to grasp how the various autobiographical fragments of Francis's life were drawn together in the face of impending death to provide an example for the brothers to emulate. Just as in the earliest period of his ministry, so at its conclusion Francis began to stress—perhaps unlike ever before—what was so important for his proclamation: the power of lived example, which words would never be able to match. The memory of a penitent life or care for the lepers had more to do with the power of example than mere storytelling.

Given the later impact of this piece of writing on the question of poverty, it would be easy to miss its main point: Francis's concern for good order among the brothers. He impressed upon the order the importance of obedience to the priesthood as well as obedience within the order itself, and he reminded the brothers of the importance of observing the daily offices. It is not hard to guess that Francis imagined challenges would come to the community after his death, for the order had already struggled with the nature of discipline within its life as well as with the authority of clergy in local parishes. Francis wanted to call the brothers to order, so it would be easy to suggest that from this perspective Francis's *Testament* bore some extremely conservative characteristics. Looking at this document alone, one would be hard pressed to describe Francis as a critic of the church, though in its reception history it did have some quite radical implications. Obedience to the church and in the church were concerns that drove Francis to his dying day.[65]

The radical credentials of his *Testament* grew out of those statements concerning the way of life of the fellowship, for example, the admonition not to accept "poor dwellings" unless "they are in harmony with the poverty which we have promised." Yet even this claim was later to cause great dissension during the controversy about poverty, for making holy poverty the measure for decision-making had its own challenges. It is not easy to understand Francis at this point. His sentences lead into one of the many tensions the religious world of the Middle Ages had to endure, for the life of the poor brothers was attractive to those born rich as well. Not that the rich necessarily wanted to take the vow and enter the order, but many did want to support the order through donations. Whoever might have wanted to grant to the community housing might also have hoped to receive a reward in the afterlife. It may not have even registered with many of the donors that such a great gift could create great tensions for those striving to honor vows to poverty that had proved so attractive to them at the outset. Truth be told, it may not have dawned on many of the Friars Minor either. This was the cutting edge of Francis's *Testament,* probably nothing more.[66]

His reference to the vows established in the *Rule* was clear evidence that in his *Testament* Francis was not striving to create any competition with the *Rule.* Rather, he explained that his new work might help the brothers to "observe in a more Catholic way the Rule we have promised to God." His *Testament* was expressly not to be a new *Rule* or another *Rule*; it was to function more like a binding explanation of the *Rule.* Holding his *Testament* in such high esteem, he instructed even the minister-general of the order not to add or take anything away from "these words," though it is true that in its context "these words" could apply to the text of the *Rule* as well as the instructions in the *Testament.* He was to read from them both at meetings of the chapter. Francis elsewhere in the *Testament* reassured his brothers that he esteemed the minister-general as his lord and intended to be obedient to him, refusing to take any step without his approval. But here he is not positioning himself under the minister-general but placing the minister-general under his own authority as binding rule-giver over him. He may well refer to himself as "Brother Francis, worthless as I am," but immediately he began to lay down regulations for the brothers: "In virtue of obedience, I strictly forbid any of my friars, clerics or lay brothers, to interpret the Rule or these words, saying, 'This is what they mean.'" It is difficult to imagine how any minister-general could have room to shape the community in the light of the will of this kind of founder.[67]

Francis's *Testament* embodied the great personal authority of the founder, but this would not be sufficient authorization from a legal perspective. It was entirely justifiable that immediately after Francis's death Pope Gregory IX made clear that only the *Rule* was legally binding, not the *Testament.* In his bull *Quo elongati,* he proclaimed on September 28, 1230, that the brothers were in no way bound to Francis's *Testament,* for it had no power in the law to bind the brothers or later generations. This was of course true. But the papal bull did nonetheless leave behind a bad taste, for rather than resolving tension it reignited ongoing and burning questions concerning the role of poverty in the order. A formal legal act drew a thick line under the charismatic enthusiasm that Francis experienced and engendered.

Almost at once after Francis's death the pope profited from Francis's sanctity. His bestowal of the status of saint on Francis was something that Francis had paved the way for in the last weeks of his life through the way he staged his own death. The performative nature of the event became the message itself: Francis died as a peacemaker who had drawn closer to Jesus on this earth than any other had. The performance required Francis to return to his hometown, where the local people received him with jubilation and praise: "The whole multitude of the people hoped that the holy one of God would die close by, and this was the reason for their great joy." Of course, this comment by Celano could sound cynical, reflecting as it did the hope of the town that they might profit from a saint's death within their walls. Even today, this small Umbrian town benefits from Francis tourism. But their joy had much deeper religious reasons too, for it was connected to Francis's longing for death, which would open up the door for Francis to take the last step toward God. Death was not his end but instead the fulfillment of life in this world and the beginning of life in the next.[68]

And the path to the next world he now began to shape. Having arrived in Assisi, he was provided accommodation and medication in the palace of the bishop, a more comfortable alternative to the hard and cold conditions in the Portiuncula. Yet even with medical support, Francis deteriorated quickly. Sensing how rapidly the end was drawing near, he requested to be carried down the hill to the Portiuncula. There he gathered the brothers around him. According to the *Second Life* of Celano, Francis gave a short speech in which he impressed on them the counsels of the Gospel. Then he pronounced a blessing on Elias of Cortona and the other brothers, with Celano not failing to draw our attention to the biblical allusions behind this action, for example, Jacob the old man who blessed his sons or Moses who blessed Israel. The brotherhood had once upon a time consisted of twelve men, like the earliest band of the apostles, who themselves were the new Israel, reflecting the twelve tribes that were blessed by Jacob and gathered around Moses. Francis's blessing was his way of placing his own movement into the narrative of salvation history as much as it was his farewell to the world. Together, Francis and the brothers sang praise to God, and Francis absolved all the brothers, those absent as well as those present, of their sins and blessed them. The peace of God that had been such a central part of his message was to shape these final moments as well. Just as he had once instructed an unknown minister to show mercy to every brother, no matter the sins he had committed, now Francis himself practiced what he preached and exercised patience and mercy.[69]

According to Celano's *Second Life*, Francis requested some bread, and he "blessed and broke it," quoting literally the words of Matthew 26:26 describing Jesus at the Last Supper. Francis's actions bore some resemblance therefore to the Eucharistic celebration, and it cannot be excluded that a Eucharist actually took place, though it could never be described in this way, for that would imply that Francis took upon himself at this moment a role only permitted to priests. Then the concluding chapters of John's Gospel were read out loud, beginning with chapter 13, where Jesus bids farewell to his disciples. Seventeen years earlier, Francis had made sure on his way to Rome that he would be counted among a group of twelve disciples and not the thirteenth as an outsider, but now it was clear that his twelve were being left behind, just as Jesus had once left his own disciples. Never previously in his life had Francis so equated himself with the person of Christ as he did through the choice of this Bible reading at his bedside. And yet its message still retained some ambiguities, for the Gospel that was read was primarily intended to offer him comfort. However, it did create a context in which the discovery of the marks of Christ on his body could later be interpreted.[70]

Then Francis lay down naked on his garment of sackcloth, and as a sign that he would soon return to dust and ashes, was strewn with ashes himself.

He died as night fell, on the evening of October 3, 1226, on the floor of the Portiuncula, where his brotherhood had first been founded. "And at the will of God it happened that his holy soul was released from his body and passed to the Kingdom of heaven at that place where, while he was still in the flesh, the knowledge of heavenly things was first given to him."[71]

A Man from Far Away

RANCIS LIVED WITH THE DEEP AWARENESS THAT death will not have the last say. He hoped for a new life, a different life. And his heirs did not stop at the description of his death either. After recounting those last moments, Celano went on to describe how Francis was laid to rest. Not surprisingly, Francis had outlined his wish that he should be buried in the Portiuncula, but this wish was to go unfulfilled. With the worry that conflict with Perugia could lead to his body being stolen, it was decided to entomb him safely within the city walls of Assisi, so he was buried in the church of San Giorgio, "where he had first learned his letters and where he later first began to preach." The massive church dedicated to his memory that today stands over his grave had not been built when he died. In 1230, his bones were secretly removed from the Portiuncula and brought up the hill to be reinterred. They remained hidden until 1818 when efforts were made to locate his sarcophagus.[1]

But even by the time his mortal remains were transferred to the church that now sits so majestically over his grave, Francis had already been canonized as a saint, which Celano includes in his *Life*. On July 16, 1228, Gregory IX could complete—not long after the beginning of his pontificate—what he had set in motion while he was still Cardinal Hugolino. Francis, whom he had protected, was now a saint, offering his protection to the pope. Yet the pope also made sure that the power that emanated from the saint did not grow excessive. In the bull *Quo elongati*, he set boundaries on the saint's influence, though they were essentially in vain, for a hundred years after his death Franciscans were still engaged in debate over the role of poverty in the life of the order. It is easy to see how difficult it was to pin Francis down.

He was to be a saint, but that meant for some a heretic or, in contemporary language, a rebel. There are so many concrete pictures that make Francis approachable, but in the end we are still trying to grasp the wind. Compliant follower of the pope, prophet of the council, determined preacher of judgment—they are all Francis too. It is just not possible to reconcile the tender poet of *The Canticle of Brother Sun* with the man who damned those who believed wrongly about the Lord's Supper. The fragmentary evidence that we have isn't easily knit together to create a picture of the whole.

Of course, there are many elements in the story that we readily recognize. The conflict with his father and his turn to the church are basic building blocks of Francis's life. Rupture with his family came before his positive decision to pursue something different. Francis's path can largely be understood in terms of generational conflict, which in his case was also social conflict, because his father's attitudes magnified the concerns about wealth and money in his own age. The growing protest with his father was, however, not transferred into protest against the church. Francis stood on the periphery of, perhaps even outside, the civic community of his day, whereas he advanced toward the center of the church. His alliance with the papacy was not an accidental outcome of his life choices—instead, it was the most consistent consequence of them. And it was this very tension that marked out his historic setting. He held up a mirror to the society of his time with particular intensity, and he saw clearly how the church could hold up a mirror to it as well. He was deeply embedded in his age, both in rejection and integration, yet he stood over it too insofar as he preached repentance, not drawing attention to analysis of the economy. His service focused on individual human beings who were prone to lose out through the workings of the thirteenth-century economy—and this has ready application to the twenty-first-century economy too.

However, any analysis falls short if we don't take into account another theme of his life, his spontaneity, which shaped him profoundly at the beginning but was still in evidence at the end. In his attempts to let his deeds and not just his words do the talking, his spontaneity led the way to his life's conclusion. Francis was not the kind of person who imagined the future conceptually or from first principles; instead, he needed advisers again and again to help him direct his spontaneous outbursts into productive paths, from rupture to rebuilding. The priest in San Damiano before whom he had thrown down the money was perhaps the first of his counselors. Bishop Guido followed after that, then the priest at the Portiuncula who explained to him Christ's commissioning sermon, then Bernhard, Hugolino, the ministers-general . . . The list of names of those he depended on to help him find clarity was long. Of course, we might reproach them for their self-interested advice, which shaped or perhaps misshaped Francis, thinking of the frustrations of the last years of his life. But in the end, they contributed significantly to his life by giving his ministry shape and longevity. Francis began a movement that in the end he was not able to control. As the brotherhood grew increasingly large, he lost the capacity and indeed the appetite to continue to lead it. Instead he chose solitude and gave up leadership, although he couldn't really release himself from involvement. This is perhaps the most problematic characteristic of his life, making the job of his counselors so difficult. His desire for autonomy is covered up in the hagiographies when they explain this tendency in terms of competition with the ministers-general or by outlining his dependence on others, both of which suggest the limits of his influence. Behind these caricatures we glimpse a man who was more shaped by what he received than what he gave.

Above all, he wanted to receive from someone in particular. He knew his life was led by God, both in the good and despite the bad. His repentance was an expression of the demands of God on his life, and the greeting of peace represented the demand to live an apostolic life, or to live according to an apostolic rule. His was a life that pointed away from himself to Christ, while at the same time he strove to honor Christ's active presence in this world, not wanting to forget the importance of resisting the devil's ever-present wiles. The presence of Christ found its climax in the Christmas celebration at Greccio, and for others more than for him in the experience of the stigmata. It is here that the most profound meaning of his life is to be understood. Whoever wanted to say something about the externals of his life ended up describing him as unprepossessing or even repulsive. But it was in exactly this way that he was happy to be the bearer of the divine message. This was itself an expression of the incarnation, which was so important to him. God, who took flesh in this world, takes the lowliest up into his service. This was the way Francis understood and presented himself. But this doesn't relieve us of the tensions he experienced, for through these means he asserted his highest authority right up until the very last words he wrote down.

This is how the fragments we have present the man. They don't always provide a complete picture. But we wouldn't expect less of a man whose personality prized spontaneity. And anyway, flat personalities are not always the most interesting ones. Through the individual pieces we sense the charisma that drew others in but that never allowed their bearer to find real peace. Fragments remain, the fragments of a life. In the distance we meet a man who was seeking but never found his purpose in life fulfilled. And a man who simply will not let us grasp him either.

Chronology

1181/82	Birth of Francis to Pietro and Pica (?) Bernardone
1193	Birth of Clare
1202/3	Francis's imprisonment in Perugia
1206	Francis's break with his father
1208 or 1209	Francis's personal experience of being called through Christ's commissioning of the apostles in Matthew 10, expounded by a priest in the Portiuncula
1209	Recognition of the brotherhood by Pope Innocent III in Rome
1211	Clare's flight from her family
1215	The Fourth Lateran Council begins in November
1216	The death of Innocent III and the election of Honorius III as his successor
1217	Restructure of the order into six provinces (presumably at the Pentecost meeting of the chapter on May 14); Francis's meeting with Cardinal Hugolino in Florence
1219/20	Francis's journey to the Middle East, where he preached a sermon before Sultan al-Malik al-Kamil
1220	Francis steps back from the position of minister-general; Peter of Catania takes on the role of leading the order
1221	Peter of Catania dies; Elias of Cortona takes on the role of minister-general May 30: Meeting known as the Chapter of Mats takes place
1223	Completion of the *Regula bullata* (the official *Rule*), confirmed by Pope Honorius on November 29; December 24/25: Celebration of the nativity in Greccio

1224	August 15–September 29: Francis fasts in La Verna and experiences the vision of the seraph; Francis is cared for in sickness at San Damiano; perhaps at this time he composes *The Canticle of Brother Sun*
1226	April/May: Francis experiences a hemorrhage in Siena, then journeys to Assisi; completion of Francis's *Testament*; October 3: The death of Francis in the Portiuncula

Glossary

Abbey:	A monastery under the independent leadership of an abbot, whose title, derived from the word meaning "father," goes back to the Rule of Benedict in the sixth century, featuring a community life shaped like a kind of spiritual family.
Albigensianism:	See Catharism.
Bishop:	A leader in the hierarchy of a church who exercises legal authority over priests and other clerics of his diocese. The bishop serves under the archbishop and the pope. Often the bishop's ecclesiastical responsibility was caught up with secular rule as well.
Canon law:	Since antiquity, the church has organized its internal life with legally binding legislation, including jurisdiction over matters like marriage, which in many places today fall under the authority of civil law. The canon lawyer Gratian assembled these laws in the twelfth century in the text *Decretum gratiani,* expanded and updated since that time in the *Corpus iuris canonici,* which had authority throughout the Middle Ages. In 1917, the Roman Catholic Church replaced this text with the *Codex iuris canonici.*
Cardinal:	Originally, cardinals were the clergy serving the main churches of the city of Rome. They have traditionally assisted the pope in the leadership of the church. In 1059, a new decree established that only cardinals could participate in the election of a pope. From the twelfth century, the title of cardinal could be awarded to dignitaries outside the city of Rome as well.
Catharism:	A twelfth- and thirteenth-century movement beginning in Provence in the south of France that taught radical ideas concerning the piety of poverty. The doctrine developed to establish a dualism between spirit and matter, God and the world. Because the Cathars' headquarters were in Albi, they were also known as Albigensians. The church proceeded against them brutally with inquisitions and a crusade (1209–29).
Chapter:	The name given to a meeting of clergy or other leaders in the church whose responsibility it was to administer the business of

their common life. At each meeting a chapter of the Bible or the rule of the order was read aloud, giving rise to the term.

Clergy: Office-bearers in the medieval church who were differentiated from the laity by their ordination vows and were therefore answerable to the requirements of canon law.

Commune: The name given to some medieval Italian cities that were the subjects of their own law (not answering to external authority), sometimes exercising rule over surrounding territory.

Crusades: Since the seventh century, the holy sites of Christendom were under Islamic rule, so in the year 1096 a crusade was called for the first time to send "armed pilgrims" to the Holy Land to expel the Islamic armies and to reconquer the area for Christ. Over the next century, crusader states emerged in the eastern Mediterranean. Militarily powerful waves of invasion proceeded against the occupiers of the Holy Land and occasionally as well against internal threats or heretics such as the Cathars.

Curia: The central administrative organ of the papacy since the eleventh century.

Custos: The leader of a group of houses within a province in the Franciscan order.

Diocese: An administrative geographical unit of the church led by a bishop.

Eucharist: A sacrament, based on the instructions of Jesus to his disciples during the Last Supper, celebrated by the bishop or priest who administers the bread and the wine to believers. During medieval debates, the belief emerged that in the element of bread, also known as the host, Jesus Christ was bodily present.

Excommunication: Exclusion from the means of grace of the church, especially the sacraments.

Feudalism: The medieval economic order in which the nobility, under the auspices of the prince, exercised authority over a given territory, the "feudum," where both free persons and slaves labored. This was a system of control built on mediated power and dependent relationships.

Friar: A member of a mendicant order. Francis insisted that the Franciscans were to be organized as a fraternity, not like a community of monks.

Guild:	An organization of tradesmen or merchants in the Middle Ages. Guilds oversaw qualifications for admission into their membership, and their members were subject to certain rights and responsibilities.
Habit:	A type of clothing adopted by monks and friars that distinguished their order.
Hagiography:	A form of biography memorializing the lives of saints that began in the early church with legends or texts that were read aloud. These texts, later expanded to become *Vitae,* or *Lives,* praised the saint to a high degree, shaping their life in terms of their holiness.
Heretic:	One who contradicts the true teaching (orthodoxy) of the church. A particular sign of heretics was their determined opposition to the received truth, in contrast to those whose error could be corrected. It is often observed how heresies in the medieval church developed as a function of claims to authority.
Holy Roman Empire:	The political entity that took shape after the collapse of the kingdom of the Franks. When the imperial crown of the Western Roman Empire was bestowed on Otto II in 962, power was thereby aligned with German claims to rule in central Europe. Following the model of the coronation of Charles the Great in the year 800, any successor as emperor was also to be crowned by the pope. The Holy Roman Empire was the result, ruling over central Europe and northern Italy, and lasting until the abdication of Francis II in 1806.
Host:	See Eucharist.
Laity:	Members of the local church who were not ordained as deacons, priests, or bishops.
Liturgy:	The performance of the Eucharist, from the Greek word *leitourgia.* The medieval church service was built around this highly symbolic representation of God's active presence in the lives of the worshippers.
Mendicants:	Orders established in the thirteenth century in which the vow of poverty was taken so seriously that their members pursued begging to provide for their physical needs.
Monastery:	A building that provided for the common life of monks, consisting primarily of the monastic church; the refectory, where they ate; and the dormitory, where they slept.

Mysticism:	A form of piety in which it was assumed that human beings could experience unity with God. Important representatives are Bernard of Clairvaux in the twelfth century and Meister Eckhart in the fourteenth century.
Neoplatonism:	An adoption and adaption of the philosophy of Plato (d. 348/347 BC). The Neoplatonism of late antiquity taught that the diversity and plurality of the sensory world emerged from the unity of the spiritual or divine reality. This contrast between spirit and matter permeated medieval thought, mediated through the writings of Pseudo-Dionysius the Areopagite (sixth century) and Augustine (354–430), feeding into the teachings of mysticism.
Nobility:	The aristocracy of medieval society. In the Middle Ages it was assumed that human beings, through birth, belonged to a particular station in life, with the chief categories consisting of the nobility, who were free, and those dependent on them, who were not. Those living in cities were also free, though not necessarily of noble birth, as were the clergy, through the merits of their ordination.
Order:	A religious organization of the Middle Ages. The first monasteries followed particular rules, though they weren't necessarily bound to one another. In 910, the monastery in Cluny based on the Benedictine Rule was founded, but it was organized as an association of several monasteries. From this beginning emerged the model of an order featuring central leadership over houses in a large area.
Orthodoxy:	The correct doctrine of belief. In principle, each Christian fellowship understands itself in terms of its orthodox teaching, which is a collection of beliefs defined by the Holy Scriptures and the councils (synods) of the church. More narrowly understood, those churches in fellowship with the patriarch of Constantinople in the eastern Mediterranean are known as Orthodox churches, especially after the split with the western churches in 1054. Apart from the Bible, their foundations are the seven councils of the ancient church from the fourth to the eighth century.
Papal bull:	A document that has been authorized with the binding administrative seal (bull) of the pope.
Penance:	The path of reentry into the church after commission of a mortal sin: blasphemy, unchastity, or murder in the ancient church. From the early Middle Ages, the categories of sin requiring penance

through auricular confession were expanded, and a predictable process was established through which the penitent expressed his contrition, offered his confession before a priest, and was given a penalty to perform. After the Fourth Lateran Council of 1215, such penance was regarded as a sacrament of the church and was required to be performed annually.

Pope:
The leader of the western Latin church. In late antiquity, the bishop of Rome emerged with this authority, based on his position as the successor of Peter who, according to Matthew 16, was the rock on whom Christ built his church, thus leading to the papacy's claims of universal jurisdiction over Christendom.

Priory:
A monastery led by a prior, who generally was subordinate to an abbot or to another figure of authority in an order.

Regular clergy:
Those clergy who lived in a community based on a rule, especially the rule of Augustine.

Relics:
The body parts of dead saints. Understood to be filled with holiness, these were distributed and often placed within the altars of churches; following the literal interpretation of Revelation 6:9, this practice would secure the protection of the church.

Sacrament:
According to Augustine a sign (in Latin *signum*) that represents a thing (*res*) that is holy, through which human beings participate in salvation. Since antiquity, the central sacraments were baptism, the Eucharist, and penance. After the death of Francis, sacraments were understood to also include confirmation, marriage, ordination, and last unction.

Saint:
In many ecclesiastical traditions, saints are those who through an exemplary life have experienced the presence of Christ in a special way. At the outset, they were martyrs but later other expressions of sanctity attested to their status as saints, especially their love of neighbor. After their death, they would proceed directly to heaven where they could hear and answer prayers, although they were not to be worshipped, that privilege belonging to God alone. In the medieval church, processes were developed to establish the saintly status of such individuals.

Scholasticism:
A style of medieval theology pursued originally by bishops and monks but adopted around the year 1200 in university settings too. Its method was to unite revelation and reason, leading to attempts to prove God's existence and methodology saturated by philosophical reasoning in service of theological questions. The

universities used Aristotelian philosophy, which had become more familiar to them through increasing contact with the Arab world.

Secular clergy: Clergy who did not live according to a rule or in community with others, instead fulfilling their vocation as individuals in pastoral ministry.

Stigmata: The five wounds of Christ inflicted by the nails in his hands and feet, as well as by the spear in his side, representing signs of his suffering, and experienced by an ardent believer.

Synod: A gathering of dignitaries of the church whose task is to make decisions on behalf of members of that church. It might represent a local region or a province, or, as a general synod, it can function as a council of the universal church.

Notes

As noted in the translator's foreword, locating information for Marion Habig's *St Francis of Assisi* and other primary texts has been standardized for the reader's convenience. The title of the text (or a summary title) is followed by the paragraph or section being quoted, with the page number after a colon.

CHAPTER 1. GETTING CLOSE TO FRANCIS

1. Appelbaum, *St. Francis of America*, 13, 82, 110, 118, 130; Francis, *On Care for Our Common Home*.

2. An explanation of the Franciscan question in English can be found in John Moorman, *The Sources for the Life of S. Francis of Assisi*.

3. Grau, "Thomas von Celano," 99–102.

4. Julian of Speyer, "The Divine Office of Saint Francis," 327; see also Julian of Speyer, "Life," 368–420. Strictly speaking, there may even be some questions concerning Francis's own writings, for the quality of their Latin varies, suggesting perhaps that he employed various secretaries over the course of his life. Thomas of Celano [hereafter referred to simply as Celano], *An Umbrian Choir Legend*, 473; Thomas of Eccleston, "Coming of the Friars Minor," 15:177.

5. There is no English translation of the *Vita brevior*; see instead Celano, *Das neuentdeckte Franziskusleben*; *Legend of the Three Companions*, 1:887. See also Celano, *Second Life*, 359; Johannes Fried, *Der Schleier der Erinnerung*.

6. *Legend of the Three Companions*, 1:887, 888. Lehmann, "Die Dreigefährtenlegende," 602, translation mine.

7. Anonymous of Perugia, "Johannes von Perugia (Anonymus Perusinus)," 573. The text of John of Perugia must be distinguished from the *Legenda Perusina*, which probably dates from the late thirteenth century but contains individual references to eyewitness accounts that possibly go back to the immediate circle of companions.

8. Francis, *The Testament of St Francis*, especially 69, where we read that God inspired Francis to write down these words "plainly and simply." Historically, however, there is great agreement that the Franciscan rule came from a gradual redactional process in which the brothers were also involved, as well as Cardinal Hugolino of Ostia. Here Francis obviously accentuates his own importance in creating the rules in order to link their validity more closely with his person.

9. See, for example, Lehmann, "Franz von Assisi," 73, who argues that the path to Francis's biography is "thorny, but signposted in such a way that one can walk it" (translation mine).

10. See Celano, *Treatise on the Miracles*, 6:404, where a man who "with the old enemy deceiving him," doubted the stigmatization of Francis.

11. This assumption is more or less shared by Feld, *Franziskus von Assisi.*

12. Luther, "Leben als Fragment."

13. The concept of perspective seems to be more appropriate for the present context than the metaphor of a "veil of memory."

14. For further on the Franciscan question, see Moorman, *Sources.*

15. Appelbaum, *St. Francis of America,* 7.

CHAPTER 2. RUPTURE

1. *Legend of the Three Companions,* 10:899, 23:913; Celano, *First Life,* 16:242.

2. See further Cusato, "Francis and the Franciscan Movement," 18; Riley, "Francis' Assisi," 400.

3. Feld, *Franziskus,* 100; *Legend of the Three Companions,* 2:891.

4. Celano, *Second Life,* 3:364.

5. Thompson, *Francis of Assisi,* 6; *Legend of the Three Companions,* 2:890; Celano, *Second Life,* 3:364.

6. Celano, *Second Life,* 3:363, 364; Celano, *First Life,* 120:334. See further Andrews, "The Influence of Joachim in the 13th Century," 221.

7. Celano, *Second Life,* 3:363.

8. Celano, *First Life,* 1:229–30, 2:230–31, 3:231–32.

9. See Celano, *Das neuentdeckte Franziskusleben,* 2, translation mine; Celano, *Second Life,* 3:363–64; *Legend of the Three Companions,* 3:891–92.

10. Celano, *Second Life,* 7:366.

11. Celano, *First Life,* 2:230; Francis, "Letter to All the Faithful," 96; Francis, *Testament,* 68. See also Hoeberichts, "The Authenticity of Admonition 27," 502.

12. Flood, *Francis of Assisi,* 100.

13. Francis, *Testament,* 67.

14. Celano, *First Life,* 7:235.

15. Celano, *First Life,* 6:233, 234, 7:235.

16. Celano, *Second Life,* 4:364; *Legend of the Three Companions,* 4:893.

17. Celano, *First Life,* 3:231–32; Feld, *Franziskus,* 108.

18. Celano, *First Life,* 4:232; Julian of Speyer, *Life,* 2:370.

19. Celano, *Second Life,* 5:365; *Legend of the Three Companions,* 6:894.

20. Celano, *First Life,* 4:232; Hoose, "Francis of Assisi's Way of Peace?" 452; Moore, *Pope Innocent III (1160–1216),* 67; Anonymous of Perugia, "Beginning or Founding of the Order," 5:35–36; *Legend of the Three Companions,* 5:894; Celano, *First Life,* 5:232–33; see also Thompson, *Francis of Assisi,* 10.

21. Bonaventure, *Major Life,* 5:232–33. On Francis's relationship with weapons, see further Hoose, "Francis of Assisi's Way of Peace?" 453; and McMichael, "Francis and the Encounter with the Sultan," 129.

22. *Legend of the Three Companions,* 6:895.

23. Celano, *Second Life,* 6:365–66.

24. *Legend of the Three Companions,* 5:894, 6:894; Celano, *First Life,* 5:233; Julian of Speyer, *Life,* 3:371; Anonymous of Perugia, "Beginning or Founding of the Order," 6:36.

25. Anonymous of Perugia, "Beginning or Founding of the Order," 4-7:34-37.

26. Julian of Speyer, *Life*, 3:372; Celano, *First Life*, 6:234; *Legend of the Three Companions*, 12:901.

27. Cusato, *Early Franciscan Movement*, 12; *Legend of the Three Companions*, 11:900-901.

28. *Legend of the Three Companions*, 11:900; Wolf, *Poverty of Riches*, 10; Rotzetter, "Die Entscheidung des hl. Franz für die Armen," 34, translation mine.

29. *Legend of the Three Companions*, 11:900-901.

30. Celano, *Second Life*, 9:370.

31. Anonymous of Perugia, "Beginning or Founding of the Order," 4:34-35.

32. Celano, *First Life*, 6:233-34, 7:235; *Legend of the Three Companions*, 7:896; Celano, *Second Life*, 9:369; *The Sacrum Commercium*, 1549.

33. Celano, *Second Life*, 8:368; *Legend of the Three Companions*, 8:897.

34. *Legend of the Three Companions*, 9:897-98.

35. *Legend of the Three Companions*, 10:898; "The Legend of Saint Clare," 280.

36. Feld, *Franziskus*, 127; *Legend of the Three Companions*, 10:898-99; Celano, *Second Life*, 12:372, 8:368.

37. Celano, *First Life*, 8:236.

38. Anonymous of Perugia, "Beginning or Founding of the Order," 7:36; Celano, *First Life*, 9:236-37.

39. Celano, *First Life*, 9:237; Anonymous of Perugia, "Beginning or Founding of the Order," 7:36-37.

40. Celano, *First Life*, 18-20:243-46; Celano, "Legend for Use in the Choir," 2:319.

41. Celano, "Legend for Use in the Choir," 2:319; Julian of Speyer, "Divine Office," 11:333; *Legend of the Three Companions*, 13:903; see also Feld, *Franziskus*, 118, where this incident is described as the first instance of a talking crucifix in Christian history.

42. Francis, *Testament*, 68; Celano, *Second Life*, 10:370, 11:371.

43. Celano, *Treatise on the Miracles of Blessed Francis*, 2:401. Note that this version of the *Treatise on the Miracles* does not include accounts that were already included in Celano's first two *Lives* of Francis, from which reference to the crucifix and the stigmata are notable omissions; Celano, *Second Life*, 11:371.

44. Celano, *First Life*, 88:303; Jordan of Giano, *Chronicle*, 1:20; Celano, *Second Life*, 10:370; "The Prayer before the Crucifix," 103.

45. Bonaventure, *Major Life*, 2:641; Celano, *First Life*, 10:237; *Legend of the Three Companions*, 16:907.

46. See Celano, *First Life*, 10-15:237-41; *Legend of the Three Companions*, 23:913.

47. Celano, *First Life*, 10:237-38, "The Legend of Saint Clare," 9:287; Anonymous of Perugia, "Beginning or Founding of the Order," 8:37; *Legend of the Three Companions*, 23:913.

48. Celano, *First Life*, 10:238, 11:238.

49. Celano, *Second Life*, 4:364.

50. Celano, *First Life*, 12:239; *Legend of the Three Companions*, 17:907.

51. Celano, *First Life*, 14:240-41.

52. Celano, *First Life*, 13:239-40. This account bears some resemblance to the story in 1 Kings 3, where a mother is in anguish at the possibility that her son would be divided in two by the command of King Solomon. Celano's account makes this interpretive layer

feasible, though it does not describe precisely the emotions of Francis's mother. *Legend of the Three Companions*, 19:908.

53. *Legend of the Three Companions*, 19:908. The office of the consuls existed from 1198 to 1212, though another office called the *podesta* (functioning like a mayor) had operated alongside the consuls from 1204, and subsequently instead of the consuls from 1212, presumably as a result of the growing power of the middle class. Celano, *First Life*, 16:242: His later retreat to the monastery of San Verecundus, however, might suggest a different interpretation of the results of the appearance before the consuls.

54. How to align the ministry of Bishops Guido I and Guido II with the life of Francis is not easy. In this book, I take it that Guido II began as bishop in Assisi in 1212, which means that the decisive events in Francis's life—the trial with his father, Clare's flight, and the trip to Rome—all took place under the episcopal leadership of Guido I. See *Legend of the Three Companions*, 19:908-9. Thompson argues that Guido "now preferred to serve as mediator between son and father, rather than acting as judge." See Thompson, *Francis of Assisi*, 14.

55. Celano, *First Life*, 15:241; *Legend of the Three Companions*, 20:909.

56. *Legend of the Three Companions*, 19:909; Celano, *First Life*, 15:241.

57. Bonaventure, *Major Life*, 5-6:643-44; Celano, *First Life*, 16:242. For further explanation of the role of clothes in premodern societies, see Rublack, *Dressing Up*.

58. Celano, *First Life*, 16:242, 17:242.

CHAPTER 3. RENEWAL

1. *Legend of the Three Companions*, 21:911.

2. *Legend of the Three Companions*, 21:911.

3. *Legend of the Three Companions*, 21:911; Celano, *First Life*, 24:248.

4. *Legend of the Three Companions*, 21:911, Celano, *First Life*, 21:246, where his decision regarding clothes was further connected to his labor at the Portiuncula.

5. *Legend of the Three Companions*, 21:911, 912, 30:919; Anonymous of Perugia, "Beginning or Founding of the Order," 12:38; Bonaventure, *Major Life*, 7:645; Celano, *First Life*, 21:246. Here Celano notes that it was the third year after Francis's conversion when he finished his work repairing churches, demonstrating congruence with the account of the Three Companions (*Legend of the Three Companions*, 27:916), which describes others joining Francis's movement two years after his conversion. The end of Francis's building work could therefore be either 1208 or 1209, though 1209 is to be preferred, given the dating of his original commission at the beginning of a calendar year.

6. Celano, *First Life*, 21:246.

7. *Legend of the Three Companions*, 22:912.

8. Francis, *Testament*, 68; *Legend of the Three Companions*, 24:913; Riley, "Francis' Assisi," 420.

9. *Legend of the Three Companions*, 23:913; Anonymous of Perugia, "Beginning or Founding of the Order," 9:37.

10. Francis, *Testament*, 68; Celano, *First Life*, 22:246, 88:303.

11. Celano, *First Life*, 22:247; *Rule of 1223*, 2:58-59, compared with *Rule of 1221*, 2:32-33.

12. See Cusato, *Early Franciscan Movement*, 69-80. See also Lapsanski, "The Autographs on the 'Chartula,'" 19; Celano, *First Life*, 22:247.

13. *Legend of the Three Companions*, 25:915; Julian of Speyer, "Life," 15:379; Jacques de Vitry, *History of the Orient*, 1610. For more on the relationship between Francis and his clothing, see Wolf, *Poverty of Riches*, 16.

14. Celano, *First Life*, 23:247; Cusato, *Early Franciscan Movement*, 52f.; Anonymous of Perugia, "Beginning or Founding of the Order," 18:41-42.

15. *Legend of the Three Companions*, 25:915-16; Celano, *First Life*, 23:247.

16. Francis, "The Blessing Given to Brother Bernard," 159.

17. Celano, *First Life*, 24:248. Although it is likely true, this observation concerning his prayer life runs counter to the narrative and intention of the earliest biographies, which stress his life of poverty.

18. Celano, *First Life*, 24:248; Anonymous of Perugia, "Beginning or Founding of the Order," 10:37-38; Jordan of Giano, *Chronicle*, 11:26, 12:28.

19. *Legend of the Three Companions*, 27:916; Celano, *First Life*, 24:248.

20. Anonymous of Perugia, "Beginning or Founding of the Order," 10:37-38; Celano, *First Life*, 24-25:248-49.

21. Celano, *First Life*, 24:249.

22. *Legend of the Three Companions*, 28-29:917-18. The question in the account of Anonymous of Perugia is left open according to the will of God, in which case less is assumed from Bernard's perspective relative to the Companions'. The argument presented here suggests that John of Perugia stresses the authority of Francis more pointedly, while the Companions in their formulation of the question maintain a tradition in which Bernard's authority is preserved.

23. *Legend of the Three Companions*, 28-29:917, 918; Anonymous of Perugia, "Beginning or Founding of the Order," 11:38. The nature of the oracle played an increasingly important role in the second wave of biographical writing in the early 1240s, and therefore perhaps suggests a secondary construction of the events. Even Francis's own words in his *Testament* (14) that Christ gave him the Gospel do not necessarily relate to the events surrounding the oracle. Celano, *First Life*, 93:307-8.

24. *Legend of the Three Companions*, 30:919. In this account, we see that Francis carried no money with him, so he had to take the money out of Bernard's pocket, though this might be a later reflection of the Franciscan community, which rejected money (see *Rule of 1223*, 4:60-61, 5:61), or perhaps an attempt by the Three Companions to maintain some distance between Francis and the movement's finances.

25. Celano, *Second Life*, 15:375.

26. *Legend of the Three Companions*, 32:920, 35:922; Celano, *First Life*, 25:249; *Legend of the Three Companions*, 1:887. The discrepancy between the versions is not resolved if, as some scholars suggest, the letter originally circulated independently of the *Legend* itself. See *Legend of the Three Companions*, 41:929, and also the title of the section: "The acceptance of four other brothers; and the ardent mutual charity of the first brothers, and of their eagerness to work and pray, and of their perfect obedience."

27. *Legend of the Three Companions*, 27:916. Innocent III had declared that monks were to be tonsured to be ordained priests, which did not apply to a brotherhood. There is some disagreement, however, of whether Francis was actually ordained as a deacon, for he read the Gospel in a liturgical setting, according to Celano, *First Life*, 86:1. Of note is that Francis

in his *Testament* both included and excluded himself from the order of clergy. See Francis, *Testament*, 67–70. Pope Lucius III (r. 1181–85) first decreed that lay preaching was forbidden during controversies with the Waldensians. See further Monti, "'Deservedly Approved'"; *Legend of the Three Companions*, 33:922, 35:922–24, 51:937.

28. *Legend of the Three Companions*, 30:919. The precise date of Silvester's entry to the fellowship is contested, whether it was before or after the establishment of the structure of the brotherhood, though it is clear that he was among the earliest of followers.

29. *Legend of the Three Companions*, 46:933. It was no coincidence either that Celano had earlier counted them as a group of seven: Celano, *First Life*, 25:249, 31:253. The first of these not to be included in the twelve was John of Perugia, who was later described by Francis as a leader among the twelve: Anonymous of Perugia, "Beginning or Founding of the Order," 31:48–49.

30. Anonymous of Perugia, "Beginning or Founding of the Order," 31:48; Thompson, *Francis of Assisi*, 25, suggests that Bernard was elected due to his superior education; *Legend of the Three Companions*, 41:929, 37:926.

31. *Legend of the Three Companions*, 35:922–23, 33:920.

32. There appear to be two distinct departures in the *Legend* (*Legend of the Three Companions*, 33:920 and 37:926), unlike the single mission in Celano. They seem consciously to reflect the ordered missionary journeys of the apostle Paul. See Celano, *First Life*, 29:252, 30:252–53, where numbers and pairings are plastic, and where the eighth man remains unnamed. See Julian of Speyer, "Life," 19:381, which reflects the later decision of the Franciscan provincial chapter of 1219 to send pairs out to the earth's four corners. Anonymous of Perugia, "Beginning or Founding of the Order," 15:40.

33. Julian of Speyer, "Life," 17:380.

34. Celano, *First Life*, 30:253.

35. *Legend of the Three Companions*, 38:926–27; Anonymous of Perugia, "Beginning or Founding of the Order," 23:44.

36. *Legend of the Three Companions*, 43:930.

37. Celano, *First Life*, 43:264–65, 42:264; *Legend of the Three Companions*, 55:939; Bonaventure, *Major Life*, IV/3:655, IV/2:654; *Legend of the Three Companions*, 55:939; *Rule of 1221*, 9:39.

38. Celano, *First Life*, 44:265–66; *Legend of the Three Companions*, 55–56:939–40.

39. Celano, *First Life*, 39:262.

40. Flood, *Francis of Assisi*, 50; "The Acts of the Process of Canonization of Clare of Assisi," 17:193; Celano, *First Life*, 39:262; Francis, *Testament*, 68; *Rule of 1221*, 7:37, 9:39, 40; *Rule of 1223*, 5:61, 6:61; Cusato, *Early Franciscan Movement*, 35; Flood, *Francis of Assisi*, 16; Cusato, "Alms-Asking and Alms-Giving," 62.

41. Francis, *Testament*, 68.

42. Francis, *Testament*, 68; *Legend of the Three Companions*, 32:920, 55–56:939; Cusato, *Early Franciscan Movement*, 14; Celano, *Second Life*, 57:412.

43. Celano, *First Life*, 32:254.

44. Celano, *First Life*, 32:254.

45. Francis, *Testament*, 68; Celano, *First Life*, 32:254. Perhaps the first chapter of the *Rule of 1221* gives some sense of the core of the original. See further Cusato, "Francis and the

Franciscan Movement," 21. Providing frequent biblical references is not a feature of the *Rule of 1223*, making it less like a traditional rule.

46. Francis, *Testament*, 68.

47. Bonaventure, *Major Life*, IV/10:653; Celano, *Second Life*, 16:376–77. Both Bonaventure and Celano use the verb *contrahere*, which can be used to describe a legal marriage vow, though it can also be used, as is likely here, to denote an illicit one. Dalarun, "Francis and Clare of Assisi," 16; *Legend of the Three Companions*, 51:936. There is some sense of Francis as representative of Christ in Bonaventure, *Major Life*, III/5:648–49.

48. Bonaventure, *Major Life*, III/10:652–53.

49. Concerning the visions of Innocent III, see further Goodich, "Vision, Dream and Canonization Policy," 153.

50. It is likely that there are two levels to the story, a diplomatic one and a hagiographical one. Celano, *First Life*, 32:254–55; Anonymous of Perugia, "Beginning or Founding of the Order," 32:49, 36:50–51. See also Monti, "'Deservedly Approved,'" 6.

51. Anonymous of Perugia, "Beginning or Founding of the Order," 32:49; *Legend of the Three Companions*, 47:934; Celano, *First Life*, 33:255.

52. *Legend of the Three Companions*, 48:934; Anonymous of Perugia, "Beginning or Founding of the Order," 33:49; Bonaventure, *Major Life*, III/9:652.

53. Celano, *First Life*, 33:255; Jacques de Vitry, "Letter of 1216," 1608.

54. Cusato, "Francis and the Franciscan Movement," 21.

55. Celano, *First Life*, 38–39:260–62; *Rule of 1221*, 37. Here Celano names them as "the Order of the Friars Minor," which appears to be another example of an early structure for their community.

56. "The Legend of Saint Clare," 1:280.

57. See Clare, "The Testament," 8:60, where she makes the only comment we have about her youth, when she lived in the "unhappy vanity of the world." It is noted, however, that this remark might be weakly supported as it fits within the stereotype of a conversion narrative. "Acts of the Process of Canonization of Clare of Assisi," 17/1:192, 18/2:193, 19/2:194–95; "The Legend of Saint Clare," 3:282.

58. "Acts of the Process of Canonization of Clare of Assisi," 17/7:193; Celano, *First Life*, 36:259; "The Legend of Saint Clare," 5/4:283–84; "Acts of the Process of Canonization of Clare of Assisi," 17/3:192; Thompson, *Francis of Assisi*, 46.

59. "Acts of the Process of Canonization of Clare of Assisi," 3/29:161. The narrative appearing here mentions Clare sucking Francis's nipples, the taste of which was so sweet to her. While we might think this implies erotic dimensions, we should recall that in Marian piety of the Middle Ages, she was often portrayed as *Maria lactans*, a breast-feeding mother, suggesting that Francis is presented here in such terms, just as elsewhere he might have been presented in Christ-like terms. *Rule of 1221*, 12:42.

60. "Acts of the Process of Canonization of Clare of Assisi," 17/3:192; Francis, "Form of Life," 76.

61. Clare, "Testament," 60; Jacques de Vitry, "Letter of 1216," 1608.

62. *Rule of 1221*, 12:42; *The Form of Life of Saint Clare (1253)*, 8/2:119–20.

63. Thompson, *Francis of Assisi*, 46; "The Legend of Saint Clare," 7–8:285–87; Godet-Calogeras, "Francis and Clare," 117, argues that Francis and Bishop Guido had planned this together as a sign.

64. "Acts of the Process of Canonization of Clare of Assisi," 13:185; "The Legend of Saint Clare," 7:286.

65. This account follows the narrative in "The Legend of Saint Clare," 285. See also "Acts of the Process of Canonization of Clare of Assisi," 12:183; "Papal Decree of Canonization," 8:265.

66. "The Legend of Saint Clare," 8:286.

67. Clare, "Testament," 25:61; "Acts of the Process of Canonization of Clare of Assisi," 12:183; "The Legend of Saint Clare," 8:287, 9:287, 24:303, 25:303. Clare's sister Beatrice and mother followed her later as well.

68. "The Legend of Saint Clare," 10:287; "Papal Decree of Canonization," 9:265.

CHAPTER 4. MISSION

1. Anonymous of Perugia, "Beginning or Founding of the Order," 19:43.

2. *Legend of the Three Companions*, 54:938.

3. Celano, *First Life*, 26:250.

4. Francis, *Testament*, 67; Francis, "Letter to a General Chapter," 107.

5. Francis, *Testament*, 68; *Rule of 1221*, 14:42; *Rule of 1223*, 3:60; Celano, *First Life*, 23:248.

6. Celano, *First Life*, 23:248.

7. Celano, *Second Life*, 4:364.

8. *Legend of the Three Companions*, 11:900.

9. *Legend of the Three Companions*, 26:916.

10. Hoeberichts, "Franz von Assisi und seine Begegnung mit Muslimen," especially 212n19.

11. Celano, *First Life*, 72:289.

12. Francis, *Admonitions*, 2:79, 4:80.

13. Francis, "Letter to All the Faithful," 97, 98; Francis, "The Second Version of the Letter to the Faithful," 69.

14. *Rule of 1221*, 21:46–47.

15. Francis, *Testament*, 67.

16. *Rule of 1221*, 23:50; Celano, *Second Life*, 108:451. It appears that this story has developed from a relatively sparse depiction of demonic possession into something more fanciful.

17. Francis, *Admonitions*, 15:83; Thomas of Split, "Chronicle," 808.

18. Francis, *Admonitions*, 14:83, 8:82.

19. Celano, *First Life*, 77:293–94, 23:247.

20. *Legend of the Three Companions*, 54:938.

21. *Rule of 1221*, 17:45.

22. Celano, *Second Life*, 163:493; Celano, *First Life*, 72:289.

23. Celano, *Second Life*, 163:493; Francis, *Testament*, 67–68; Francis, "Letter to St Anthony," 164.

24. Francis, "Letter to St Anthony," 164; *Rule of 1223*, 5:61.

25. Thomas of Split, "Chronicle," 808; Bonaventure, *Major Life*, IV/4:655; *Rule of 1221*, 21:46–47.

26. *Legend of the Three Companions*, 58:942–43; *Rule of 1221*, 17:44.

27. *Legend of the Three Companions*, 54:938; Celano, *First Life*, 62:281.

28. Celano, *First Life*, 62:281.

29. Celano, *First Life*, 63:281.

30. Celano, *First Life*, 63:281, 282.

31. Jacques de Vitry, "Letter of 1216," 1608–9.

32. Celano, *Treatise on the Miracles*, 13:408; Bonaventure, *Major Life*, II:630–787, I/1–6: 635–40; Vauchez, *Francis of Assisi*, 74.

33. Bonaventure, *Major Life*, II/1:753; Celano, *Treatise on the Miracles*, 40–41:419–20.

34. Celano, *First Life*, 50:271.

35. Celano, *First Life*, 48:269–70, 68:285, 65:283, 66:283–84.

36. Vauchez, *Francis of Assisi*, 75; "Assisi Compilation," 67:170–71, 84:187–88. See also Celano, *Second Life*, 30:388.

37. Celano, *First Life*, 16:242. See also Sorrell, *St Francis of Assisi and Nature*, 42–44, where Sorrell suggests that it was during Francis's life as a hermit that we see the beginnings of his relationship with nature. Francis, *Admonitions*, 5:80–81; Celano, *First Life*, 80:296; Celano, *Second Life*, 165:494.

38. Verhey: "Ursprüngliche Unschuld," 98, translation mine; Celano, *First Life*, 80:296. We note, however, that it still wasn't widely understood in Francis's day that bees produced honey; rather, it was commonly assumed that honey was like a divine dew. Jordan of Giano, *Chronicle*, 12:28.

39. Celano, *Second Life*, 165:494–95.

40. Sorrell, *St Francis of Assisi and Nature*, 89–92. See also Armstrong, *Saint Francis*.

41. Celano, *Second Life*, 165:495.

42. See further Armstrong, *Saint Francis*, 44–46, who points out not so much the hagiographical elements but the surprising attention given to Francis by the birds. Celano, *First Life*, 58:277–78. This episode is the only one in which Celano expressly says that it was reported to him by Francis and his brothers.

43. Celano, *First Life*, 58:277, 278.

44. Celano, *First Life*, 58:278.

45. *Little Flowers of St Francis*, 1337; Celano, *Treatise on the Miracles*, 26:413–14, 29:414, 31:414.

46. Celano, *Second Life*, 213:533; *Legend of Perugia*, 43:1022.

47. *Legend of Perugia*, 44:1023, 100:1076–77.

48. Translation by Bezzant and Leppin.

49. Francis, *Praises of the Virtues*, 134. As this is a song of praise, we must be careful not to expound it with only biographical questions in mind.

50. See Thompson, *Francis of Assisi*, 124, who suggests tendentiously that if Francis saw animals as possessed by demons, he would not include them in the canticle.

51. See further Sorrell, *St Francis of Assisi and Nature*, 103. Further to the canticle's Trinitarian form, see Kinsella, "How Great a Gladness," 64: "The *Canticum* takes nature back to

the very ground of the Godhead in the Trinity. Nature is the visible, material, and incarnational expression of the Trinity itself." See also *Rule of 1221*, 31.

52. Celano, *First Life*, 81:297.

53. See further Hoose, "Francis of Assisi's Way of Peace?" 464; Celano, *First Life*, 55:274; Julian of Speyer, "Life," 34:394; Jordan of Giano, *Chronicle*, 10:25-26. For further reflection on the role of martyrdom in hagiographical writing since antiquity, see Tolan, "The Friar and the Sultan," 64; Cusato, *Early Franciscan Movement*, 106.

54. Jordan of Giano, *Chronicle*, 9:24, 7:24, 8:24, 10:25-26; Roncaglia, *St Francis of Assisi and the Middle East*, 31. Compare this suggestion with the statement in Francis, *Admonitions*, 6:81.

55. Celano, *First Life*, 55:274-75; Julian of Speyer, "Life," 34:394.

56. Celano, *First Life*, 55:274; Celano, *Treatise on the Miracles*, 33:415-16; Celano, *Das neuentdeckte Franziskusleben*, 52.

57. Celano, *First Life*, 56:275-76; O'Callaghan, *Reconquest and Crusade in Medieval Spain*, 70-76; O'Callaghan, "Innocent III and the Kingdom of Castile and Leon," 332-35.

58. Other contemporary scholars have attempted to reconstruct two journeys to Morocco. See, for example, Johnson, "St Francis and the Sultan," 149.

59. Roncaglia, *St Francis of Assisi and the Middle East*, 26n46, who comments on how to weigh various sources, and acknowledges that the sultan did meet a monk at around the time that Francis voyaged. Vauchez, *Francis of Assisi*, 87; Warren, *Daring to Cross the Threshold*, 31. Vauchez points out the similarities between the homiletic logic of Francis and the crusaders: Vauchez, *Francis of Assisi*, 93. For reflection on interpreting this tension, see Hoose, "Francis of Assisi's Way of Peace?"

60. Vauchez, *Francis of Assisi*, 92; Moore, *Pope Innocent III (1160-1216)*, 107.

61. "St Francis and the Sultan of Egypt," 1615; Celano, *Second Life*, 30:388-89. Hoose, "Francis of Assisi's Way of Peace?" 458, argues that Francis's attitude toward the crusades was typical of his day. See also Warren, *Daring to Cross the Threshold*, 35f.; Johnson, "St Francis and the Sultan," 151.

62. Johnson, "St Francis and the Sultan," 151; Jacques de Vitry, "Letter of 1220," 1609; Jacques de Vitry, *History of the Orient*, 1612; Bonaventure, *Major Life*, IX/8:703; Ernoul, "Chronicle," 605-6.

63. Jacques de Vitry, *History of the Orient*, 1612. For more on the linguistic issues, see Thompson, *Francis of Assisi*, 68; Jordan of Giano, *Chronicle*, 10:25-26. It could be that the arresting party thought that Francis was an envoy from the enemy, and that the sultan's entourage would contain a translator.

64. Jacques de Vitry, *History of the Orient*, 1612; Ernoul, "Chronicle," 606-7; Celano, *First Life*, 57:277.

65. Bonaventure, *Major Life*, IX/8:704.

66. Jacques de Vitry, *History of the Orient*, 1612-13; Hoose, "Francis of Assisi's Way of Peace?" 467.

67. For the reception history of Francis's encounter with the sultan, see Tolan, "The Friar and the Sultan." The Franciscans were the first order to include explicit guidelines concerning mission in the *Rule of 1221*, 16:43-44.

68. *Rule of 1221*, 16:43-44; Jacques de Vitry, *History of the Orient*, 1612; Francis, "Letter to a General Chapter," 105.

CHAPTER 5. ORDER

1. Abdelkawy Sheir, "Legend of Prester John," 238.

2. Jacques de Vitry, "Letter of 1216," 1608.

3. See further Moore, *Pope Innocent III*; Moore, *Pope Innocent III (1160–1216)*. For the history of interpretation concerning Innocent III, see Powell, *Innocent III*.

4. See "Constitutions of the Fourth Lateran Council of 1215."

5. See further Cheney, *Pope Innocent III and England*, 294–356. Previously Innocent III had also made vassal states of Portugal in 1210 and Aragon in 1204. See García y García, "Innocent III and the Kingdom of Castile," 342.

6. Thomas of Eccleston, "Coming of the Friars Minor," 15:182, though if it is true, it is difficult to explain why Vitry does not mention Francis in his account of the incident, despite his mention of Francis extensively in a letter from Genoa: Jacques de Vitry, "Letter I (1216)," 579.

7. John of Salisbury, *Memoirs of the Papal Court*, 65.

8. Biller, *The Waldenses*.

9. It should be pointed out, however, that the dualistic tendencies among the Cathars are nowhere to be seen in the teachings of Francis, but instead we have noted the ways in which Francis's doctrine of creation highlighted God's close engagement with the material world.

10. Celano, *First Life*, 281; Julian of Speyer, "Life," 28:388.

11. Stephen of Bourbon, "Reverence for Priests," 1605–6.

12. Francis, *Testament*, 67.

13. Francis, "Letter to All Clerics," 101. See also Landini, *Causes of the Clericalization*, 49; Francis, "Letter to All Clerics," 101–2; Francis, "Letter to a General Chapter," 104.

14. Francis, *Admonitions*, 86.

15. Francis, *Praises of the Virtues*, 133.

16. Francis, *Praises of the Virtues*, 133; *Rule of 1221*, 46.

17. For the full Latin text of the bull, see Moore, *Pope Innocent III*, 72–73, translation mine. For the resolutions of the council in English, see "The Canons of the Fourth Lateran Council of 1215"; Lombard, *The Sentences*, I.1.1:5–6.

18. See "The Canons of the Fourth Lateran Council of 1215."

19. *Rule of 1221*, 20:46.

20. See canon 1 in "The Canons of the Fourth Lateran Council of 1215"; Bradshaw and Johnson, *The Eucharistic Liturgies*, 224.

21. Francis, "Letter to a General Chapter," 105.

22. In later Lutheran teaching, it was made clear that Christ is present in the actions of the Eucharist, not in any remaining elements. For canons of the council, see "The Canons of the Fourth Lateran Council of 1215." Francis, "Letter to All Clerics," 101. From this instruction, we can understand the account in Celano that Francis gave to his brothers receptacles to store the host, namely a pyx or ciborium, in order that they might handle the elements with due reverence. See also Celano, *Second Life*, 201:522–23.

23. Hoeberichts, "The Authenticity of Admonition 27," 505. Francis did not use the term *eucharistia* but instead *sanctissimum corpus et sanguis Domini nostri Jesu Christi*; Francis, *Admonitions*, 1:78.

24. Francis, "Letter to a General Chapter," 104.

25. Francis, "Letter to a General Chapter," 105–6.

26. Francis, *Testament*, 67; Francis, *Admonitions*, 1:78–79; Francis, "Letter to a General Chapter," 106.

27. Francis, "Letter to All Superiors of the Friars Minor" 113; Francis, *Testament*, 67.

28. See "The Canons of the Fourth Lateran Council of 1215."

29. Celano, *Second Life*, 202:523–24.

30. See further Leppin, *Martin Luther*, 33–37; "The Canons of the Fourth Lateran Council of 1215."

31. Berg, Lehmann, and Freyer, introduction to *The Rule of 1221*, 69; see also the introduction to the *Vermächtnis für Klara und ihre Schwestern*, 63; *Legend of the Three Companions*, 923; see the prologue to *Rule of 1221*, 31, 32.

32. Flood, *Francis of Assisi*. For the most recent Latin edition, see Schlageter, "Die Chronica," 39. Jordan of Giano, *Chronicle*, 15:30; *Legend of Perugia*, 80:1055–56.

33. See further Thompson, *Francis of Assisi*, 91; *Little Flowers of St Francis*, 18:1339–43; Jordan of Giano, *Chronicle*, 18:34–36; Francis, *Die Opuscula*, 300, translation mine. See also Flood, *Francis of Assisi*.

34. Anonymous of Perugia, "Beginning or Founding of the Order," 44:56.

35. In examining the source material, Kruse has demonstrated that narrating the biography of Hugolino has challenges similar to narrating the story of Francis, which itself does not provide many concrete details concerning Hugolino. See Kruse, "The Changing Role of Hugolino," 438–64; Francis, *Testament*, 69; *Rule of 1223*, 64.

36. Celano, *First Life*, 314. Of course it might be that the relationship between Francis and Hugolino was not initiated by Francis but fell to Hugolino as a member of the Curia responsible for orders, who as cardinal and later pope was responsible for keeping an eye on heretical movements as well. Anonymous of Perugia, "Beginning or Founding of the Order," 44; Celano, *First Life*, 219; *Legend of the Three Companions*, 61:945–46. Celano glances over the fact that Hugolino had hoped to convene a meeting of both Dominic and Francis, esteemed leaders of the recently founded mendicant orders, though there is no record of any such meeting ever happening. See Celano, *Second Life*, 148–50:481–83; *Legend of the Three Companions*, 62:947–48. It also might explain why Hugo refused to give Francis permission to travel to France: Jordan of Giano, *Chronicle*, 11–13:26–29.

37. Manselli, *St. Francis of Assisi*, 197, although Manselli acknowledges that Hugolino does intervene to refuse permission for Francis to travel to France. Celano, *First Life*, 315, 316.

38. *Legend of the Three Companions*, 61:946; Celano, *First Life*, 74:290; Anonymous of Perugia, "Beginning or Founding of the Order," 45:57.

39. *Legend of the Three Companions*, 66:950.

40. Francis, *Testament*, 31–33:69; Francis, "Letter to a Minister," 110; compare *Rule of 1223*, 7:62 with Francis, "Letter to a Minister," 110–11.

41. *Rule of 1221*, 2:32; *Rule of 1223*, 2:58, 8:62.

42. *Rule of 1221*, 5:35; *Rule of 1223*, 8:62.

CHAPTER 6. RETREAT

1. For a more detailed exploration of this, see Flood, *Francis of Assisi*, 25.

2. *Rule of 1221*, 1:31, 8:38.

3. See, for example, Bonaventure, "Sermon 3," 100, or Bonaventure, "Excerpts from Other Works," 19:847–48; *Rule of 1221*, 8:38–39.

4. *Rule of 1221*, 8:38; see lines 2801–4 in Goethe, *Faust*, 83; *Rule of 1221*, 8:39. It appears that the role of money was so deeply embedded in the early narrative of the movement, enabling the renovation of churches, that Bernard's responsibility for the common purse was not something worthy of rebuke but instead something that the community learned to appreciate: *Rule of 1223*, 4:61.

5. *Rule of 1223*, 5:61; *Rule of 1221*, 7:37.

6. Francis, *Testament*, 21:68; *Rule of 1223*, 7:62.

7. Celano, *Second Life*, 200:522.

8. Francis, *Admonitions*, 5:81, 14:83, 7:81, 16:83–84, 8:82, 9:82.

9. Francis, *Admonitions*, 19:84, 17:84; Francis, "Letter to a General Chapter," 104, 108.

10. Francis, *Praises of the Virtues*, 133; *Rule of 1223*, 6:61.

11. Francis, *Testament*, 68.

12. *Rule of 1221*, 22:47; see further Brown, *The Body and Society*.

13. Celano, *Second Life*, 116:459.

14. Francis, *Admonitions*, 10:82.

15. Celano, *First Life*, 51:272; *Legend of the Three Companions*, 15:904–5; *Rule of 1221*, 3:34; *Rule of 1223*, 3:60.

16. *Rule of 1221*, 13:42; Francis, "Religious Life in Hermitages," 72; Celano, *Second Life*, 114:457. See further Cedillo, "Habitual Gender," 76, on the comparison of Eve and Mary.

17. Celano, *Second Life*, 112:455; *Rule of 1221*, 12:42; *Rule of 1223*, 11:64.

18. Anonymous of Perugia, "Beginning or Founding of the Order," 20:43, 16:40; *Rule of 1221*, 13:42.

19. For the emphasis on veneration of the angels, see especially Celano, *Second Life*, 197:520; Celano, *First Life*, 45:267; Francis, "Letter to All the Faithful," 94; Francis, "Letter to a General Chapter," 107. It is difficult to judge what Francis really meant when he wrote that he hadn't prayed the Office often enough, given its genre as confession of sin. But it certainly does not imply that Francis laid no value on the Liturgy of the Hours, even though it is true that because of poor health he was not able to attend regularly. Francis, "The Paraphrase of the Our Father," 159–60.

20. Francis, "The Office of the Passion," 141; see also Francis, *Testament*, 68, and *Rule of 1223*, 3:59–60. The lay brothers also contributed by praying the Lord's Prayer and the prayer for the dead. Francis points in several places to the liturgical practice of Rome, suggesting he didn't see his own rite as a replacement. Francis, "Office of the Passion," 142; Francis, "Salutation of the Blessed Virgin," 136.

21. Francis, "The Canticle of Exhortation to Saint Clare and Her Sisters," 6:41; *Rule of 1221*, 1:31; Francis, *Testament*, 67.

22. Francis, *Admonitions*, 6:81, 5:81; Schmucki, *Beiträge*, 484, translation mine.

23. Francis, "Letter to All the Faithful," 93; Celano, *First Life*, 84–86:299–301, 84:300.

24. Celano, *First Life*, 87:302.

25. Celano, *First Life*, 86:301. The Latin word used here by Celano for "deacon" is *levita*, derived from the word *Levite*.

26. For the quotation ascribed to Leo, see the introduction to Francis, "The Parchment Given to Brother Leo," 99; Francis, *Praises of God*, 125.

27. Francis, *Praises of God*, 125.

28. See McGinn, "Was Francis of Assisi a Mystic?" 151, who argues that though Francis displays some characteristics of the mystical tradition, in the end Francis can't in the most technical definition of the term be described as a mystic, in opposition to Oktavian Schmucki's position. Hoeberichts, "The Authenticity of Admonition 27," 522; Francis, *Admonitions*, 27:86.

29. Augustine, *Confessions*, 21. Francis wants to draw special attention to the language of fear, given his deliberate adaptation of Luke 11:21—where the language of fear does not appear—in Admonition 27.

30. Francis, *Admonitions*, 5:8081, 1:78.

31. Francis, *Admonitions*, 1:78; Francis, "Letter to All the Faithful," 3, for a clear connection with the Eucharist. Francis, "Letter to All the Faithful," 96. We note how this text in the "Second Version of the Letter to the Faithful" is almost an exact repeat of these sentences in the first abbreviated version. Compare Francis, "Second Version of the Letter to the Faithful" to "The First Version of the Letter to the Faithful." On Francis's mysticism, see Cedillo, "Habitual Gender," 75, which argues that the use of female imagery for men is an attempt to avoid same-sex erotic associations; and also McGinn, "Was Francis of Assisi a Mystic?" 150.

32. *Rule of 1223*, 8:62; see further Landini, *Causes of the Clericalization*, 36: "Francis himself was by no means an organizer"; Jordan of Giano, *Chronicle*, 11:26–27.

33. Francis, *Admonitions*, 3:79, 80; Francis, "Letter to Brother Leo," 118–19. We note in the first line of the letter that Francis has written his name in contemporary Italian, a mixture of Latin and Middle Italian: "Francesco."

34. *Legend of the Three Companions*, 57:941; Jacques de Vitry, "Letter of 1216," 1608, 1611. It is worth noting that Habig's translation does not make explicit what the Latin states. See further Flood, *Francis of Assisi*, 117. See *Rule of 1221*, 18:45, where both annual dates are mentioned.

35. Jacques de Vitry, "Letter of 1216," 1608; Flood, *Francis of Assisi*, 120; Jordan of Giano, *Chronicle*, 1–3:20–21; *Legend of the Three Companions*, 62:947. In the *Rule of 1223*, 8:62, the word *religio* functions effectively as a synonym for the order.

36. Jordan of Giano, *Chronicle*, 5:22–23.

37. *Rule of 1221*, 18:45–46; Jordan of Giano, *Chronicle*, 16; Thomas of Eccleston, "Coming of the Friars Minor," 6:126; Bonaventure, *Major Life*, 10:660.

38. Jordan of Giano, *Chronicle*, 11:26–27. Francis is likely to have appointed two replacements for him, not just one, despite the argument that from 1217 Peter of Catania was his deputy. *Rule of 1221*, 7:38. This regulation is based on the instruction from 1 Peter 4:9; *Rule of 1223*, 3:60.

39. Francis, "Letter to a Minister," 110.

40. *Legend of Perugia*, 12:988; Celano, *Second Life*, 67:419; 91:436; 182:507, 143:477–78.

41. Jordan of Giano, *Chronicle*, 9:24–25, 17:33–34.

42. *Rule of 1223*, 1:57; Francis, "Letter to a General Chapter," 103, 104, 107, 108; *Rule of 1223*, 8:62.

43. Francis, "Letter to a General Chapter," 103.

44. *Little Flowers of St Francis*, 8:1318–20; Francis, *True and Perfect Joy*, 165.

45. Julian of Speyer, "Life," 67:414; Francis, "Letter to a Minister," 110; Celano, *Second Life*, 144:478; Francis, "Religious Life in Hermitages," 72–73; Celano, *First Life*, 94:308.

46. Brother Elias, "On the Stigmata," 1895. It is assumed that the text is reliable, making the reports of Francis's death here in relation to other reports more difficult.

47. Trexler, "Stigmatized Body of Francis of Assisi," 485–87.

48. *Legend of the Three Companions*, 69–70:953–54; Celano, *First Life*, 113:326, 95:309.

49. Roger of Wendover, "Chronicle," 10–13:600–601; Celano, *First Life*, 94:308.

50. Celano, *First Life*, 95:310. It is surprising, then, that there is no report of this incident by the Three Companions, given that Rufinus was one of the authorities they relied on. Celano, *Second Life*, 135–38:472–74, 135:472; see Robert Kiely, "Further Considerations of the Holy Stigmata of St Francis."

51. Celano, *Treatise on the Miracles*, 6:404.

52. Celano, *Treatise on the Miracles*, 6–8:404–5.

53. Several early accounts separate these events. See further McGinn, "Was Francis of Assisi a Mystic?" 160; *Legend of the Three Companions*, 69:953; Celano, *First Life*, 94:309.

54. Thomas of Eccleston, "Coming of the Friars Minor," 13:162.

55. Schmucki, *Beiträge*, 484, 490; Schmucki, *Stigma of St. Francis of Assisi*, 207–9, 214.

56. See also McGinn, "Was Francis of Assisi a Mystic?" 158; Daxelmüller, *"Süße Nägel der Passion,"* 117; Yoram, *Body, Blood and Sexuality*, 96; Feld, *Franziskus*, 265–67.

57. Celano, *Second Life*, 129:468. Francis, of course, practiced a severely ascetic life, but attests that it was scourging and fasting that produced the wounds, not other kinds of physical self-harm. Bösch, *Franz von Assisi*, 29, translation mine.

58. Trexler, "Stigmatized Body of Francis of Assisi," 486. His interpretation in the end assumes some measure of invention in the account of Elias.

59. *Pace* Trexler, "Stigmatized Body of Francis of Assisi," 486; Brother Elias, "On the Stigmata," 1895; see further Dooren, "Stigmatization of St Francis."

60. See also McGinn, "Was Francis of Assisi a Mystic?" 158; Brother Elias, "On the Stigmata," 1895; Muessig, "Signs of Salvation," 68.

61. *Legend of the Three Companions*, 69:953; Brother Elias, "On the Stigmata."

62. See further *Legend of Perugia*, 39:1016–18; Celano, *First Life*, 97:311, 105:319.

63. "Assisi Compilation," 83:184; Celano, *First Life*, 98:312, 101:316; Celano, *Second Life*, 215:535.

64. Celano, *First Life*, 105:319; Thompson, *Francis of Assisi*, 133–36; Francis, *Testament*, 69.

65. Francis, *Testament*, 67–70.

66. Francis, *Testament*, 68.

67. Francis, *Testament*, 69.

68. Celano, *First Life*, 109:322–23.

69. Celano, *First Life*, 108:322, 107:320–21, 110:323; Celano, *Second Life*, 216:535.

70. Celano, *Second Life*, 217:536; Celano, *First Life*, 110:323.

71. Celano, *Second Life*, 214:534; Celano, *First Life*, 110:324, 105:320.

CODA. A MAN FROM FAR AWAY

1. Jordan of Giano, *Chronicle*, 50:57.

Bibliography

PRIMARY SOURCES

"The Acts of the Process of Canonization of Clare of Assisi." In *The Lady: Clare of Assisi; Early Documents,* edited by Regis J. Armstrong, 139–96. New York: New City, 2006.

Anonymous [John] of Perugia. "The Beginning or Founding of the Order and the Deeds of Those Lesser Brothers Who Were the First Companions of Blessed Francis in Religion." In *Francis of Assisi: Early Documents; The Founder,* edited by Regis J. Armstrong, J. A. Wayne Hellmann, and William J. Short, 29–58. New York: New City, 2000.

———. "Johannes von Perugia (Anonymus Perusinus), Anfang oder Grundlegung des Ordens." In *Franziskus-Quellen: Die Schriften des Heiligen Franziskus, Lebensbeschreibungen, Chroniken und Zeugnisse über ihn und seine Orden,* edited by Dieter Berg, Leonhard Lehmann, and Johannes-Baptist Freyer, 571–601. Kevelaer, Germany: Butzon & Bercker, 2009.

"The Assisi Compilation (1244–1260)." In *Francis of Assisi: Early Documents; The Founder,* edited by Regis J. Armstrong, J. A. Wayne Hellmann, and William J. Short, 111–230. New York: New City, 2000.

Augustine. *Confessions.* Translated by R. S. Pine-Coffin. London: Penguin, 1961.

Berg, Dieter, Leonhard Lehmann, and Johannes-Baptist Freyer. Introduction to *The Rule of 1221.* In *Franziskus-Quellen: Die Schriften des Heiligen Franziskus, Lebensbeschreibungen, Chroniken und Zeugnisse über ihn und seine Orden,* edited by Dieter Berg, Leonhard Lehmann, and Johannes-Baptist Freyer, 69. Kevelaer, Germany: Butzon & Bercker, 2009.

———. Introduction to the *Vermächtnis für Klara und ihre Schwestern.* In *Franziskus-Quellen: Die Schriften des Heiligen Franziskus, Lebensbeschreibungen, Chroniken und Zeugnisse über ihn und seine Orden,* edited by Dieter Berg, Leonhard Lehmann, and Johannes-Baptist Freyer, 63. Kevelaer, Germany: Butzon & Bercker, 2009.

Bonaventure. "Excerpts from Other Works." In *St Francis of Assisi: Writings and Early Biographies; English Omnibus of the Sources for the Life of St Francis,* edited by Marion A. Habig, translated by Benen Fahy, 833–51. London: SPCK, 1979.

———. *Major Life.* In *St Francis of Assisi: Writings and Early Biographies; English Omnibus of the Sources for the Life of St Francis,* edited by Marion A. Habig, translated by Bene Fahy and Damien Vorreux, 627–787. London: SPCK, 1979.

———. "Sermon 3 on St. Francis Preached at Paris, October 4, 1266." In *The Disciple and the Master: St. Bonaventure's Sermons on St. Francis of Assisi,* edited and translated by Eric Doyle, 97–104. Chicago: Franciscan Herald, 1983.

Brother Elias. "On the Stigmata." In *St Francis of Assisi: Writings and Early Biographies; English Omnibus of the Sources for the Life of St Francis,* edited by Marion A. Habig, translated by John R. H. Moorman, 1894–95. London: SPCK, 1979.

"The Canons of the Fourth Lateran Council of 1215." Fordham University, Internet History Sourcebooks Project. https://sourcebooks.fordham.edu/basis/lateran4.asp, accessed December 6, 2022.

Clare. "The Testament." In *The Lady: Clare of Assisi; Early Documents*, edited and translated by Regis J. Armstrong, 59–65. Hyde Park: New City, 2006.

"Constitutions of the Fourth Lateran Council of 1215." Papal Encyclicals Online. https://www.papalencyclicals.net/councils/ecum12-2.htm#5, accessed December 4, 2022.

"The Earlier Rule (the Rule without a Papal Seal) (1209–1221)." In *Francis of Assisi: Early Documents; The Saint*, edited by Regis J. Armstrong, J. A. Wayne Hellmann, and William J. Short, 63–86. New York: New City, 1999.

Ernoul. "Chronicle." In *Francis of Assisi: Early Documents; The Saint*, edited by Regis J. Armstrong, J. A. Wayne Hellmann, and William J. Short, 605–7. New York: New City, 1999.

The Form of Life of Saint Clare (1253). In *The Lady: Clare of Assisi; Early Documents*, edited by Regis J. Armstrong, 106–26. New York: New City, 2006.

Francis. *The Admonitions*. In *St Francis of Assisi: Writings and Early Biographies; English Omnibus of the Sources for the Life of St Francis*, edited by Marion A. Habig, translated by Benen Fahy, 77–87. London: SPCK, 1979.

———. "The Blessing Given to Brother Bernard." In *Francis and Clare: The Complete Works*, edited and translated by Regis J. Armstrong and Ignatius C. Brady, 159. New York: Paulist, 1982.

———. *The Canticle of Brother Sun*. In *St Francis of Assisi: Writings and Early Biographies; English Omnibus of the Sources for the Life of St Francis*, edited by Marion A. Habig, translated by Benen Fahy, 127–31. London: SPCK, 1979.

———. "The Canticle of Exhortation to Saint Clare and Her Sisters." In *Francis and Clare: The Complete Works*, edited and translated by Regis J. Armstrong and Ignatius C. Brady, 40–41. New York: Paulist, 1982.

———. *Die Opuscula des Hl. Franziskus von Assisi: Neue textkritische Edition*. Edited by Kajetan Eßer. Grottaferrata: Editiones Collegii S. Bonaventurae ad Claras Aquas, 1989.

———. "The First Version of the Letter to the Faithful." In *Francis and Clare: The Complete Works*, edited and translated by Regis J. Armstrong and Ignatius C. Brady, 62–65. New York: Paulist, 1982.

———. "'Form of Life' and 'Last Will' for St Clare." In *St Francis of Assisi: Writings and Early Biographies; English Omnibus of the Sources for the Life of St Francis*, edited by Marion A. Habig, translated by Benen Fahy, 74–76. London: SPCK, 1979.

———. "Letter to a General Chapter." In *St Francis of Assisi: Writings and Early Biographies; English Omnibus of the Sources for the Life of St Francis*, edited by Marion A. Habig, translated by Benen Fahy, 102–8. London: SPCK, 1979.

———. "Letter to All Clerics." In *St Francis of Assisi: Writings and Early Biographies; English Omnibus of the Sources for the Life of St Francis*, edited by Marion A. Habig, translated by Benen Fahy, 100–101. London: SPCK, 1979.

———. "Letter to All Superiors of the Friars Minor." In *St Francis of Assisi: Writings and Early Biographies; English Omnibus of the Sources for the Life of St Francis*, edited by Marion A. Habig, translated by Benen Fahy, 112–14. London: SPCK, 1979.

————. "Letter to All the Faithful." In *St Francis of Assisi: Writings and Early Biographies; English Omnibus of the Sources for the Life of St Francis*, edited by Marion A. Habig, translated by Benen Fahy, 91–99. London: SPCK, 1979.

————. "Letter to a Minister." In *St Francis of Assisi: Writings and Early Biographies; English Omnibus of the Sources for the Life of St Francis*, edited by Marion A. Habig, translated by Benen Fahy, 109–11. London: SPCK, 1979.

————. "Letter to Brother Leo." In *St Francis of Assisi: Writings and Early Biographies; English Omnibus of the Sources for the Life of St Francis*, edited by Marion A. Habig, translated by Benen Fahy, 117–19. London: SPCK, 1979.

————. "Letter to St Anthony." In *St Francis of Assisi: Writings and Early Biographies; English Omnibus of the Sources for the Life of St Francis*, edited by Marion A. Habig, translated by Benen Fahy, 162–64. London: SPCK, 1979.

————. "The Office of the Passion." In *St Francis of Assisi: Writings and Early Biographies; English Omnibus of the Sources for the Life of St Francis*, edited by Marion A. Habig, translated by Benen Fahy, 140–55. London: SPCK, 1979.

————. "The Paraphrase of the Our Father." In *St Francis of Assisi: Writings and Early Biographies; English Omnibus of the Sources for the Life of St Francis*, edited by Marion A. Habig, translated by Benen Fahy, 159–60. London: SPCK, 1979.

————. "The Parchment Given to Brother Leo." In *Francis and Clare: The Complete Works*, edited and translated by Regis J. Armstrong and Ignatius C. Brady, 99–100. New York: Paulist, 1982.

————. *Praises of God*. In *St Francis of Assisi: Writings and Early Biographies; English Omnibus of the Sources for the Life of St Francis*, edited by Marion A. Habig, translated by Benen Fahy, 123–26. London: SPCK, 1979.

————. *The Praises of the Virtues*. In *St Francis of Assisi: Writings and Early Biographies; English Omnibus of the Sources for the Life of St Francis*, edited by Marion A. Habig, translated by Benen Fahy, 132–34. London: SPCK, 1979.

————. "Religious Life in Hermitages." In *St Francis of Assisi: Writings and Early Biographies; English Omnibus of the Sources for the Life of St Francis*, edited by Marion A. Habig, translated by Benen Fahy, 71–73. London: SPCK, 1979.

————. "Salutation of the Blessed Virgin." In *St Francis of Assisi: Writings and Early Biographies; English Omnibus of the Sources for the Life of St Francis*, edited by Marion A. Habig, translated by Benen Fahy, 135–36. London: SPCK, 1979.

————. "The Second Version of the Letter to the Faithful." In *Francis and Clare: The Complete Works*, edited and translated by Regis J. Armstrong and Ignatius C. Brady, 66–73. New York: Paulist, 1982.

————. *The Testament of St Francis*. In *St Francis of Assisi: Writings and Early Biographies; English Omnibus of the Sources for the Life of St Francis*, edited by Marion A. Habig, translated by Benen Fahy, 65–70. London: SPCK, 1979.

————. *True and Perfect Joy*. In *Francis and Clare: The Complete Works*, edited and translated by Regis J. Armstrong and Ignatius C. Brady, 165–66. New York: Paulist Press, 1982.

Jacques de Vitry. *History of the Orient*. In *St Francis of Assisi: Writings and Early Biographies; English Omnibus of the Sources for the Life of St Francis*, edited by Marion A. Habig, translated by Paul Oligny, 1609–13. London: SPCK, 1979.

————. "Letter I (1216)." In *Francis of Assisi: Early Documents; The Saint*, edited by Regis J. Armstrong, J. A. Wayne Hellmann, and William J. Short, 578–80. New York: New City, 1999.

————. "Letter of 1216." In *St Francis of Assisi: Writings and Early Biographies; English Omnibus of the Sources for the Life of St Francis*, edited by Marion A. Habig, translated by Paul Oligny, 1608–9. London: SPCK, 1979.

————. "Letter of 1220." In *St Francis of Assisi: Writings and Early Biographies; English Omnibus of the Sources for the Life of St Francis*, edited by Marion A. Habig, translated by Paul Oligny, 1609. London: SPCK, 1979.

John of Salisbury. *Memoirs of the Papal Court*. Edited and translated by Marjorie Chibnall. London: Nelson, 1956.

Jordan of Giano. *The Chronicle*. In *XIIIth Century Chronicles: Jordan of Giano, Thomas of Eccleston, Salimbene Degli Adami*, edited by Marie-Thérèse Laureilhe, translated by Placid Hermann, 1–77. Chicago: Franciscan Herald, 1961.

Julian of Speyer. "The Divine Office of Saint Francis." In *Francis of Assisi: Early Documents; The Saint*, edited by Regis J. Armstrong, J. A. Wayne Hellmann, and William J. Short, 327–45. New York: New City, 1999.

————. *The Life of Saint Francis*. In *Francis of Assisi: Early Documents; The Saint*, edited by Regis J. Armstrong, J. A. Wayne Hellmann, and William J. Short, 361–420. New York: New City, 1999.

Legend of Perugia. In *St Francis of Assisi: Writings and Early Biographies; English Omnibus of the Sources for the Life of St Francis*, edited by Marion A. Habig, translated by Paul Oligny, 957–1101. London: SPCK, 1979.

"The Legend of Saint Clare." In *The Lady: Clare of Assisi; Early Documents*, edited by Regis J. Armstrong, 272–329. New York: New City, 2006.

Legend of the Three Companions. In *St Francis of Assisi: Writings and Early Biographies; English Omnibus of the Sources for the Life of St Francis*, edited by Marion A. Habig, translated by Nesta de Robeck, 885–956. London: SPCK, 1979.

Little Flowers of St Francis. In *St Francis of Assisi: Writings and Early Biographies; English Omnibus of the Sources for the Life of St Francis*, edited by Marion A. Habig, translated by Raphael Brown, 1267–1530. London: SPCK, 1979.

Lombard, Peter. *The Sentences: Book 1; The Mystery of the Trinity*. Translated by Giulio Silano. Medieval Sources in Translation 42. Toronto: Pontifical Institute of Mediaeval Studies, 2007.

Moorman, John R. H. *The Sources for the Life of S. Francis of Assisi*. 2nd ed. Farnborough, UK: Gregg, 1966.

"The Papal Decree of Canonization (1255)." In *The Lady: Clare of Assisi; Early Documents*, edited by Regis J. Armstrong, 262–71. Hyde Park: New City, 2006.

"The Prayer before the Crucifix." In *Francis and Clare: The Complete Works*, edited by Regis J. Armstrong and Ignatius C. Brady, 103. New York: Paulist, 1982.

Roger of Wendover. "Chronicle." In *Francis of Assisi: Early Documents; The Saint*, edited by Regis J. Armstrong, J. A. Wayne Hellmann, and William J. Short, 596–601. New York: New City, 1999.

The Rule of 1221. In *St Francis of Assisi: Writings and Early Biographies; English Omnibus of the Sources for the Life of St Francis,* edited by Marion A. Habig, translated by Benen Fahy, 27–53. London: SPCK, 1979.

The Rule of 1223. In *St Francis of Assisi: Writings and Early Biographies; English Omnibus of the Sources for the Life of St Francis,* edited by Marion A. Habig, translated by Benen Fahy, 54–66. London: SPCK, 1979.

The Sacrum Commercium; or, Francis and His Lady Poverty. In *St Francis of Assisi: Writings and Early Biographies; English Omnibus of the Sources for the Life of St Francis,* edited by Marion A. Habig, translated by Placid Hermann, 1531–96. London: SPCK, 1979.

Schlageter, Johannes. "Die *Chronica* des Bruders Jordan von Giano: Einführung und kritische Edition nach den bisher bekannten Handschriften." *Archivum Franciscanum Historicum* 104, nos. 1–2 (2011): 3–64.

Stephen of Bourbon. "Reverence for Priests." In *St Francis of Assisi: Writings and Early Biographies; English Omnibus of the Sources for the Life of St Francis,* edited by Marion A. Habig, translated by Paul Oligny, 1605–6. London: SPCK, 1979.

"St Francis and the Sultan of Egypt." In *St Francis of Assisi: Writings and Early Biographies; English Omnibus of the Sources for the Life of St Francis,* edited by Marion A. Habig, translated by Paul Oligny, 1614–15. London: SPCK, 1979.

Thomas of Celano. *Das neuentdeckte Franziskusleben des Thomas von Celano.* Edited by Leonhard Lehmann, Johannes Schneider, and Jacques Dalarun, translated by Leonhard Lehmann and Johannes Schneider. Sankt Ottilien: EOS-Verlag, 2017.

———. *First Life.* In *St Francis of Assisi: Writings and Early Biographies; English Omnibus of the Sources for the Life of St Francis,* edited by Marion A. Habig, translated by Placid Hermann, 225–355. London: SPCK, 1979.

———. "The Legend for Use in the Choir." In *Francis of Assisi: Early Documents; The Saint,* edited by Regis J. Armstrong, J. A. Wayne Hellmann, and William J. Short, 319–26. New York: New City, 1999.

———. *Second Life.* In *St Francis of Assisi: Writings and Early Biographies; English Omnibus of the Sources for the Life of St Francis,* edited by Marion A. Habig, translated by Placid Hermann, 357–543. London: SPCK, 1979.

———. *Treatise on the Miracles of Blessed Francis.* In *St Francis of Assisi: Writings and Early Biographies; English Omnibus of the Sources for the Life of St Francis,* edited by Marion A. Habig, translated by Placid Hermann, 545–54. London: SPCK, 1979.

———. *The Treatise on the Miracles of Saint Francis.* In *Saint Francis: Early Documents; The Founder,* edited by Regis J. Armstrong, J. A. Wayne Hellmann, and William J. Short, 395–468. New York: New City, 2000.

———. *An Umbrian Choir Legend.* In *Francis of Assisi: The Founder; Early Documents,* edited by Regis J. Armstrong, J. A. Wayne Hellmann, and William J. Short, 469–82. New York: New City, 2002.

Thomas of Eccleston. "The Coming of the Friars Minor to England." In *XIIIth Century Chronicles: Jordan of Giano, Thomas of Eccleston, Salimbene Degli Adami,* edited by Marie-Thérèse Laureilhe, translated by Placid Hermann, 79–191. Chicago: Franciscan Herald, 1961.

Thomas of Split. "Chronicle." In *Francis of Assisi: Early Documents; The Founder,* edited by Regis J. Armstrong, J. A. Wayne Hellmann, and William J. Short, 807–8. New York: New City, 1999.

SECONDARY SOURCES

Abdelkawy Sheir, Ahmed Mohamed. "The Legend of Prester John versus the Peace Negotiations between the Muslims and the Crusaders in Damietta (1218–1221/615–618 AH)." In *Relations between East and West: Various Studies; Medieval and Contemporary Ages*, edited by Ahmed Ali El-Sayed, Luciano Gallinari, and Abdallah Abdel-Ati Al-Nagar, 224–47. Cairo: Dar al-Kitab al-Gamey, 2017.

Andrews, Frances. "The Influence of Joachim in the 13th Century." In *A Companion to Joachim of Fiore*, edited by Matthias Riedl, 190–266. Leiden: Brill, 2017.

Appelbaum, Patricia. *St. Francis of America: How a Thirteenth-Century Friar Became America's Most Popular Saint*. Chapel Hill: University of North Carolina Press, 2015.

Armstrong, Edward A. *Saint Francis, Nature Mystic: The Derivation and Significance of the Nature Stories in the Franciscan Legend*. Berkeley: University of California Press, 1973.

Biller, Peter. *The Waldenses, 1170–1530: Between a Religious Order and a Church*. Aldershot, UK: Ashgate, 2001.

Bösch, Paul. *Franz von Assisi—neuer Christus: Die Geschichte einer Verklärung*. Düsseldorf: Patmos, 2005.

Bradshaw, Paul, and Maxwell Johnson. *The Eucharistic Liturgies: Their Evolution and Interpretation*. Collegeville, MN: Liturgical, 2012.

Brown, Peter. *The Body and Society: Men, Women, and Sexual Renunciation in Early Christianity*. London: Faber & Faber, 1998.

Cedillo, Christiana. "Habitual Gender: Rhetorical Androgyny in Franciscan Texts." *Journal of Feminist Studies in Religion* 31, no. 1 (2015): 65–81.

Cheney, Christopher R. *Pope Innocent III and England*. Päpste und Papsttum 9. Stuttgart: Hiersemann, 1976.

Cusato, Michael F. "Alms-Asking and Alms-Giving as Social Commentary and Social Remedy." In *The Rule of the Friars Minor, 1209–2009: Historical Perspectives, Lived Realities*, edited by Daria Mitchell, 59–79. St. Bonaventure, NY: Franciscan Institute, 2010.

———. *The Early Franciscan Movement (1205–1239): History, Sources, and Hermeneutics*. Spoleto: Franciscan Institute, 2009.

———. "Francis and the Franciscan Movement (1181/2–1226)." In *The Cambridge Companion to Francis of Assisi*, edited by Michael J. O. Robson, 17–22. Cambridge: Cambridge University Press, 2012.

Dalarun, Jacques. "Francis and Clare of Assisi: Differing Perspectives on Gender and Power." *Franciscan Studies* 63 (2005): 11–25.

Daxelmüller, Christoph. *"Süße Nägel der Passion": Die Geschichte der Selbstkreuzigung von Franz von Assisi bis heute*. Düsseldorf: Patmos, 2001.

Dooren, Kees van. "The Stigmatization of St Francis: Fact or Fiction?" In *Verum, pulchrum et bonum*, edited by Yoannes Teklemariam, 155–83. Rome: FS Servus Gieben, 2006.

Feld, Helmut. *Franziskus von Assisi: Der Namenspatron des Papstes*. 3rd ed. Darmstadt: Wissenschaftliche Buchgesellschaft, 2014.

Flood, David Ethelbert. *Francis of Assisi and the Franciscan Movement*. Quezon City, Philippines: Franciscan Institute of Asia Contact Publications, 1989.

Francis, Pope. *On Care for Our Common Home: The Encyclical Letter Laudato Si*. Mahwah, NJ: Paulist, 2015.

Fried, Johannes. *Der Schleier der Erinnerung: Grundzüge einer historischen Memorik*. Munich: C. H. Beck, 2012.

García y García, Antonio. "Innocent III and the Kingdom of Castile." In *Pope Innocent III and His World*, edited by John C. Moore, 337–50. Aldershot, UK: Ashgate, 1999.

Godet-Calogeras, Jean-François. "Francis and Clare and the Emergence of the Second Order." In *The Cambridge Companion to Francis of Assisi*, edited by Michael J. O. Robson, 115–26. Cambridge: Cambridge University Press, 2012.

Goethe, Johann Wolfgang von. *Faust: Der Tragödie erster Teil*. Stuttgart: Reclam, 1980.

Goodich, Michael. "Vision, Dream and Canonization Policy under Pope Innocent III." In *Innocent III and His World*, edited by John C. Moore, 151–63. Aldershot, UK: Ashgate, 1999.

Grau, Engelbert. "Thomas von Celano: Leben und Werk." *Wissenschaft und Weisheit* 52 (1989): 97–140.

Hoeberichts, Jan. "The Authenticity of Admonition 27 of Francis of Assisi: A Discussion with Carlo Paolazzi and Beyond." *Collectanea Franciscana* 75 (2005): 499–523.

———. "Franz von Assisi und seine Begegnung mit Muslimen." In *Das Charisma des Ursprungs und die Religionen: Das Werden christlicher Orden im Kontext der Religionen*, edited by Petrus Bsteh und Brigitte Proksch, 206–41. Vienna: Lit, 2011.

Hoose, Adam L. "Francis of Assisi's Way of Peace? His Conversion and Mission to Egypt." *Catholic Historical Review* 96, no. 3 (2010): 449–69.

Johnson, Galen K. "St Francis and the Sultan: An Historical and Critical Reassessment." *Mission Studies* 18, nos. 1–2 (2001): 146–63.

Kiely, Robert. "Further Considerations of the Holy Stigmata of St Francis: Where Was Brother Leo?" *Religion and the Arts* 3, no. 1 (1999): 20–40.

Kinsella, Sean Edward. "How Great a Gladness: Some Thoughts of Francis of Assisi and the Natural World." *Studies in Spirituality* 12 (2002): 61–67.

Kruse, John V. "The Changing Role of Hugolino dei Conti di Segni (Gregory IX): A Hermeneutical Tool for Understanding the Lives of Francis." *Miscellanea Francescana* 108 (2008): 438–64.

Landini, Lawrence C. *The Causes of the Clericalization of the Order of Friars Minor, 1209–1260, in the Light of Early Franciscan Sources*. Chicago: Facultate Historiae Ecclesiastice, 1968.

Lapsanski, Duane. "The Autographs on the 'Chartula' of St Francis of Assisi." *Archivum Franciscanum Historicum* 67 (1974): 18–37.

Lehmann, Leonhard. "Die Dreigefährtenlegende." In *Franziskus-Quellen: Die Schriften des Heiligen Franziskus, Lebensbeschreibungen, Chroniken und Zeugnisse über ihn und seine Orden*, edited by Dieter Berg, Leonhard Lehmann, and Johannes-Baptist Freyer, 602–53. Kevelaer, Germany: Butzon & Bercker, 2009.

———. "Franz von Assisi: Mystik zwischen Selbstbewusstsein und Kirchengehorsam." In *Die Kirchenmystik der Mystiker: Prophetie aus Gotteserfahrung*, edited by Mariano Delgado and Gotthard Fuchs, 69–103. Fribourg/Stuttgart: Academic Press Fribourg / W. Kohlhammer, 2004.

Leppin, Volker. *Martin Luther: A Late Medieval Life*. Translated by Rhys S. Bezzant and Karen Roe. Grand Rapids, MI: Baker, 2017.

Luther, Henning. "Leben als Fragment: Der Mythos von der Ganzheit." *Wege zum Menschen* 43 (1991): 262–73.

Manselli, Raoul. *Franziskus: Der solidarische Bruder*. Freiburg: Herder, 1989.

———. *St. Francis of Assisi*. Translated by Paul Duggan. Chicago: Franciscan Herald, 1988.

McGinn, Bernard. "Was Francis of Assisi a Mystic?" In *Doors of Understanding: Conversations in Global Spirituality*, edited by Steven Chase, 145–74. Quincy, IL: F. S. Ewert Cousins, 1997.

McMichael, Steven J. "Francis and the Encounter with the Sultan (1219)." In *The Cambridge Companion to Francis of Assisi*, edited by Michael J. O. Robson, 127–42. Cambridge: Cambridge University Press, 2012.

Monti, Dominic. "'Deservedly Approved by the Roman Church': The Context for Papal Recognition of Francis's *Forma Vitae*." In *The Rule of the Friars Minor, 1209–2009: Historical Perspectives, Lived Realities*, edited by Daria Mitchell, 3–31. St. Bonaventure, NY: Franciscan Institute, 2010.

Moore, John C. *Pope Innocent III (1160/61–1216) and His World: To Root Up and to Plant*. Aldershot, UK: Ashgate, 2003.

———, ed. *Pope Innocent III and His World*. London: Routledge, 2016.

Muessig, Carolyn. "Signs of Salvation: The Evolution of Stigmatic Spirituality before Francis of Assisi." *Church History* 82, no. 1 (2013): 40–68.

O'Callaghan, Joseph F. "Innocent III and the Kingdom of Castile and Leon." In *Pope Innocent III and His World*, edited by John C. Moore, 317–35. Aldershot, UK: Ashgate, 1999.

———. *Reconquest and Crusade in Medieval Spain*. Philadelphia: University of Pennsylvania Press, 2004.

Powell, James M., ed. *Innocent III: Vicar of Christ or Lord of the World?* 2nd ed. Washington, DC: Catholic University of America Press, 1994.

Riley, Paul V. "Francis' Assisi: Its Political and Social History, 1175–1225." *Franciscan Studies* 34 (1974): 393–424.

Roncaglia, Martiniano. *St Francis of Assisi and the Middle East*. 3rd ed. Cairo: Franciscan Center of Oriental Studies, 1957.

Rotzetter, A. "Die Entscheidung des Hl. Franz für die Armen: Zum kirchlichen und gesellschaftlichen Ort der franziskanischen Lebensraum." *Franziskanische Studien* 64 (1982): 27–53.

Rublack, Ulinka. *Dressing Up: Cultural Identity in Renaissance Europe*. Oxford: Oxford University Press, 2010.

Schmucki, Oktavian. *Beiträge zur Franziskusforschung: Zum 80. Geburtstag*. Franziskanische Forschungen. Edited by Ulrich Köpf and Leonhard Lehmann. Kevelaer, Germany: Butzon & Bercker, 2007.

———. *The Stigmata of St. Francis of Assisi: A Critical Investigation in the Light of Thirteenth-Century Sources*. St. Bonaventure, NY: Franciscan Institute, St. Bonaventure University, 1991.

Sorrell, Roger D. *St. Francis of Assisi and Nature: Tradition and Innovation in Western Christian Attitudes toward the Environment.* New York: Oxford University Press, 1988.

Thompson, Augustine. *Francis of Assisi: A New Biography.* Ithaca, NY: Cornell University Press, 2012.

Tolan, John. "The Friar and the Sultan: Francis of Assisi's Mission to Egypt." *European Review* 16 (2008): 115–26.

Trexler, Richard C. "The Stigmatized Body of Francis of Assisi: Conceived, Processed, Disappeared." In *Frömmigkeit im Mittelalter: Politisch-soziale Kontexte, visuelle Praxis, körperliche Ausdrucksformen,* edited by Klaus Schreiner, 463–97. Munich: Fink, 2002.

Vauchez, André. *Francis of Assisi: The Life and Afterlife of a Medieval Saint.* Translated by Michael F. Cusato. New Haven, CT: Yale University Press, 2012.

Verhey, Sigismund. "Ursprüngliche Unschuld: Franziskus von Assisi spricht mit den Vögeln und mit anderen Tieren." *Wissenschaft und Weisheit* 42, nos. 2–3 (1979): 97–106.

Warren, Kathleen. *Daring to Cross the Threshold: Francis of Assisi Encounters Sultan Malek Al-Kamel.* Eugene, OR: Wipf & Stock, 2003.

Wolf, Kenneth B. *The Poverty of Riches: St Francis of Assisi Reconsidered.* Oxford: Oxford University Press, 2003.

Yoram, Nitza. *Body, Blood and Sexuality: A Psychoanalytic Study of St. Francis' Stigmata and Their Historical Context.* Studies in History and Culture 4. New York: Peter Lang, 1992.

Index